TUNNELLING TO FREEDOM

"The cell doors were flung open and we were marched out into the prison yard to find six guards lined up with rifles. We continued our march in single file to the far end and halted with our backs to the wall, facing the riflemen.

"I thought of the little baby I had never seen ... of the thousand and one things I wanted to tell my wife.

"'Chins up,' whispered Neil.

"I prepared myself for the awful, red-hot, sizzling, sudden pain of the crashing bullet..."

———◆———

Sergeant John Fancy, a navigator in the RAF, was shot down during a bombing raid in northern France on the 14th of May 1940. He was captured and held prisoner by the Germans until the end of the war, during which time he made sixteen attempts to gain his freedom. He escaped three times but was recaptured on each occasion. After the war he established a market garden in the Yorkshire Wolds, eventually moving to South Devon, where he died in September 2008, aged 95.

TUNNELLING TO FREEDOM

JOHN FANCY

Aurum Press Ltd
7 Greenland Street
London NW1 0ND
www.aurumpress.co.uk

First published by Panther Books Ltd 1957
This edition published by Aurum Press Ltd 2010

A catalogue record for this book is available from the British Library

ISBN 978 1 84513 514 0

Typeset in Berling by David Fletcher Welch
Plate section designed by David Fletcher Welch
Printed in the UK by CPI Bookmarque, Croydon, CR0 4TD

DEDICATION

To all R.A.F. ex-P.O.W.s whose unfailing good humour and
courage in adversity made all things possible.
JOHN FANCY No. 524851. W.O.I.
"FANCE."

CONTENTS

ACKNOWLEDGEMENTS

Aurum Press would like to thank John Fancy's family for their help in producing this book, particularly his daughter Jan Bryon-Edmond and granddaughter Brydgette Bryon-Edmond.

INTRODUCTION

By Air Commodore Graham Pitchfork, MBE, FRAeS

During the late afternoon of 4 September 1939, the RAF mounted its first bombing raid of the Second World War. Of the fifteen Blenheim Mark IV bombers that took part, four were shot down in the target area near Wilhelmshaven, a coastal town in Lower Saxony, and ten of the aircrew lost their lives. The observer and the air gunner of one of the Blenheims survived, although badly injured, and were taken into captivity, the first Allied airmen to become prisoners of war (POWs). A few months later, Sergeant John Fancy joined them as a guest of the Third Reich. When Germany surrendered five years later in May 1945, they were repatriated together with 13,020 other British and Dominion Air Force former prisoners.

During his captivity, John Fancy became a huge irritant to his captors who were forced to expend a great deal of time, effort and manpower curbing his misdemeanours. An inveterate escaper, he was one of the most determined airmen in captivity, whose sole aim in life was to gain his freedom.

John Fancy was born on 9 March 1913, in the vicarage of Lund, near Driffield in Yorkshire, and educated at Hymer's College, Hull. He studied land management and worked at Scarborough in the Parks and Gardens Department but decided to join the RAF at the end of 1935. He trained as an aircraft fitter but, with war imminent, he volunteered to be a pilot. Due to a minor eyesight defect, he was selected as an air observer (navigator) and completed his training in December 1939.

In January 1940 he joined No.110 Squadron, based in Suffolk and equipped with the Blenheim bomber. In late February twelve Blenheims were gifted to Finland, and Fancy and his crew were detailed to ferry one of the aircraft. Wearing civilian clothes, and with the aircraft bearing the blue swastika markings of the Finnish Air Force, they stopped to refuel in Scotland and neutral Norway. They were guided to a frozen lake at Juva where they landed and the aircraft were handed over. After a few days instructing the Finnish crews, they were flown to Stockholm in a Finnish Airlines Junkers transport. Two weeks later they returned to Suffolk.

During the spring of 1940 Fancy flew a number of sweeps over the North Sea, and in April he attacked the Norwegian airfield at Stavangar. After the German invasion of the Low Countries, the Blenheim squadrons turned their attention to supporting the British Expeditionary Force in its rearguard actions in northern France.

Following the German Blitzkrieg into the Low Countries and France on 10 May 1940, the RAF's light bombers based in France suffered crippling losses, so the Blenheim squadrons based in England were thrown into the battle. The key targets were the bridges over the River Meuse at Maastricht and Sedan. Twelve aircraft of No.110 Squadron were tasked to attack the bridge at Sedan on the 14th, one of them navigated by Seargeant John Fancy, who that morning had found out that his wife was expecting their first child. The force was subjected to intense anti-aircraft fire and to attacks by German fighters but Fancy and his crew bombed the bridge successfully. However, five of the twelve aircraft were shot down, including Fancy's as it left the target, to crash-land in the grounds of a chateau.

Fancy suffered burns and was wounded by exploding ammunition but he was able to drag his injured pilot, Pilot Officer Duggie Wright, free. Their gunner, Leading Aircraftman Bill Speed, was uninjured and he would figure largely in Fancy's escaping activities in the months ahead. The three men were soon surrounded by German troops and their long captivity began.

As he laid waiting to be transferred to hospital, Fancy made up his mind that he "would return home at the first opportunity". It was a desire that increased throughout the privations of captivity and by the end of the war he had made sixteen attempts to gain his freedom, either by tunnelling, absconding from outside working parties, cutting through the camp's perimeter wire, or jumping from moving trains.

During training it was impressed on all aircrew that it was their duty to escape but told that the longer they delayed their attempt, the smaller would be their chance of success. They were advised that an escape attempt should be made as soon as possible after capture since, in the early stages, they would almost certainly be in the hands of front-line troops or local police forces who had no specialist knowledge of guarding or imprisonment. As prisoners were moved to Germany, they would come under the control of more competent guards until arriving in a prison camp, an establishment that was specifically designed and organised to keep them in captivity. The dangers of delaying an escape attempt are graphically illustrated by the statistics: over 5,000 men "evaded" capture or escaped in transit – just 29 succeeded in making a successful escape from a German prisoner-of-war camp. Once a man had escaped from the camp, he became an evader, but he faced the almost insurmountable problem of being deep inside German territory with no hope of any outside assistance, unlike those who came down in the occupied countries where many heroic members of the local population were willing to offer assistance, which allowed the evaders to avoid capture and return home via one of the escape lines.

At the beginning of the war all prisoner-of-war affairs were the preserve of the German High Command, the *Oberkommand der Wehrmacht (OKW)*, and the camps were run entirely by army personnel. However, *Feldmarschall* Hermann Goering, Commander-in-Chief of the Luftwaffe, was determined that the detention of air force prisoners should come under his control and, in due course, separate camps were established for them. Despite his many faults, Goering still held a certain sense of chivalry dating from his experiences in the First World War. He was also concerned that his own captured aircrew would be well treated by the Allies, and these two considerations shaped his attitude towards the imprisonment of Air Force personnel.

By July 1940, two Air Force camps had been established. *Durch-gangsler der Luftwaffe (Dulag Luft)*, at Oberursel near Frankfurt, became the initial reception and interrogation centre for all captured airmen. The first permanent camp, *Stalag Luft I*, was at Barth-Vogelsang on the Baltic coast but this camp soon filled up. In October 1941, Goering ordered a new camp to be constructed but it was not until March 1942 that the very large camp at Sagan, *Stalag Luft III*, was completed. This became the main camp for all air force prisoners, although separate compounds were established for officers and NCOs. John Fancy would find his way there in due course.

First he spent a few weeks in hospital recovering from his wounds before he was transferred to *Dulag Luft* where he was processed, which included interrogation. Within days he was aboard a cattle truck and heading for Lamsdorf on the Czechoslovak frontier where he was introduced to life as a POW. Within a few weeks, the RAF prisoners were transferred to *Stalag Luft* I at Barth-Vogelsang and Fancy started to think of escape but realised that, for the time being, his damaged leg would prevent an attempt. Nevertheless, whilst exercising to regain his fitness, he was busy noting the habits of the guards and the layout of the camp, and gathering as much intelligence as possible. It was to be the pattern of his life for the next five years.

As his strength and mobility returned he made his first attempt for freedom with his gunner Bill Speed. They joined an outside working party repairing roads and they made a dash for freedom as others created a diversion. Within minutes they were recaptured and spent the next 21 days in solitary confinement in the "cooler". Fancy was to spend many more weeks in solitary, almost one eighth of his time as a POW. By the time he returned to the main compound, he had resolved to pursue his new "hobby" to the bitter end and he set about investigating the camp's defences. He soon met up with other like-minded colleagues, and they discussed the possibility of digging a tunnel.

Fancy, using a strong all-metal table knife as his primary tool, soon assumed the role of chief digger. After three weeks the tunnel became flooded and had to be abandoned but within weeks a second was started. With just a few feet to go before the tunnellers reached the surface and a chance to make their bid for freedom, the guards discovered the entrance. However, the prisoners had learned many lessons and gained valuable experience.

These early activities of Fancy and his colleagues, albeit unsuccessful, highlighted the valuable contribution that POWs could continue to make by their disruptive conduct in the camps and their escape attempts. It only needed a small party to escape for a national alarm to be initiated, and for many thousands of Germans to be diverted to scour the country, men who would otherwise have been available for other essential duties in the defence of their homeland. This nagging and continuous requirement whenever prisoners were at large was a type of sabotage and it remained a constant weapon which allowed the prisoners, as a force, to continue to contribute to the war effort. This important duty did not escape John Fancy's attention.

———◆———

Of the many insights contained in Fancy's account, amongst the most fascinating are those relating to the POWs' psychology and the sense of community in the prison camps. The life of a POW was of course strictly regimented and often harsh, but everyone was in the same predicament and like-minded men were able to come together and work for each other in an effective and rewarding way against a common enemy. Camps became sophisticated and unusual social places where men of vastly different backgrounds were thrown together. Their collective knowledge, initiatives, experiences, cultural backgrounds and attitudes created a unique society that most of us will never experience, and therefore have some difficulty understanding.

It was in this environment that John Fancy started to adopt a more considered and organised approach to his attempts. This is well illustrated by his next effort to break out of Stalag Luft I. Winter, particularly in Eastern Europe, was the close season for escaping activities, an attitude that was shared by both captives and guards. Only the boldest POW would seek to turn this to his advantage. Fancy, with Bill Speed again alongside, did just that. They waited for a foul night in November 1940 and headed for the wire perimeter. They had cut their way through most of the wire entanglement when a searchlight caught them. Lucky not to be shot, they duly spent another twenty-one days in the cooler.

This experience, in the depth of winter, would deter almost anyone, but not Fancy and Speed. Having been caught trying to go under the wire, they next decided to make an attempt over the wire and, once again, take advantage of a foul winter night. Their audacious plan was to get under a sentry box and then scale the wire. They chose a night of heavy snow and in these dreadful conditions, almost certainly as uncomfortable for the guards, they managed to scale the wire. At his fifth attempt, John Fancy was finally free. The two men headed for the coast and set off to walk to Sweden over the frozen sea. Having walked all night, for a distance of 20 miles, they were spotted by a searching aircraft. This amazing winter effort was rewarded with a four-week stretch in the cooler.

During the early years of his captivity, Fancy's escape attempts were almost entirely his own idea, with no attempt to co-ordinate his efforts with those of others. Naturally other POWs made their own attempts but success under these circumstances was negligible. It was almost two years into the war before Flight Lieutenant Harry Burton (later Air Marshal Sir Harry Burton) made the first successful escape, and by the end of 1941 just two men had made a "home run".

In one camp in 1942, over 40 individual tunnels were being constructed at the same time. None succeeded, and had all that effort gone into one or two co-ordinated efforts, the chances of success would have been much greater. The many individual efforts often jeopardised the safety of fellow prisoners and other escape attempts. During the searches carried out by guards after a failed attempt, other projects and materials were discovered, negating weeks, or even months, of laborious and careful work. Furthermore, when an escape attempt was discovered or foiled, it was not uncommon for certain facilities and benefits, including food parcels, to be withdrawn from the whole camp.

It became apparent to the POWs that, if they were to have any chance of success, they would need to establish a formal organisation through which their escape attempts could be properly planned and co-ordinated. Hence the formation of "escape committees", which started to appear in 1941.

The numerous efforts had made it clear that escape was an extension of a military operation and, under the control of the escape committees, it was conducted in such a way. Gathering, collating and interpreting intelligence was essential, as was detailed briefing. The organisation had to be capable of producing tools to aid an escape and the appropriate materials, be they maps, clothing or forged documents. It was in these departments that the huge variety of talents amongst the prisoners (or *kriegies* as they called themselves, after *Kriegsgefangene*, the German word for a POW) played such an important role. Many worked under the guise of making theatre stage sets or costumes, printing camp newspapers, gardening, education classes and other·activities. In this way, they could disguise many of their clandestine tasks, some on an almost industrial scale, in support of escape. These activities had an important indirect value since everyone involved, including those who would not be part of the escape attempt, experienced a sense of community spirit and a great boost to their morale.

With the agreement of the Stalag Luft I escape committee, John Fancy's next two attempts were underground. As "chief engineer" and main digger, he made good progress in a tunnel until the "goons" (guards) suddenly appeared and Fancy was marched off for another three-week spell in the cooler. Needless to say, as the POWs gained experience with each attempt, so did the camp authorities, who became increasingly effective in tracing and foiling escape attempts.

———◆———

With the RAF bombing campaign gathering momentum throughout 1942, the Luftwaffe-controlled prison camps started to fill rapidly. The huge purpose-built Stalag Luft III at Sagan had been opened early that year. The German authorities took the opportunity to move some of the more troublesome POWs to this "escape-proof" camp. It was no surprise when Fancy found himself heading for the Senior Non-Commissioned Officer's (SNCO's) compound at Sagan.

Fancy looked upon his transfer as a new challenge. He was soon tunnelling through the sandy soil. The tunnel was almost complete when the goons discovered it and so his latest attempt had failed. To most men, these constant and cruel disappointments, often with success tantalisingly close, would be crushing blows and many would decide to settle for the relaxed life and wait for the war's end. To a few men, Fancy included, these setbacks made them even more determined and they re-doubled their efforts. He was soon back in another tunnel but this too was discovered. Another, dug from under the latrines, collapsed and Fancy was dragged clear to be greeted by the chief goon and marched off for another month's solitary confinement.

In early summer 1943 Fancy was on the move again, this time to Heydekrug, a camp in East Prussia near the Lithuanian border. The POWs felt they were miles away from civilization, and indeed it would be difficult to imagine a more desolate spot. The camp was built on sand and had been opened in early June 1943, and was the main camp for Air Force NCOs. Nearly all the NCOs from the Central Compound at Sagan arrived in batches of 200 and Fancy was amongst the first. However, his introduction to the camp was delayed since his first three weeks were spent in the cooler – a punishment for jumping from a train.

By the summer of 1943, escape committees in all prison camps had become increasingly effective and some of the long-serving POWs had become highly skilled. For some, apart from their brief period as aircrew, surviving prison, goon-baiting and escape were the only skills they possessed. They had also adjusted to the unique living environment and they were better able to cope with the rigours of prison life. Fancy was not only one of the longest-serving POWs, but one of the most experienced in the tunnelling business. Having been given the exalted title of "the Mole" by his captors he was appointed to lead the digging of a tunnel.

This was a most sophisticated attempt and incorporated many of the features that were employed during the famous Great Escape at Sagan the following year. Fancy describes this escape attempt in detail in this book. Suffice to say, a number of men got away, including Fancy who had a series of amazing adventures during his two weeks of freedom. After stealing a boat, he and his companion had sailed 30 miles towards Sweden, when they were spotted and soon arrested. Fancy added another twenty-eight days of solitary to his ever-increasing tally.

A feature of his time at large was the bravery and support he received from some of the local population. One can only have the greatest admiration for these gallant "helpers" in the occupied territories, who gave their support despite knowing that they would pay the ultimate price if they were discovered.

———◆———

The escaping scene took a dramatic turn following the mass escape from *Stalag Luft III* on the night of 24 March 1944. The escape of 76 men from a 336-foot tunnel caused a huge country-wide manhunt that involved many thousands of soldiers, diverted from operational areas. There was also a series of brutal repercussions, the most dastardly being Hitler's order to execute 50 of the recaptured airmen. Furthermore, the Führer made it clear that any future escape attempts would be treated with the utmost severity. The Senior British Officers in the numerous POW camps were briefed accordingly and, with the tide turning in favour of the Allies, they ordered a cessation in escape activities.

The tunnels at Heydekrug and Sagan encapsulated an amazing array of talent, skill, ingenuity and sheer bloody-mindedness, not to mention courage. We can only marvel at their achievements, sadly at such a great loss.

———◆———

The "Hitler Order" and the Allied invasion of France changed the attitude of most prisoners towards escape but, despite the risks, John Fancy and his escape-minded colleagues decided to start another tunnel. Heydekrug was the furthest eastern camp and a long way from western armies so Fancy's plan was to escape to the east and link up with the Russians. However, with the advance of the Soviet armies the Germans decided to evacuate the camp and in July the prisoners were ordered to get ready to leave. Fancy quickly converted his tunnel into a large chamber, which was completed two days before the order to evacuate the camp was given.

A number of prisoners were sealed into the chamber the night before the evacuation and once they were confident that the camp had been evacuated they broke free. After numerous adventures, and having covered 50 miles, they were captured. It soon became apparent that they were in the hands of one of Hitler's extermination squads, and they were only spared following the intervention of a staff officer. Nevertheless, this proved to be a temporary reprieve and over the next few days, Fancy and his fellow escapers faced three mock executions by firing squad. After more days in solitary confinement they began a rail journey in cattle trucks, travelling west. An attempt to slip away resulted in more time in the cooler but they were soon herded back onto cattle trucks and taken to the POW camp at Fallingbostel.

Conditions were harsh in all German POW camps but Fallingbostel was recognised as one of the worst. With the marches arriving from the east, the conditions in the increasingly overcrowded camp became desperate. The onset of winter merely increased the scale of the prisoners' depravation and ordeal. With the collapse of the camp command, Fancy once again turned his mind to escape but the risks of being loose in a chaotic situation with ill-disciplined German diehards roaming the countryside were too great. Finally, on the morning of 19 April 1945 British troops rolled into the camp and Fancy's ordeal was over.

———◆———

Five years after taking off on a three-hour sortie, John Fancy finally arrived back in England. His health had suffered considerably during his time as a POW and he spent three months in RAF hospitals recovering before he was invalided from the service in August 1945 as a warrant officer. Whilst in hospital in Lancashire he met his five-year old daughter for the first time. For his conduct as a POW and his persistent attempts to escape, he was mentioned in dispatches.

Fancy returned to the Yorkshire Wolds and established a market garden near Driffield and three greengrocers in Scarborough. A countryman and good at sports, particularly tennis, he was also a keen artist and he took great pride in his gardens. After the death of his wife he moved to Slapton in South Devon to be near his daughter. He was a great favourite in the village and had his own seat at the bar in the two local pubs.

In 1992, John Fancy was invited to a celebration for the 75th Anniversary of the Finnish Air Force, held in London, when the Finnish Ambassador presented him with the Winter War Medal.

John Fancy, a remarkable and gallant man, died on 16 September 2008, aged 95.

———◆———

Tunnelling to Freedom was first published by Panther Books in 1957 and became an instant bestseller. The text is reproduced here in full exactly as it appeared in the original edition, except for the standardisation of spellings and punctuation.

An amazing and compelling story, it is a great tribute to the determination, courage and sense of duty of John Fancy and his fellow kriegies. He would be the first to admit that he was just one of many and his book also honours the thousands of servicemen who for much of the war could only contribute to the Allied effort by causing the Germans as much trouble as possible.

AUTHOR'S PREFACE

In my efforts to escape from German P.O.W. camps over a period of almost five years, during which I sampled many different compounds throughout Germany, Poland, and East Prussia, I made sixteen separate attempts: either by tunnelling; cutting my way through masses of barbed wire; climbing over the wire; from outside working parties; or from moving trains. My escape activities landed me in the cooler for a total of thirty-four weeks – one-eighth of my total imprisonment.

I tramped Germany, East Prussia, Lithuania, and Latvia, plodded forty miles over the frozen Baltic sea, and rowed a small boat for thirty-five miles over the same sea, and on one occasion tramped through several miles of horrible bogland in pitch darkness. My captures landed me in several of the worst type of civil prisons, from one of which I escaped for a short while. Once I was put in a Russian saboteur prison after being rescued from the extermination squad which had captured me. From this prison, while waiting for an escort, I was led out before a firing squad on three successive days.

To find my way I depended almost exclusively upon a small pocket compass and a hand-made map. I once received direction from an unwitting German soldier. Most of my food I begged from rich and poor of the local inhabitants, and met many extraordinary characters. At one farmhouse I landed just in time to hear the B.B.C. news broadcast on a forbidden radio. The only thing I stole was a boat, and the only damage I did was to break open a shed to steal the boat.

The story reveals the fortitude of R.A.F. P.O.W.s in German hands and embraces a host of faithful P.O.W. friends without whose help these adventures could not have been attempted; many whose names I have forgotten will recognise themselves, and their help, as they read from one event to another. My special partners in many crimes were: Bill Street, Jock Sterling, Neil Prendergast, Paddy Flynn, Harry Leggett, and George Grimston, not forgetting the untiring efforts of the escape committee.

I must thank the many suffering Lithuanians, and Latvians who, in great danger and at grave risk to themselves, spontaneously gave to me a small share of their meagre food supplies to help me on my way. Without this I must have died on the open road. It is only fitting to remember and thank the Red Cross for the many parcels that maintained life and hope in many thousands of P.O.W.s in enemy hands.

I have to thank my sister, Mrs. Howes, for the long days and nights she has sat at her typewriter unravelling my writing to produce the story in readable typescript and to my wife for her long-suffering patience, during the many hours of my struggle to write the story.

While as an amateur tunneller – I must have tunnelled in all one thousand feet with an all-steel table knife – I gained the service nickname of "the Mole", I cannot make the least claim to being a writer. In fact, for ten years I had struggled to put my story into readable form and never got very far, until at last by a chance introduction I met Mr. C. Le-B. Allbeury, a writer and fellow-citizen of Scarborough, who freely relieved me of my burden. Without his sound advice, patient criticisms, and readily given help, the task would never have been completed. The result is solely due to his help.

Finally, I trust all my old P.O.W. friends will read the story, which is as much theirs as mine, and I wish them, each and every one – in P.O.W. terms – a full set of bed boards, a well-packed straw mattress, and one Red Cross parcel every week for the remainder of their lives.

JOHN FANCY

CHAPTER ONE

If anyone had told me in the days when I flew model aeroplanes in the fields around my home that one day I should be fighting for my life as co-pilot and navigator in a real warplane while it bucked and kicked like a wild west bronco as though determined on its own destruction, I should have thought they had been reading one of Jules Verne's futuristic conceptions. Yet truth is, indeed, stranger than fiction, for that is exactly what happened.

Like many young men of my age I joined the Royal Air Force during its 1935 expansion; partly for the change of scene, and partly for the excitement I hoped it would provide, but I was doomed to disappointment. I became a member of the ground staff and it was only by pestering the authorities that I was at last recommended for a course of flying training in 1938. When war broke out the following year I was well on in my training for night bombing, but was suddenly switched to training needed for day bombing. In November 1939 I was posted to 110 Squadron at Wittisham in Suffolk and took part in many operations, mostly routine, although once I was one of the navigators flying a squadron of Blenheims to Finland. I was transferred to Lossiemouth for a while in the spring of 1940, and had my share of excitement over Norway. I had just started some leave on May 10, 1940, when I was hurriedly recalled by telegram to Wittisham.

I arrived at Stowmarket soon after midnight to find a shuttle service of trucks operating to pick up the chaps and return them to the 'drome, where I landed amid an air of suppressed excitement. We were all on permanent standby and already one party had been out on a raid over the Dutch frontier just as the Germans were breaking through.

After an early breakfast on the 11th we were away to bomb the beaches of Holland where transport planes were unloading enemy troops by the thousands; the beaches were thickly littered with troops, supplies, and transport planes, an ideal target I thought. This is where we show the swine what we think of their bombing of defenceless neutral cities. And didn't we paste them! Our sticks of bombs devastated whole areas, yet they still went on unloading transports of men and materials, while we returned for a hurried meal and another load of trouble for the ant-like swarms of Germans below.

Up to now, except for sporadic rifle fire, we'd had it all our own way, but Jerry was quick to react with his mobile flak. He gave us a warmer and unexpected reception on this trip, and we received quite a peppering – losing two planes. In the evening, mess conversation took on a sober tone; Jerry had broken through into Holland and Belgium on little more than an ultimatum, 108 Squadron had lost several planes, and most other Blenheim Squadrons in the command had lost two or more; it was a time for sober reflection. But authority did not reflect for long; on the 12th we were again on our way to the beaches to give them another pounding and to receive one ourselves. We met a solid wall of bullets and flak; they had lost no time strengthening their defences – on this trip we lost another plane.

The Germans had now occupied several Dutch airfields and we could expect fighter interference as well as ground defence, and my afternoon trip of the same day was switched to Amsterdam Airport. Here, they threw everything they had at us; it was like flying through a gigantic firework display while the plane was buffeted like a sheet of paper in a whirlwind. And although we unloaded right over the target, I couldn't see how we could make a safe return – we lost two more planes and the rest of us were punctured with holes like riddles.

On the way home, I remarked to Duggie,

"I don't see how we can keep up this pace for much longer."

"If and when it's got our number on it, that's ours!" he replied.

With each new day, fresh crews were flying in replacement planes, and the mess became full of strange faces. Far too many of the old familiars were missing for my comfort of mind. My room-mate Paddy Martin was still with us; Grim Parker, Taffy Evans, Fernley, and Lamb just about made the total of the old originals.

On the 13th, bless my luck, I was on rest, so I spent the morning writing letters, and the afternoon playing tennis with Fernley. 108 Squadron raided the Maastricht Bridge on the Dutch-Belgian frontier, a hellish spot – from which one half of the squadron failed to return.

Dawn of the 14th ushered in a beautiful day, not a cloud to be seen, and after breakfast we wandered over to the crew room to learn our fate for the day. We were to bust the bridges at Sedan. Apparently the Germans were bypassing the Maginot line and pouring round the Northern end into France. We were due out after lunch; our task to disrupt their lines of communication. We stayed on in the crew room working out courses and discussing general tactics, then lounged outside enjoying the sunshine.

"Isn't it peaceful here, Bill?" I ruminated aloud.

"It's hard to believe there's a war over there in full cry, and some poor bastard is probably going through hell."

"You're right ... and that poor bastard might be one of us in a few hours' time," replied Bill.

"Let's think of strawberries and cream, or blondes and fast cars, or just plain beer," I suggested cheerfully, without feeling too cheerful myself. "Why not buy another old car? We can always fiddle a drop of black-market petrol. Then we won't have to rush around to catch the truck back from Ipswich when Paddy goes a-courting in his flying bedstead." But Bill wasn't a bit interested, so we ambled over for lunch.

Take-off was at one-thirty p.m. and at one-fifteen we were ferried over to dispersal, tested the engines for starting, stowed our gear, and sat in our plane waiting for the Squadron Leader to taxi out. Punctually at one-thirty we taxied out in our turn and joined formation with our leader over the airfield. Then we set course for a point on the French coast, where we expected to rendezvous with a fighter escort for the overland flight.

As we climbed to six thousand feet I thought I had never before flown on such a beautiful day. There wasn't a cloud to be seen, visibility was perfect. The sort of flying weather for a honeymoon, but hardly my choice for an inland bombing mission.

I had received a letter from my wife that morning informing me I was to become a father, so I was feeling quite elated with the idea as I sat beside Duggie.

I caught a final glimpse of England as the North Foreland shyly disappeared under our starboard wing and we nosed out across the Channel for the Continent. In a matter of minutes the low coastline of northern France came into view and we crossed at a point northeast of Dunkirk. I searched the skies around but no trace of the promised fighter escort could be seen. I was just thinking they might be engaged somewhere else on their way over when the Commander's voice came over the 'phone, "No point in hanging around, chaps, we'll press on; good hunting!"

Our course took us along the Franco-Belgian frontier and, knowing the Germans were well into the Belgian interior, I quite expected we should meet some opposition before reaching our target – we did, as I've good reasons to remember. We were approaching Valenciennes when the sky changed to a positive forest of white puffs from exploding flak, and some other poor devils were passing through it, possibly a French flight or even our escort in a spot of trouble.

We received orders for the formation to detour south and avoid the area. After fifteen minutes' flying we still hadn't quite escaped and were flying over a wooded patch north of Mezières when the Germans opened up on the formation. We were now only five minutes from the target when the Squadron Commander gave orders to break formation and attack in flights.

The flak was getting very heavy and they were getting our range and height with disconcerting accuracy. Duggie broke away and began weaving about to shake them off, but we received a buffeting I'll never forget before we finally got clear.

"Not so good, eh, Duggie?" I murmured. "The Jerries must have their skates on; our latest report didn't place them anywhere near this area. We'd better look out at Sedan, they may already be there waiting to welcome us."

"I'll run in from the south. We'll have a looksee and you can spot the bridges. Pick out the best one!" said Duggie.

By this time Sedan came into view five miles away on our left, and looking down as we crossed the roads I could see thousands of people streaming away south and east. "What do you make of it, Duggie?" I asked. "Looks like an evacuation. I wonder if Jerry has arrived?"

"Don't know," mumbled Dug. "But I'll soon find out. Bill! Keep your eyes peeled aloft, we're going in."

Duggie turned North over the town and I laid flat down in the nose to get a better view of the bridges. The area seemed strangely empty, no traffic about and no flak coming up. Then I spotted the bridges and pointed out the main one to Duggie. "That's the one, looks like we've beaten 'em to it. Round we go."

Duggie banked round on a close circuit to come in on the bombing run, when a yell from Bill: "Look out to port!" made us both jump. Duggie heaved back on the stick and a flight of three Blenheims shot past right under our nose.

"Phew! That was a near squeak," he gasped as he levelled out.

I could see our numbers two and three still sticking to us like a couple of lurchers so I made contact with them.

"We are now going in to bomb. We will cross the bridge at a narrow angle, so drop your bombs in a stick when the bridge is in your sights. Don't forget we're at six thousand feet."

We are turning in now and I have my eyes glued to the bomb-sight, a couple of corrections to Duggie, "Left … Left … Steady … hold her there." The bridge now appears to be gliding along my bomb-sight drift-bars as it steadily reaches the cross-wire, my aiming line, I press the bomb release, one, two, three, four.

"Bombs away," I shouted, confident of a hit.

They glided down, then, smack; the first hit the water about twenty yards from the bridge, the second right alongside, the third was a peach, right plumb on the bridge almost at midstream, and the fourth twenty yards away on the opposite side.

It was like practising on a bomb range. I turned and watched the other results. Our number two landed a direct hit with his first bomb, and the other three closely overshot the bridge. Number three crept progressively nearer with his first three bombs and his fourth landed right in the middle of the road where the bridge joined the bank. It was a highly satisfactory result, especially as we had all shared in the demolition of the bridge. I voiced Duggie's thanks over the 'phone and hoped our efforts would cause the enemy a considerable hold-up.

I was just in the act of setting course for home, when glancing below I saw a long straight road, just north of Sedan, running through thickly wooded country, and travelling along it towards the town was a long line of troop-carrying vehicles. Turning excitedly to Duggie, I shouted, "Look down there, Dug. Jerry troops."

Duggie looked and immediately dived. "My kingdom for some bombs," he cried. They were a perfect target for a shoot-up.

At three thousand feet he opened fire with the front guns raking right along the column, then at five hundred feet he levelled out and we shot our way past them while Bill joined in over the side with his turret guns. We watched the Jerries diving for cover in all directions as several of the trucks were blazing merrily. I thought of the good pals I'd lost and tasted the sweetness of vengeance. It was good while it lasted and we turned away feeling like little dogs with several tails.

Our spot of ground strafing had carried us several miles from

Sedan and I was searching for a good landmark from which to set a new course when several gun flashes became visible from a clearing below; simultaneously with my discovery there occurred a terrific crash beside me, followed by a searing pain down my right leg. The nose of the plane had virtually disappeared, and the cockpit was filled with acrid smoke.

Duggie and I were choking and half blind; the plane lurched and swayed violently and we were tossed about like dice in a cup before the throw. I couldn't see a thing before me, but I managed to grope my way back to where Duggie was grimly fighting to keep the plane, now a bucking bronco, under control.

We had received a direct hit and the blast had removed my helmet together with earphones and goggles, but I heard Duggie shout, "It's no good, chaps, I can't do a thing."

The hatch, I must get the hatch open! I scrambled up and wrenched it open; it cleared the smoke from the cockpit.

And then I knew we were doomed.

Black smoke was pouring from both engines and the wings were blazing furiously. We must get out, the heat was unbearable, anything was better than this, we would be cooked alive! But what use was a parachute now? We were at only eight hundred feet when it happened, since when the ground had been racing up to meet us while she dived out of control – a crash was inevitable!

I grabbed my mouthpiece, as there was no other means of contacting Bill in his turret, and yelled, "Bill, Bill, brace yourself, we're going to crash any second." Duggie's face was as of a soul in torment as he grimly struggled to haul the plane back to obedience. He hadn't seemed to realise that both engines were useless, and it was only at that moment that realisation forced itself upon me. There was nothing we could do. From the moment the shell struck us to this fearful moment of realisation only seconds in time had passed. I just had time to think "I'll never see my little baby now. Why didn't I write that letter this morning?" when the burning plane struck the top of a tree a glancing blow and pivoting round to the opposite direction, levelled out to hit the deck with a horrible crunch.

It was a moment to defy detailed description or even recollection. All I remember was the noise of breaking metal and woodwork and the fearful heat when the flames broke with a new ferocity as the plane struck the earth; lurched, rolled, and bounced, ploughing a great furrow for a further thirty to fifty yards. I was thrown about inside the fuselage like a shuttlecock and injured myself with every throw against some broken part of the plane, until at last, she came to rest leaving a trail of wreckage behind her – and then what seemed a terrifying silence.

A silence one could feel, an almost deathly silence that compelled me to hold my breath in case the sound of my breathing intruded to break the spell of my entry into a new and unknown world.

The exploding ammunition and the roaring flames of the burning wings and petrol brought me to my senses. I felt as though every bone in my body were broken. I staggered to my feet and was scrambling through the hatch when I suddenly realised Duggie wasn't following me. I turned to see what was wrong and found him struggling to free one foot that was jammed behind the rudder bar. He was in intense agony and the horrible thought passed through my mind that he would be burned alive.

I hung head downwards through the hatch and tried to unfasten his boot-straps. I just couldn't. Then, God only knows how, but somehow, I got his foot out and left his boot behind.

We then turned to look for Bill, we had heard no sound from him, horrible thoughts passed through my mind. What would I find? I scrambled on to the fuselage almost unaware of my own burns and injuries, and tried to kick my way through his entry hatch, but it wouldn't budge. Surely there was some way in? We couldn't possibly just leave him to burn whether he was dead or alive.

Duggie shouted that the tail unit had broken away, carrying with it a large portion of the fuselage. It was only a small gap and Duggie was too big to crawl through. There was no time to lose, and the heat was now almost unbearable; the tanks might explode at any moment, so I wriggled my thin body inside and found Bill, more dead than alive from the fumes of the burning batteries, with his feet entangled in the rudder control cables. I coughed and spluttered with the fumes, and my eyes streamed with water, but I got him free and struggled back with him. Then with Duggie's help I dragged him feet first through the hole.

We carried him a good distance clear of the plane, and only just in time. We had no sooner laid him down than the tanks blew up with a roar like a bursting bomb. Pieces of wreckage flew in all directions and ignited petrol spewed around the area and enveloped the plane in a shroud of fire. We dragged Bill to a place of safety away from the blazing inferno and waited for him to revive in the fresh air. He was just beginning to realise the situation when we were alarmed by loud shouts.

Soon we were surrounded by enemy troops menacingly pointing their fixed bayonets, poking at us with automatic rifles and yelling their heads off for us to put up our hands. We were almost beyond taking notice of their threats, but we made a token effort of surrender by half raising our hands.

This turn of events was not at all to my liking, but I knew we had no chance of escape even if the troops hadn't turned up. So we accompanied them to a large house two hundred yards away among some trees, where we did a check up on our injuries. Duggie had one side of his face burnt and a sore ankle; Bill, apart from being almost asphyxiated, hadn't a scratch, and I had numerous shrapnel wounds down my right leg and odd pieces of aircraft here and there. Both my hands were rather burned and rapidly becoming the size of footballs, and most of my hair had been singed from my head. But as cause for congratulations, we hadn't a broken bone among us.

Duggie and I looked like a couple of nigger minstrels, our faces were so black from the smoke that blew into the noseless cockpit from the burning engines. Duggie was calling himself all the names under the sun for getting us into this mess, and every few minutes breaking out with renewed apologies. I had to keep telling him not to be such a clot as we were all in the same mess, and still very much alive. Bill couldn't suppress an occasional laugh, due more to nerves than amusement. I was feeling pretty sick now the excitement and action had abated, and my leg had gone quite numb so that I was obliged to sit down, guards or no guards.

The guards then searched us for hidden arms, and offered us a drink of water for which I was most grateful owing to my raging thirst. Their offer of water and my thanks seemed to bring about a considerable lessening of tension between captors and captives and, although we had no common language between us, we managed to learn we had crashed close by a forward wireless unit with the house as headquarters.

Then a young officer arrived and addressed us in broken English, obviously pleased to try it out and impress the young guards. He began very high-handedly: "For you the war is over" then he went on to explain we wouldn't be prisoners for long, in three weeks they would be in England and then three weeks afterwards the war would be over and we could go home. He was quite serious in all this and treated our derisive laughter as a form of hysteria due to shock following the crash.

Meanwhile the guards kept a close eye on us, fearful lest we made a bolt for liberty, but I was in no condition for bolting and preferred to sit leaning against the wall to rest my aching body and leg.

An hour and a half had passed since we were shot down and I began to feel hungry, but there was no sign of food forthcoming. I could have done justice to a few bars of the chocolate we had left behind in the plane.

Both Duggie and I still had our watches and despite our buffeting these were still going, and for some reason, no doubt nerve reaction, we kept looking at them; goodness knows why, there was no train to catch!

CHAPTER TWO

At five-thirty p.m. a couple of trucks rolled up in a cloud of dust and we climbed aboard; Duggie with two guards in one, and Bill and I with two guards in the other. We set off for heaven knows where, bumping along rough country lanes to the curious stares of a passing troop of riflemen mounted on bicycles, and pulling aside to allow columns of motorised troops to pass who yelled all kinds of unintelligible remarks to our guards, of which we understood only "Englander."

As we passed through several deserted villages I thought the trip would never end until, at last, we drove into a farmyard and were directed into a large barn. It was still daylight outside but as soon as the doors were closed the place was pitch dark, and we found it full of Frenchmen sprawled everywhere. No portion had been allocated to my party so we just stumbled over the sleeping bodies and scrambled in as best we could.

Our arrival caused a general commotion as we stumbled among the Frenchmen lying there. We couldn't see an inch before us and might have gone treading on sleeping bodies all night only we heard voices speaking English. Bill shouted, "Who the hell are you blokes?" and received the reply, "Don't be so bloody curious, come over here. We won't eat you."

We made our way over the grumbling Frenchies and located a

couple of English types: they were Sergeant Winkler, pilot of a Fairey Battle, and Sergeant Smally, his observer. They made room for us and we sat down to exchange news. They had been shot down during a flight from a French base, and the Frenchmen around us were captured in the Maginot Line. What they said to emphasise *in* is quite unprintable! We settled down hoping to sleep.

For me, it was a night of pain and thirst. There was nothing to relieve my pain, but I did get a delicious drink of wine from a fatherly Frenchman's water bottle. I spent the night full of anxiety for my wife, wondering how soon the authorities would inform her I was alive. It is surprising how a young man, free to come and go at liberty among his own people, develops ideas of what he would do or wouldn't do should he fall into enemy hands! I was no different to any others. I was full of beans and big ideas. They wouldn't do this to me!

But here I am, in enemy hands; wounded, burnt, in pain, hungry, thirsty, bundled about like a bag of firewood, thrown into a dark shed among men I know nothing about, wondering what is to happen next. I feel revealed to myself for the first time, and though not dispirited, I am a very chastened mortal, and would give anything to be waiting in a bus queue in the pouring rain somewhere near my home.

When dawn broke and thin strips of daylight shone through the cracks of the door, I was able to assess my surroundings better. Our plight seemed more hopeless than ever.

It was three-thirty p.m. the previous day when we hit the decks and lost our liberty; it was now six-thirty a.m. and nothing had been done for us in the way of food, drink, a wash, bedding, or first-aid dressings for our damaged bodies; very different to our treatment of enemy prisoners. The barn measured roughly fifty feet by twenty feet and contained two hundred men; all Frenchmen except we five British, and all unwashed, unshaved, and as ragged as highway tramps.

They opened the doors at eight o'clock and beckoned Duggie and I outside. I had the utmost difficulty in standing upright and my two faithful friends had to help me along. There was an ambulance waiting in the yard, and we were allowed to wash at the handpump with only our handkerchiefs to dry on before Duggie and I scrambled inside. Then, with a cheery wave to Bill and our two new pals, the ambulance moved off. We saw no more of Bill for almost four months.

The journey lasted twenty minutes, about eight miles. The last two were along a drive through a thick wood, and came to a halt before a large country house, which we later discovered was a field dressing station.

Here they dressed our burns, and painted my leg with something that burned me horribly; I could have yelled for the few minutes it lasted. But I must say the doctor was very kind and gentle.

After this treatment we sat on the front steps gloating over the continual stream of casualties passing in and out, for the Germans were getting a battering somewhere near at hand. I remarked to Duggie, "If I go much longer without eating I shall pass out."

We sat there from nine to eleven a.m., when an orderly brought each of us a plate of soup; brownish looking stuff with a smell I can only describe as of unwashed old socks, but it was something to fill the aching void so we wolfed it down. Later on I came to know this Wehrmacht Suppe all too well and I shunned it whenever possible; for tummy rumblings and rude noises it leaves green peas and ginger cake standing at the post.

The soup finished, we were anxiously waiting for the first course, when we were bundled into our ambulance. Our one guard who had been in close attendance, locked us in and climbed up beside the driver. We naturally thought of being returned to Bill, but we travelled northwards instead.

Poor old Duggie was still lashing himself at intervals for having got us into this pickle and nothing I said could comfort him; it made things worse when he realised we were leaving Bill behind. He was already getting escape ideas and suggested busting a window and bolting. I urged him to have a go if he felt like it but to leave me behind, as I'd only be a serious burden to him.

13

It was a hideous journey, as we stopped every few hundred yards to allow troop convoys to pass on the narrow roads; it lasted until late evening. There were no signposts on the narrow by-ways but I had a feeling we were travelling through Belgium. Alas for Duggie's chance of escape, the guard kept peeping through the shutter between driving cab and ambulance which had never once been closed, to assure himself of our continued presence.

Finally, after seven o'clock, we drove into Neuchâteau and were led into a schoolroom where a bed of straw had been laid on the floor around the walls, and we joined eight other wounded prisoners – two French, three Dutch, and three Belgians – we two English made up quite a cosmopolitan party. The guards, and an interpreter, with an N.C.O. in charge, occupied an adjoining room.

The interpreter was a most benevolent-looking, bumptious, imposing, self-important, aged gentleman, and every one of these adjectives is necessary to describe him; in fact, he could never be described in words. He had an air that left no doubt in one's mind that he was the pivotal point in the German war machine, and in some respects, not without justification, because if his French and Dutch were as good as his English, which I never doubted, then he was an extraordinary person.

"You English airmen, yes?" he began. We replied that we were, then, "What are your names? ... What are your numbers? ... What is your unit? ... Where were you flying from? ... What were you doing when you were shot down?" and a lot more similar questions.

We gave our names and numbers, but refused to answer any further questions. He very politely informed us, "You are not being very helpful... It is stupid of you not to tell me these things ... How can I let your people know that you are safe if you do not tell me?"

To which I replied wearily, "They'll find out."

Most interpreters I met later would have expressed their annoyance in some petty form of violence, but this nice important old gent just stamped away leaving us in peace. Our evening meal consisted of two rock-hard biscuits each, like the old fashioned three by two inch Spratt's dog biscuit, with a scraping of jam and a mug of German tea, which beggars description and for which I never acquired a taste.

It was the first solid food I'd tasted since my bacon and eggs before taking off thirty-two hours earlier. It would keep me going a while longer. I was dog-tired from loss of sleep and blood, to say nothing of the presence of numerous pieces of shrapnel and bits of aeroplane still in my legs. My wounds, which were still bleeding and kept sticking to my trouser-leg, were a continual source of discomfort. I sank gratefully back on the straw without covering, gave Duggie a weary "Good night" and composed myself for sleep.

Except for the sudden jolts of pain each time I moved my leg during sleep, and the mutterings and groanings of my wounded room-mates, I passed a fair night and felt a little better next morning, but we were a sorry bunch indeed. At daylight, a new batch of wounded prisoners arrived bringing our total to twenty. Then breakfast came, a wedge of black bread thinly covered with margarine, and more of the vile tea – how I hated the muck.

We could hardly complain at the poor fare and accommodation. Perhaps if we'd warned Hitler of our intended visit he would have reserved the best hotel in Berlin. Instead, we were uninvited guests, whose boisterous arrival had not only knocked the place about some-what, but who had most inconveniently arrived at the moment he was engaged in a militarised lawsuit with all his neighbours, and worse still, gate-crashed the country without visas, or even an apology.

I was already becoming annoyed at this shabby treatment, and determined to express my disapproval by planning to return home at the first convenient opportunity. I realised the uselessness of applying for passports and crowns for convoy in the usual way and decided to side-step this formality and find other means, even if it meant tunnelling half-way across Europe and opening the first cross-Channel tunnel.

This is slightly wide of my actual achievements, nevertheless, they were formidable.

For the moment, this project would have to wait until I could get my right leg and both hands into action again, and build up my strength, though how to manage this on my present diet I failed to see.

Throughout the morning we discussed recent events and the possibilities for the future with one of our Dutch room-mates who could speak a little English, to the accompaniment of noisy German planes overhead. We learnt of the rapid, non-stop German advance through Holland and Belgium, and of the fearful atrocities perpetrated by German paratroops on the unarmed helpless Dutch civilians.

The immediate outlook was certainly pretty grim. At noon we were ordered into the school yard, given a bowl of soup from a field-kitchen, issued with one blanket per man, loaded into trucks, and driven to the station where we were immediately transferred to a covered cattle-truck and locked in.

The exertion of climbing into and out of the transport from the school to station, and again into the cattle-truck, had tested my strength to breaking point, and unless I could obtain medical attention very soon I was going to be in bad shape. Already my leg was ninety per cent useless and smelled so that I feared it would become gangrenous. I could no longer use it, and with my thickly bandaged hands it was most difficult to help myself. It was rather like trying to eat, drink, dress, and undress, wearing a pair of boxing gloves; in fact, Duggie had to assist me in every possible way.

After an hour's delay the truck was hitched up to a passenger train and we started on our way. All we could see outside through the cowled slits in the ventilators was the side of the track, so that we had no idea of our destination, nor in which direction we were travelling.

There were frequent and prolonged halts when we could hear the passengers banging the doors as they mounted or left the train, and at six in the evening we halted at a large station.

Here we were counted and led to the end of the platform behind a workman's shed which did service as a latrine – you may imagine my difficulties, if not my embarrassment. We were a sorry sight as we helped each other along the platform to the canteen to receive our evening meal of a thick slice of black bread, a piece of liver sausage, and a mug of *ersatz* coffee instead of the hateful tea.

There were so many troops and civilians speaking German that I concluded we must be in Germany. Although they stared at us out of curiosity they made no demonstration of ill-will. I've no doubt we did look a disreputable crowd, all unshaven, in torn and dirty rags, fed up and far from home, bandaged and limping.

I searched around for the name of the station but all evidence had been removed. Duggie complained at the lack of sanitary arrangements and they stuck an old tin in the corner of the truck for our relief during the night and then locked us in again.

On we went into the unknown and soon the conversation ceased. Everyone lay silently seeking a comfortable position on the thin layer of straw in the hope of a night's sleep. Listening to the intermittent clack, clack, of the wheels over the rail points, I judged we were travelling at no more than a leisured crawl, and my thoughts again wandered to my wife, hoping she had been told of my safety and would make the best of it for our unborn baby's sake.

Then I thought of my pals at the squadron and wondered how many more of them had become casualties.

Then I suddenly remembered, that just before the shell hit us, Bill had shouted over the intercom that our number three had been hit by flak, and would have crashed within a mile of us. They were a new crew, had arrived the day before our raid, and I didn't even know their names.

Poor devils! Their first trip and it had to end like that! That meant only one of my flight returned – returned *if* he had dodged the flak and fighters on the long trip home. A thing no lone bomber could ever hope to achieve. My thoughts rambled far and wide until I must have fallen into the sleep of exhaustion.

The next thing I knew, the train had halted at a large and noisy station. It was broad daylight and my watch showed that it was eight o'clock. I stirred cautiously, but oh! every movement was an agony. I felt less tired but terribly hungry and my tongue was like a piece of emery paper.

There was a rattle of bolts, and the door opened to reveal a young German N.C.O. complete with briefcase and revolver holster, reading from a sheet of paper.

He poked his head inside and called, "Mr. Wright and Mr. Fancy. Will you come please!" We clambered out with the aid of the young German and he seemed such a polite young man I ventured to ask him where we were. He replied: "This is Cologne. You are coming with me to hospital at Frankfurt-on-Main."

This was welcome news, and I cheered up enough to thank him and smile at Duggie. With my arm round Dug's shoulder we followed him down a subway and on to another platform, and after a large bowl of the inevitable soup we embarked on a long Pullman train for the run down the beautiful Rhine Valley. To sit back in the luxuriously upholstered seat and watch the scenery was the nearest approach to any degree of civilised comfort I had experienced since leaving Wattisham – Wattisham! How I wished myself there at that moment.

With the warm soup inside me I felt in better shape to appreciate the glorious countryside around me, and to face up to the future.

Our interpreter was again of the talkative type, and I must admit, very civil; he spoke excellent English. He informed us there was a prison camp not far from Frankfurt called "Dulag Luft", to which all air force prisoners were taken when first captured. Here they received clothes, toilet articles, and extra food provided by the Red Cross, before being sent to other permanent camps. I didn't like the word "permanent", but he painted such a glowing picture of Dulag Luft, the luxury holiday-camp, I could hardly wait to get there.

We passed through Bonn into the Rhine Valley of the tourists' posters while the interpreter pointed out places of interest; the ancient castles perched on the hilltops and the terraced vineyards running down the hillsides to the river's bank made the scenery most beautiful and eased the tumult in my brain.

At twelve-thirty we pulled into Coblenz and here the interpreter obtained for us Frankfurter sandwiches and coffee, another real treat.

Then on to Mayence through ever-changing, rugged scenery where we crossed the Rhine and headed eastward along the south bank of the Main, and arrived at Frankfurt-on-Main at six-thirty in the evening. The interpreter 'phoned from the station and in half an hour a truck arrived and, after a seven-mile drive, we arrived at the hospital of the Convent of an Order the name of which I have forgotten – more to my shame!

CHAPTER THREE

The sister who received us, though she spoke no word of English, showed us every sign of sympathy and kindness. I was assisted up some stairs and conducted into a small room containing bed, chair, locker, and a small table. The Sister then led me across the corridor to a bathroom, produced razor, soap, and towel, and pointed to my beard; then, realising my helplessness owing to my bandaged hands, she threw up her hands and laughed merrily.

I shall always believe her laugh was an attempt to draw from me a smile. She removed some of the bandages to free my fingers and left me to get on with the job. It was a painful business removing my four days' growth, and by the time I had finished she returned with a suit of pyjamas.

Motioning me to undress, she filled the bath with water and helped me to scramble over the side. Then she scrubbed me from head to toe until I glowed pink like a schoolboy. I felt I was back in the hands of my own mother; she was so gentle and tender as she indicated I was not to get my hands wet. She carefully washed my injured leg and chest, never once dragging on the pieces of metal now visible in the flesh. What wonderful women they are!

I looked such a gory mess before I entered the bath, and now I was as clean and fresh as a small child. It was the first chance I'd had to examine my wounds; the knee seemed worst, it had completely seized up. I felt a new man after I'd donned my pyjamas and crept between lovely cool sheets.

Still smiling cheerily, my ministering angel returned with a tray containing two covered dishes, a plate, knife, fork, and spoon. She removed the covers with a flourish like a magician displaying his favourite trick; and the smell! It was like nothing in this world. One dish contained asparagus in white sauce, the other, fried meat balls and mashed potatoes covered with a delicious gravy. The memory of that first meal lingered on for many a long day.

I was lying back thinking all was well in the world at last and wondering about Duggie, when a doctor came. He gave me a thorough examination, but when he tried my knee I couldn't suppress a yell. I gathered from his expression he was most apologetic, and I smiled my forgiveness. He removed the sticky mess from my hands most skilfully, redressed them, put a dressing on my chest punctures indicating they would prevent the sheet dragging on the pieces of metal, and swathed my leg in loose gauze and bandages. Then he motioned me to lie down and sleep.

I slept like a log throughout the night, and at seven-thirty next morning was awakened by another Sister who gave me tea – the real thing – porridge, and white bread and jam. Then followed a wash, and I was told to dress in hospital trousers, jacket and greatcoat, assisted by an orderly.

At nine o'clock I was assisted downstairs and into a waiting car, and driven to a general hospital at Frankfurt.

After waiting an hour my leg and chest were X-rayed and I set off on a shopping expedition with my attendant orderly and the driver. I sat with the driver watching the moving crowds and my observations led me to conclude the war had not affected Frankfurt; the people were well dressed, and the shops displayed an abundance of merchandise with a fair selection of goods.

Shopping completed, we returned to the Convent and I was assisted into bed. It was now lunch time and I felt peckish and although I could hear all the evidence of people eating, no-one appeared with a tray for me. When Duggie appeared wiping the gravy from his lips I told him it was a dirty trick, to which the blighter agreed and then informed me I was due for an operation at two-thirty.

In due course the Sister arrived with a mobile anaesthetic unit, and an orderly with white shirt and rubber sheet. I donned the shirt and prostrated myself on the rubber sheet, and in two ticks was away in the land of dreams.

I remembered no more until late evening when I heard the door opening. It was the Sister, and seeing me awake she popped out and returned with a bowl of thin soup. During her absence I had done a spot of exploring as I could feel no life in my leg. My hand told me there was something there and I felt re-assured. Thank goodness, I still had my leg. For one horrible moment I thought they might have taken it off. It was a possibility that had haunted me ever since I first discovered it had begun to smell.

The Sister produced a dish containing innumerable small pieces of shrapnel and pieces of aeroplane, all removed from my leg and other parts of my anatomy. I couldn't recognise any particular component such as a propeller or engine piston, yet I had been carrying quite a bit of extra weight around for the past few days – no wonder my walking speed had slowed down!

Then Duggie rolled in to see how I was getting along, and produced a couple of cigarettes.

"Well, you dirty traitor. So you've been holding out on me!" I exclaimed, sensing a plot already afoot. "Come on, where did you get them?"

"Ah! There's plenty where these came from – Dulag Luft, my dear sir," he replied mysteriously. "It's only a mile away and we've had some sent up."

"We've? Who's we?" I asked eagerly.

"There are another six R.A.F. types in here. All from French bases," he replied.

It was the first smoke I'd had since before leaving England five days ago, and it didn't taste too good, due possibly to the amount of anaesthetic still in me. It reminded me my pipe had survived the crash and was still in my jacket pocket, so I persuaded Duggie to find out if pipe tobacco was also part of the service at the fabulous "Dulag Luft".

I was confined to bed for a full week and found life very boring, so I enquired if there were any English books ... yes, there was one ... an ancient and massive tome ... a history of the great fire of London. It was rather an old chestnut, and a case of "Hobson's choice", but I read it from cover to cover, and later on no-one dare mention the fire of London to me.

It was my own fault. Whenever I became hard up for something to air my knowledge on, I would resort to the fire of London.

During my week in dry dock the German interrogation officer from Dulag Luft arrived to ask a few questions. He plied me handsomely with cigarettes during the questioning, and I felt proud of the answers I provided in return for his hospitality.

I promoted the long deceased "John Peel" to "Group Captain" in charge of a fighter station at "Peckham" equipped with "Tiger Moths", and transferred my own bomber station from Wattisham to the precincts of Lord Haw-Haw's naval dockyard city at Filey.

One memorable day during the second week of my stay I inherited a wheel-chair, formerly used by a pilot now transferred to Dulag Luft, and got someone to push me along to the conservatory. Here the mobile cases collected during the day to chat over experiences and how they intended to escape when well enough.

It was here I met Flt. Lt. Clancy, a burly Canadian who, having baled out of his damaged aircraft somewhere over West Germany, found himself suspended by his parachute for a whole day and night between two tall pine trees forty feet from the ground and unable to reach a branch from any direction.

Feeling fed up, thirsty and hungry, he took his courage in both hands, pressed his harness release, and crashed to the ground, injuring his spine and rattling every bone in his body. He used to say, "If ever I get back to dear old Canada, I'll make a living selling matches in the gutter rather than leave there ever again."

Then there was Flt. Lt. Madge, a golf-mad Scotsman, who on the morning of his last raid was appointed Flight Commander. His hands and arms were shockingly burned, and his sole worry was whether he'd ever be able to play his beloved game again.

I made a rapid and satisfying recovery, and was soon able to join the others in a steady walk around the gardens while the accompanying Sisters strove to explain the names of plants and shrubs, and proudly displayed their vegetable garden. It was on one of these jaunts I discovered the place really was guarded. I knew from my X-ray trip there was a guard on the entrance gates, but realised only now that we were surrounded by a formidable fence of barbed wire.

During my first week in hospital I sent off a postcard to my wife briefly stating that I was safe, and the next week wrote her a letter-card explaining my circumstances in more detail, so that I now hopefully looked forward to receiving a reply. As things turned out my hopes were a little premature. It was several months later when I received my first letter from home.

My convalescence ended all too soon. It was a period when I saw the Germans as human beings, a period I should remember with gratitude for many long months ahead, perhaps years. But at the end of six weeks, I said goodbye to those noble and gentle Sisters and thanked them for all their kindly ministrations. As I shook hands with the Sister-in-Charge, a dear old soul with snow-white hair and a beautifully carved face, expressing all the pain and sorrow in the world in her eyes, I saw the tears trickling down her wrinkled cheeks.

She knew better than I the troubles in store for the world and Germany in particular; she also knew what we were heading for, and her tears were not only for us few strangers but for our loved ones at home and those in trouble throughout the whole world. I would have given much for the gift of languages to tell her what was in my heart.

I was out of danger but I had to contend with a stiff leg for a further nine months. It was time to move on, and one morning a party of guards arrived to escort five of us, Duggie, myself, and three others, to a further, yet unknown destination. Friends Clancy and Madge remained behind for further treatment. No transport was provided for the short distance to Dulag Luft but I enjoyed my limp along the road to the camp.

So this was the Dulag Luft luxury holiday camp! It looked a dreary place to me as we approached nearer and nearer. There were four or five long wooden huts inside a compound surrounded by masses of barbed wire with guard-boxes at each corner, guards at the entrance and guards patrolling the outer perimeter. We waited outside while an entrance guard reported to his officer and when the gates were opened we were ushered in to meet our fellow prisoners, or so we thought. Instead we were locked in separate cells in the detention block.

Time passed and eventually I was visited by a slimy, smooth type, German interrogator. He handed me a long questionnaire which he requested me to fill in and sign. It included such questions as, types of aircraft flown ... name of home station ... station Commander ... Flight Commander ... what mission was I on when shot down, and a whole lot more I cannot remember.

He left me to complete it alone, and when he returned and found I had made a great cross the size of the paper he became most annoyed. He showed me a completed form supposedly filled in and signed by Duggie, although I knew damned well it wasn't his. He wanted to know why I was so stupid ... how could my people be informed if I refused to give him the necessary information, and then the usual gimp ... "then you will stay here unable to enjoy the company of your comrades and share their good food, until you become more reasonable."

So! I thought, this is where the beasts show their teeth and bring out the whip! I replied, "You have all the information necessary, and as I had a good breakfast this morning I don't feel hungry, thank you!"

I quite expected him to blow up and start bashing me about with his revolver-butt. Instead, he warned me, "You will be extremely sorry for this!", stamped out, and banged the door behind him.

I must credit him with sticking to his word. I did remain in my cell, and I did not enjoy the company of my comrades, nor their so-called good food.

I stayed there until the following morning, when I was released with Duggie and taken to the store, issued with toilet kit and two blankets, and managed to scrounge a jacket to replace my own tattered garment.

"How did you come on, Duggie?" I enquired.

"Same as you, by the look of things," he replied. "That was a very neat statement you completed."

"Yes," I agreed. "Almost as good as yours."

I now met for the first time some of my fellow-prisoner types who made up the permanent staff at the camp, of whom it was rumoured that, by ingratiating themselves into favour with the authorities, they had landed themselves into nice soft jobs. They certainly didn't appear short of any of the good things that could help to smooth a prisoner's life. To me, the place smelled suspiciously of unwholesome rackets.

This was the camp that first received all Red Cross supplies when dispatched from Geneva. Theoretically it enabled each new R.A.F. prisoner passing through Dulag Luft – a prisoner dispersal camp or clearance centre – to receive replacements of clothing, toilet articles, and personal necessities which he may have lost when shot down or left behind at base before leaving on his mission. In addition to this there was some food, and a few luxuries such as cigarettes, tobacco, matches, stationery, a pipe, and many other small but highly appreciated accessories to start a prisoner on his way to a permanent prison camp.

Dulag Luft, at that time, was the only R.A.F. prisoner transit camp, and I'm afraid these Red Cross supplies were very grudgingly and sparingly distributed, and often not at all, by these prisoners sitting tight in cushy jobs.

I was one of those who received nothing from the Red Cross supplies, and only one day's prison ration, when Duggie and I, included in a batch of fifty, moved off on the day of our release from the cells, to another camp.

All along the line of camps I became acquainted with some very strong language to describe the suspicious practices at Dulag Luft. We did manage to get a mug of English tea and some white bread and jam from the Robbers' Den, as it became known, before collecting our belongings and loading into the lorries for the run to Frankfurt; but now I must forget Dulag Luft and return to my story.

CHAPTER FOUR

At the station, we loaded into cattle trucks, and although we were twenty-five to a truck we weren't overcrowded. After a whole day ambling through the countryside to cover one hundred miles, we were dumped in a sort of no-man's land by the side of the railway line with not a building in sight; we were marched a mile or two to a camp consisting of an assortment of oddly shaped huts, surrounded by high barbed-wire fences; and although we stayed there for several days I never learnt the name of the place.

Here we joined several hundred more prisoners of various Allied nationalities – a truly cosmopolitan gathering – living under conditions such as I had never before experienced nor thought possible, but with which, unfortunately, I was soon to become fully and intimately acquainted.

Our party was made up of all ranks from Squadron Leader to Aircraftman, and here they segregated us; officers to one compound, and other ranks to another. This meant losing a fine pal, for Duggie was an officer and I a sergeant. We had hoped, especially as we had lost Bill after the first night, to stick together throughout the period of our captivity in Germany, but the German swine had other ideas; this was the parting of our ways.

We shook hands, wished each other the best of luck and sadly went our separate ways.

I joined twenty other chaps and was directed to a hut, already tenanted by more than a hundred other prisoners: some British, some French, some Belgians and others – to be greeted by a scene of utter confusion and a malodorous cacophony of dis-harmonic smells. I have a particularly sensitive nose and in consequence suffered extreme discomfort.

In the centre of the hut stood a large metal stove that gave off a great heat from its outside surfaces, and a fair number of the original settlers were trying to toast their slices of black bread by sticking them on the hot metal. The scorching bread filled the air with a foul-smelling blue smoke that stung my eyes and almost choked me. The idea, I learned, was to harden the bread. It was more difficult to chew and lasted a good deal longer.

The hut was fitted with three-tier bunks separated by narrow alleyways, with the lucky ones near the stove. Mine was on the second tier in a dark corner, and in very few minutes I set up home without the luxury of sheets or other bedding comforts.

Later I received a large sack which I filled with straw, and two coarse blankets; these with my razor and two blades, soap, towel, and a spare pair of socks, made up my sole possessions.

Searching among the many faces I was struck by the appearance of two chaps standing by the stove; both were mere skeletons, with long pale faces and blond, almost snow-white hair. They were Sgt. Forsyth (Blondie) and L.A.C. Jones (Jonah). In the years that followed I came to know them intimately and, it transpired, their seemingly emaciated appearance was their normal condition; but to me, seeing them for the first time and in those circumstances, the effect was startling.

I was a long time getting to know the other inmates; but among them it pleased me to find a couple from my own station back home, who enjoyed a certain unique notoriety; they were, Georgie Booth, and Larry Slattery, the first two R.A.F. prisoners, shot down during a raid on the second day of hostilities in 1939. It was now the end of

June 1940 and they were considered by the Germans quite distinguished prisoners and not any less by us as distinguished and easily distinguishable kriegies – our name for airmen prisoners.

They were hungry for home news and I told them all I knew, including my own various missions, who were casualties, who of the old gang were still operational, and any other changes likely to interest them.

The food ration at this dump was unspeakably inadequate, neither food nor filling. It consisted of a tin of watery vegetable soup, a dainty wedge of black bread, and a still daintier ration of fat, our daily ration to last twenty-four hours. It was such indigestible muck that it required twenty-four hours for the digestion to cope with it.

At the end of six days in this hell-hole, rumours circulated of a move, and next morning I was once more on the march – or rather limp!

We were a party of eighty-five, all the British non-commissioned airmen on the camp. We returned to our original point of disembarkation by the side of the railway line, were loaded in prisoners' specials – cattle trucks – and eventually hooked up to a passing goods train.

We rattled along over a flat and desolate countryside with frequent and prolonged stops for a couple of days and nights; passing through Breslau and Oppeln, and ending up at the small town of Lamsdorf, near the Czechoslovak frontier.

We were checked and rechecked to make sure all were present and after the inevitable footslog arrived at the British Army Troops' Camp at Stalag 8.B. I had lost my two faithful friends and as I had travelled up with Georgie and Larry, I found it comforting to have them beside me as we gazed at the maze of compounds within the camp. This looked like the real thing.

During the day we were searched, interrogated, shorn of all hair from our heads down to the bare wood, which annoyed me intensely as it was nicely growing again after being burnt off, photographed with our numbers in large figures spread across our chests, which we could never remember and the Germans never forgot, and herded into one large hut in a small compound, while the neighbouring army chaps greeted us with: "So this is where the Air Force was during Dunkirk!"

We stared at them uncomprehendingly, as we knew nothing of the debacle on the French and Belgian beaches, and it was a few days later before we heard full details.

There was a large number of captured British troops in the compounds joined to ours and they were feeling pretty bitter about things in general; they thought they had been badly let down by the R.A.F. at Dunkirk, and they cursed the French up hill and down dale. Maybe they were justified; we generally make a hash of our opening land battles.

The accommodation and food were no better than I already knew except that I had my own dixie to collect my soup. I was allotted a top tier bunk of three and as no-one volunteered to swop I had fun and games with my stiff leg trying to get up and down. I made a friend of my opposite number across the alleyway, a fighter pilot named Pavey.

He had a venomous hatred of all Germans and spent hours hurling insults at the guards through the wire. Fortunately they didn't understand, and whenever I reminded him, he said it relieved his feelings and he didn't care a trump if they did understand.

I was never outside my own small compound, but I could see the camp stretching for miles with compound after compound. I heard it was originally designed as a residential camp for workers, on a projected scheme for local industries; probably salt mines and other unpleasant occupations.

I do know there was a detention compound with an extra large cell-block, usually well patronised by over-exuberant airmen. The place was a mass of barbed wire, and littered with sentry-boxes; it also maintained kennels of well-trained Alsatian dogs to deter would-be escapees.

It was here I enjoyed my first experience of *Die Kultur* and the sadistic workings of the German mind. Every time there was a heavy raid over Germany – night or day – we, airmen in particular, were routed out at bayonet point to endure one hour of P.T. to the accompaniment of our ribald laughter, jeers, and cat-calls which desperately annoyed the Germans – they would even get a bit rough with anyone they caught in the act.

Many of the guards at Stalag 8.B. were unreasonably nervous and sensitive to British ragging. They just couldn't take it and didn't know how to react; and we'd just about got each one nicely weighed up where we could hurt him most on his weak spots, when orders went round for another move.

I had been there only three weeks and found it most disappointing to have to leave now I'd found which guard I could torment with the things he hated most.

I mustn't forget to tell you that I was now becoming quite fluent in German, and found it a pleasant distraction to bait the beasts, in spite of seeing our most daring baiters being carted off daily to the cooler as a reprisal.

Coinciding with the new move, it was rumoured the new camp had been specially prepared for R.A.F. prisoners only, and was situated near the Baltic coast. It looked as though Jerry was cooking up something special for us, and I didn't like the look of it at all. My thoughts were now centred on a means of escape and while the new camp might be escape-proof and thus stall my hopes, it would be premature to attempt it in my present condition.

No, I had debated the matter in my mind for a long time, and did not intend to make a move until all the requisite factors were present. I must wait and see.

The whole eighty-five of us were loaded into the usual prisoners' specials. They became our home for the next three days and nights; we slept in goods depots, and stopped here and there for the distribution of food and drink, and for toilet purposes. Cigarettes were non-existent so I tried a few dried tea-leaves in my pipe; three puffs were enough, never again.

I had no special pal as yet, so made the most of the chaps in my small party, composed of Sergeants Pavey, Robson, Luter, Merton, Sands, and Hart, of whom more anon.

The route carried us through Berlin, but our hopes of seeing the capital remained unfulfilled owing to the darkness. It seemed an endless trip, and everyone had his own guess for the ultimate destination, none of which was within a hundred miles of correct, for we finally detrained at the small town of Barth, several miles west of Stralsund on the Baltic coast.

I couldn't blame the locals for their curious stares as we ambled the two miles to our new home; for Stalag 8.B., by cropping our heads for purposes of ready identification, had also turned us into creatures of another world.

All they could see were eighty-five airmen from the country of Shakespeare, Christopher Wren, Sir Isaac Newton, and Winston Churchill, with bald heads, noble handle-bar moustaches, Santa Claus beards, dressed in rags, tired, weary, and not too clean, wearing an assortment of footwear – and these represented, so far as they knew, the cream of the greatest Empire on earth!

CHAPTER FIVE

Seen from a nicely calculated focus, like a painted lady, our new special quarters caught my interest at first sight and retained it right up to reaching the gates.

It was a pleasantly situated little camp surrounded by scenery to please the eye of an artist, and supervised exclusively by Germany's crack Luftwaffe Guards – the equivalent of the British R.A.F. Regiment – who seemed, at first, much more friendly towards us than our hitherto-known rifle guards.

The Lager (post or encampment) Commandant, Leut. Peeber, welcomed us with a pretty little speech – in English – in which he hoped we would feel happy once we settled down, as he wished to do everything possible for our well-being and comfort, to which one of our wags interrupted, "Can you send me home, please?"

Peeber had a sense of humour and seemed amused at the question and replied, "I'm sorry, but I'm afraid that is not possible at the moment, but in due course no doubt, it will be done." We all laughed, rather sneeringly I'm afraid, but it augured well for the future.

We were conducted to our billets, and informed that in half an hour soup would be served in the Dining-Hall. DINING-HALL, mark you.

I found this new angle of treatment for P.O.W.s a pleasant reflection, but kept my fingers crossed anticipating the snags.

From the first moment of hearing about this specially prepared camp for R.A.F. prisoners I had considered two possibilities: either they had constructed an impregnable fortress to make escape impossible; or Geneva had heard about our earlier inhuman treatment and were interesting themselves on our behalf, and Jerry authorities, seeing the red light ahead, were trying to curry favour with Britain to encourage a round-table talk. This would draw us out of the war, and leave her free to smash Russia after settling matters with France, Holland, Belgium, and other – as she considered then – smaller fry.

Even our billets conformed to new and more civilised ideas of construction. Each of the three billets (huts) in our compound consisted of a long central corridor with four rooms of different sizes leading from each side; the largest contained nine two-tier bunks arranged around the walls, a stove for heating and cooking, and a maid-of-all-work table and several forms, the smallest had only four two-tier bunks with stove, table, and forms.

The result was a cosy and more family-like arrangement. My original party of seven, plus a chap called Eastick, moved into a ten-bunk room, leaving the two vacant ones nearest the door, staked our claims by dumping our small collection of kit on each one's selected bunk, and made our way to the high-sounding dining-hall at the end of the compound.

Here there were more surprises. We found a large hall set out with tables and forms, and a service hatch on one side leading into a semi-detached cookhouse. First we queued to receive new soup bowl, plate, mug, and knife, fork, and spoon – this seemed to me impossible, it felt like being prepared for execution – then queued for the steaming hot soup, served by German cooks, and retired to the tables to eat it in style.

There was a loud buzz of discussion over these unexpected luxuries being thrust upon us so suddenly, and everyone had his own theories to account for it. I thought the reason stuck out a mile. If we were made comfortable, our hosts reasoned, we would write home and tell our folk how nice the Germans were, we would not cause them any trouble as prisoners, and it would lessen the risk of escaping kriegies – more than likely.

Hitler and his gang had already been informed that British P.O.W.s were a most unco-operative crowd and refused to be subjugated by his sadistic guards, which meant he would need an army to keep us in subjection, but if he eased his *Kultur* it might release more of his guards for the battle-fronts.

As this place had all the appearance of a permanent residence, we removed the bed-boards from the empty bunks and fixed them as shelves for our few belongings, filled our mattress-sacks with straw, laid out our blankets, and made ourselves, "at home".

Reading clockwise from the stove, there was Vincent Luter – Lute to everyone – a Portsmouth man with a gloomy expression of impending doom, but a sterling character with a heart of gold; above Lute was Denis Eastick, a youngster from Norwich whose character was still in the formative stage, and who was rather temperamental.

Next came Charles Pavey – Pave – the blithe spirit from Beckenham with that poisonous hatred of all Germans, who occasionally went completely round the bend, and would waste his whole ration of letter-cards to write stinking epistles about the Germans, calling them pig-dogs, swine out of hell, bastards, sons of Jew prostitutes, and many other names far too colourful to write here. He knew they would never pass the censor and would be destroyed, and that he would finish up more often than not with seven days or more in the cooler. But Pave came out, always looking well and as cheerful as ever, and as soon as he got a few more cards to write home, back he went to the cooler. Nothing we could suggest would stop him.

I bunked above Pave, then, next in line, was Charles Merton – Mert – a Londoner, as broad across the shoulders as he was tall, and possessed of superhuman strength. He was an irrepressible character and eventually gravitated to the cookhouse, to lead Emanuel, the German leading cook, a dog's life.

Above Mert lived Fred Robson – Robbie – another Beckenham character, whose only likeness to Pave, his fellow townsman, was his delight in discussing the highlights of Beckenham, its women, and its low dives, but the right sort of man to have nearby in a spot of trouble.

Then there was John Sands – Sandy – addicted to a Sherlock Holmes pipe and strong tobacco when procurable, and mad about his little M.G. car at home – his sole topic of conversation – but he did become the ration king, responsible for the issue of rations to all in the compound, faithfully discharging this duty over a long period.

Finally, above Sandy, we have the most colourful character of all, Charles Hart – Chas – from Wilton in Wiltshire; a talented musician, actor, and fluent linguist from whom I learnt to speak German, and an outstanding personality in any company. Whenever he got an idea for a new play or a new piece for orchestration he became completely oblivious to the whole world.

He produced our early plays and concerts, taught our instrumentalists, wrote all the music, and formed the orchestra, in which I played the drums on a scrubbing board – the beginning and end of my musical career.

As Chas spoke fluent German he became our first Liaison Officer. He would entertain us for hours, reclining on his bunk with one long leg hanging over the edge, reading from a purloined German newspaper, either the *Algemeine Zeitung* or the *Völkischer Beobachter* in true-to-life German style with all the histrionic by-play, and arm waving so truly Germanic, announcing all the glorious German victories against a world of enemies, won, it F that is, as airmen go – in our late twenties; anyone over thirty was considered quite a patriarch.

I had no illusions concerning my captors. I accepted my improved and luxurious quarters, the more plentiful and better-quality food, and any other comforts they cared to offer, still with a jaundiced eye, but I still considered the country beyond the barbed wire had more to offer to my liking than anything inside the compound. One of these days, given the chance, I would prove my preference beyond any doubt.

At the moment I still had my stiff leg, and was giving it all the exercise possible, by patrolling the interior perimeter warning wire, to bring it into working order ready for a bid into the wide and open spaces beyond. I spent a great deal of my time wandering round the compound getting a thorough knowledge of the camp layout, and as much as I could see of the surrounding country.

We were the first tenants of this small compound. At one end there were two wash-houses and two latrines, and our three huts, then an open grass area the size of a small football field, and at the other end the dining-hall and cookhouse. Along one side were the German guard-room and their quarters, the administration offices and stores, the sick-quarters, and the cell-block, known as the cooler. All this was contained within a surrounding fence of twin barbed wire criss-crossed so that a rat would have difficulty squeezing through, reaching ten feet high.

Calling this the inner fence, there was another similar fence, the outer one, leaving a six foot corridor between them; this corridor was filled in with coiled barbed-wire entanglements, making in all a six-foot wide, ten-foot high, wall of murderous wire between the P.O.W.s and the outside country.

In addition to this precaution there were sentry-cabins built high up on stilts at regular intervals, each manned by two guards armed with machine-guns and searchlights, commanding a view of every inch of the compound night and day.

Then, inside the compound at a distance of six feet from the main fences, a single strand of barbed wire three feet from the ground, nailed to posts, ran round the interior perimeter as a warning wire. This meant that no-one approached nearer to the main wire than six feet at any point. To pass that wire, or even to lean against it, meant death from a hail of bullets from the machine guns.

As an extra precaution, a roving patrol of armed guards roamed the area outside the main fences.

Adjacent to our compound, on the side of the administration offices, there was another compound similar to ours, and said to be ready to accommodate P.O.W.s of commissioned rank; and sure enough, a week following our arrival, along came a party of officers.

The road leading into the camp ran parallel to the end of the compound, and thus behind the wash-houses and latrines. As soon as the news spread that the newcomers were on the way from the station we all rushed to that end to greet them, and to prove that the machine-gun cabins were not there for ornamentation the guards began shouting and threatening with their guns whenever anyone touched the warning wire.

Of course, I was there among the crowd, hoping and hoping. And, sure enough, there was Duggie, right in front of the party. We followed along the wire and I shouted, "Hello, Duggie, where have you been all this time?" and he replied "Stuck in that dump where you left me, while you lucky devils have been lolling it off in this Butlin's camp."

Here's a sample of some of the illuminating backchat bandied to and fro across the wire. "Oh! It's lovely here, rationed to two women a week, free beer, and unlimited cigarettes … allowed outside two nights a week … got a date with a blonde Fräulein at the local Biergarten tomorrow night, she's hot stuff too, daren't strike a match near her … hope you haven't forgotten your table manners, you'll need 'em here … night porters to put you to bed if you come in blotto." And so it went on until they passed out of hearing and disappeared into their own compound.

We were still a party of only eighty-five strong and by the time the officers settled down in the next door compound we just about knew each other, and the time had come to elect a leader.

The choice fell on Flt. Sgt. Hall – Nobby – and Nobby was a man of many good points but, unfortunately, diplomacy in treating with the enemy was not one of them, and after many fractious meetings with the Germans on points of camp discipline, he fell from favour, the Commandant severing diplomatic relations and refusing to deal with him.

Flt. Sgt. Ross – Chiefie – was then persuaded to step into the breach, until a leader, acceptable to both parties, could be found. Eventually Sgt. Deans – inevitably called Dixie – was elected and accepted by the Commandant and diplomatic relations were re-opened; the choice could not have been better.

Dixie, a Scot, earned the unqualified gratitude of every kriegie in his care during his four years of leadership, for his firm, but tactful handling of many ticklish situations. He spoke fluent German, and was treated with great respect by the Germans, guards and officers alike.

At the end of three weeks, a new batch of thirty R.A.F. types arrived; everybody rushed to the wire scanning the faces seeking old friends, and as soon as they entered the compound we pounced on them for the latest news. How long would it last? … how were things at home? And a thousand other similar questions.

They were then escorted by friends and acquaintances to their billets and introduced to the amenities of prison camp, Stalag Luft I. The two vacant bunks in my room were taken over by Ken Murray, a Londoner, and Ginger Flowers, a Devonian, and what a hell of a time they had for the first few days, for we pumped them dry for war news, particularly flying news, and every aspect of home affairs.

I had now been a prisoner for fourteen weeks but, owing to my various migrations from one transit camp to another, none of my letters from home had yet caught up with me. During this period I had written three cards, and it was probable they hadn't reached home owing to the chaotic state of affairs in Western Europe.

Being now, seemingly in a permanent camp and with a monthly ration of two letter cards and four postcards, I began a regular correspondence hoping that at least the odd one would get through to inform my wife and family of my well-being.

Several factors were aiding the recovery of my mental and physical condition apart from the improved quantity and quality of the food at this new camp. First, but not least, was my timely admission to the Convent hospital, where the causes were surgically removed and the road opened for a cure. Here the main ingredient for my recovery was undoubtedly the infusion of hope provided by the kindness and Christian love for all men of those wonderful Sisters. Then, of course, I must remember the help and encouragement I received from Duggie. And little by little, though only here and there, I noticed traces of humanity in the Germans' conduct towards me and I found this mentally helpful.

And finally, on a day when I was without a pal, I ran into as fine a set of pals as any man could wish for, and whatever the future held, there was little I could complain of, considering I was a prisoner of war, concerning my treatment at this camp.

The fact was, my health had so improved that I was able to undertake more extensive exercises in preparation for an attempt at escape in the near future – my leg was the one drawback.

Meanwhile at the camp, arrangements were in hand to produce a series of concerts and other forms of entertainment; educational classes and lectures were being organised, and I made a daily routine of French and German lessons.

Then, like a gift from the Gods, the Germans offered opportunities for small parties to work on local jobs *outside* the camp. It was something out of the blue I had never dreamed of; if they'd reserved a seat on a neutral plane to fly me home I couldn't have been more surprised. It offered a splendid opportunity to spy out the surrounding neighbourhood. I promptly entered my name in capital letters.

Then one fine morning, with five other chaps and two guards, I went fruit pulling at a local market-garden; I not only filled the baskets, but filled my pockets and my belly for it was the first fruit I'd tasted since leaving England.

It had been a fine day, and while enjoying the outing I had mentally photographed the roads and countryside to begin making my local map for future reference. The outing also taught me that my leg was far from being strong enough for a break followed by a hike of possibly several hundred miles.

When collecting stores from the German quarters it was a common thing for our party to meet a party of officers on a similar mission. One day they indicated that two of them wanted to join a working party, but as officers were taboo on such parties they would have to revert to the ranks and would we make a swap? So it was one day during a visit to the toilet attached to the stores, two of our chaps entered as "other ranks" and marched away as officers, and two officers were reduced to the ranks and returned with us to the compound.

Next morning they joined a working party and went out to a road repairing job. They made their break all right but had the bad luck to be spotted immediately and were soon recaptured.

This unfortunately resulted in the Germans stopping all working parties and confining everyone to camp. They went nearly crackers when they found how they'd been duped.

It was a bitter blow to my hopes for several weeks, but then fortune smiled again; the civilian contractors for the job had come to a standstill for lack of labour and, after representations to the Commandant, working parties were again organised. No officers and no N.C.O.s were allowed, and airmen were permitted only after the closest check. Good enough. If I were to escape through this channel then I would have to become an airman – and this would require advance planning.

At the end of my sixth week at Barth a further batch of new kriegies arrived, and there among them, I spotted the grinning mug of my old wireless-operator Bill Street. Good old Bill! The very pal I'd been waiting for. Bill the optimist, humorist, prepared to chance anything once, the missing link with my former life, had turned up at the very moment I had glimpsed the outside world and began to itch for my freedom. Bill's return renewed my hopes for the future. His arrival meant more than luck, it was an omen. The Gods were watching, and God helps those who help themselves.

There were no empty bunks in my compartment, and as I couldn't expect anyone to change he was fixed up next door. I was eager for his story and between us there was much to relate. After our separation, he was one of a long column of P.O.W.s who marched for a fortnight from place to place re-laying railway lines and mending roads that had been damaged by our own planes. We talked for hours and by the time I had filled him in with the possibilities of the present layout "Lights out" was sounded.

CHAPTER SIX

Bill was as keen as I to get away, and so long as we could be included together we agreed to join any working party going outside. We realised if we were seen too often together it would arouse suspicions, so outside the hut we separated. Neither of us was a big man, which we considered an advantage, although Bill was as strong as an ox and quite fearless, while I was decidedly thin but fairly fit and toughish, and my leg now ready for the test.

At the end of a fortnight we had accumulated a fair stock of bread conserved from our daily rations, a little cheese, and a cob of fat.

We managed to get together on a road-mending party and each day carried with us our "iron rations" in case the chance of a break presented itself.

There were ten kriegies and two armed guards in today's party, and the transport carried us four miles from the camp to a stretch of road under repair running through a thick forest. It was our job to load stone into relays of trailers ready for a tractor to tow to the place under repair.

I quietly nudged Bill. "Have you got everything? It looks a lovely day for a stroll. If we get the chance, do we take it?"

"You bet, and I'd like to take that tractor driver for a ride at the same time. I hate his blasted guts!"

None of us unduly exerted himself, and as the previous scare was now a thing of the past, even the guards relaxed and sat around smoking.

Normally we finished work at four-thirty so we decided to bolt at about four o'clock; this would give us the advantage of early darkness.

Quietly and as casually as possible we arranged for the other chaps to spread out a bit so that we could trickle nearer the edge of the forest and slip away unnoticed. Everything was going nicely in our favour, all we needed was a five-second distraction for the guards and we would vanish.

Suddenly a couple of our chaps began threatening each other, and as the commotion diverted the attention of the guards we dashed into the woods. Unfortunately we had overlooked the tractor driver a hundred yards away; he shouted the alarm, and the chase was on with Bill and me the quarry.

I had over-estimated the strength of my leg and before I could reach full cover of the woods a bullet smacked into the nearest tree, followed by the shout, "*Halt.*"

I was still a good target so I halted instantly with my hands in the air while I could hear Bill dashing hell for leather through the woods. One guard with his rifle at his shoulder and the bastard tractor-driver with his shovel covered the other chaps, while the other moved towards me keeping me covered and then marched me back to the road.

The party re-assembled and remained covered by the guards' rifles until the transport arrived to return us to camp. You may easily guess my thoughts as I waited; if that bullet had hit me I should have been number one V.I.P. at a funeral service! It was pitiful to watch the guards' dumb pantomime as they attempted to explain the trouble they were in for letting Bill escape.

I gathered they were in the fertilizer right up to the chin. They were really windy and nervous and kept saying, "*Arrest geben, ja, ja, nicht gut,*" indicating that they, as well as we, would be in the cooler together.

I'm sure it never occurred to them that two different parties would try the same thing in the same place. But there it is, it was my business to escape if possible and theirs to stop me.

I was already thinking in terms of next time, and wondering how far Bill had travelled. As soon as we returned to camp I was immediately escorted to the Commandant to account for my crime against the Third Reich and received a severe dressing down.

"How could anyone wish to leave his beautiful camp? ... didn't I know I could be sent to the most dreadful places for attempting to escape? ... and what about my unfortunate companion? ... he would most certainly be shot, as there was no possible chance of leaving the country!" By the time he had finished he almost had me weeping on his shoulder. "You can have twenty-one days in the cells to cool off!" and away I went to the cooler.

At lunch time next day I heard someone enter the cell next door and as soon as the door slammed closed I heard Bill's cackling laugh mocking his jailers.

"Hard luck, Bill," I yelled.

"Well, here we are again! Now what do you know about that?" he replied, still as cheerful as ever.

There was only a thin partition between the two cells and we passed the time discussing events. Bill got through the woods and covered about eight miles of open country then built himself a hideout for the night of corn sheaves in the middle of a field. He was captured in his hideout next morning, having, as he put it, overslept!

The only drawback to being in the cells was the confinement. Off-duty guards often came to peep at us through the spy-holes. I'm sure they thought us mad. But then the whole British race, who never seem to recognise defeat however hopeless the situation, are always thought mad – at least by the Germans.

We played the craziest tricks on the peeping Toms, by banging on the spy-hole with our fists as soon as an eye appeared, or sitting quiet in a corner where the eye couldn't reach us, when they would rush off in a panic for the keys, fling open the door and find us sitting there like lunatics counting our fingers.

There was no remission for good conduct and at the end of the twenty-one days we were returned to the compound amid a noisy welcome from room-mates and friends. All outside working parties had ceased and everyone was confined to the compound. This decreased our popularity with our own chaps because I've no doubt many of them harboured similar ideas via this closed channel.

The Germans definitely mistrusted us – it was too bad! We'd have to find other means. It was too funny to find the interpreters popping in and out at the oddest moments as though they were old friends enquiring after our health. Just to see if Mr. Street and Mr. Fancy were still there.

By setting our feet on the path of escape we had, at least, broken the trail and tested the treatment for re-captured escapees; and I intended to pursue the course to the bitter end – success, or failure! I felt consecrated to a new hobby and began seriously investigating the camp's defences. I reasoned that as all working parties had ceased, thereby closing this avenue, nothing remained but to escape direct from the compound itself, but how? That was the question to fill my thoughts night and day until I found an answer.

As I saw it, there were four well-nigh impossible ways. Number one: through the open gate. That would require a foolproof disguise – and where was that to be found? – fluency in the German language – difficult but not impossible – and opportunity – meaning easily fooled guards. At present I could not fulfil any of the requirements.

Number two: over the mass of entangled wire – not to be recommended except in very special circumstances, such as a power-cut plus a blinding snowstorm, or a black fog during hours of darkness plus protection from the barbs.

Number three: through the wire – this method would require a powerful pair of wire-cutters to cut through six feet of closely packed wire, plus a pitch black night, a power cut for the searchlights, and a thunderstorm to muffle the noise. Numbers two and three invited a hail of bullets into one's hide, and I had already found that my body was not bullet-proof.

Number four: under the wire – a tunnel. This method offered a measure of security while the escapee passed from inside to outside the compound. It represented a matter of only six feet but every inch overland carried a thousand deaths.

It was a point to be considered. There would be risks at the exit, but then every moment of life these days carried a risk, P.O.W. or civilian. Incidentally, at the point of exit, man's best friend is the P.O.W.'s worst enemy, and once one picks up his scent he will be looking over his shoulder for at least forty-eight hours.

These vicious dogs patrol inside and outside the compound every night, and during the day members of the internal security force, nick-named "Goons" or "ferrets", make sudden visits to the compound and tear the place apart in their hunt for subversive activities.

The Germans may lose every war they begin, but they certainly go to a lot of trouble to retain a prisoner once they capture him. Taking it by and large I reckon it requires at least one healthy German to keep one British P.O.W. behind the wire or in hospital and behaving himself.

No, it was hopeless. I could see no means of a surface escape, and the confinement was torturing me. My active nature revolted at the meaningless daily routine which brought my restless body to a halt at the warning fence and limited my thinking powers to one obsession, how to get beyond that surrounding wire! It was driving me crackers.

I imagined barbed wire round the edge of my soup bowl. In my sleep I fought Alsatians up and down the six-foot corridors of impregnable wire. I once dreamt I had made friends with a Goon who one night led me safely out of the compound to a cave stocked with food in a river bank, but every time I wanted some food or to leave the cave, great savage dogs barred my way.

Eventually the cave became a tunnel and I was crawling to freedom when I came face to face with the dogs who changed to Goons and when I turned round to go back I met more Goons. Then a great noise started and I woke with Bill shaking me. "Come on, Fancy. It's everyone outside, the blasted Goons are here on a nocturnal search!" I scrambled into my overcoat and made for outside, glad of an interruption.

I felt sadly discouraged at the sight of that mountain of barbed wire, machine-gun and searchlight boxes, exterior armed patrols and their dogs, not forgetting my uncertain leg; for although I could now fully bend the knee, many of the leg muscles still required re-education. I began to break from my shell of secrecy and sought ideas from a select gang of other restless spirits.

There was Bill, of course, ready at all times to take a chance at anything in the wind, Neil Prendergast, Harry Leggett, Bill Garriock, Paddy Flynn, George Grimston, Arthur Parfitt, as well as Pave and Mert from my own room.

Neil, tall and slim, an untiring worker, whose mind was firmly fixed on a return home by any means.

Harry, short and stocky, absorbed in the German language, and later to become a valued member of the escape committee.

Bill Garriock, a small and very slim Irishman, whose appearance belied his enormous reserves of energy, always unstintingly available in any escape bid.

Paddy, a tall gangling Irishman, with a burning hatred of all things German, just waiting for the least chance of a tilt at the stupid bastards.

George Grimston, whose exploits you will hear more about, and Arthur, a phlegmatic character, full of Yorkshire grit who never lost his temper, he used to say to anyone seeking to bandy words with him, "You can't insult me. I'm too dumb!"

These and many others were my partners in crime, always ready and willing in any good cause, whether in baiting our captors or helping an escape effort.

CHAPTER SEVEN

After days of intensive discussion we evolved a plan and decided to go ahead – a tunnel it should be. None of us knew anything about tunnelling, so we set about the task without any preconceived notions of how it should be done.

At this stage we had no organised escape committee so we informed Dixie, our camp leader, of the plan, hoping for his sanction. He listened non-committally to the end, then replied, "If you want to go home that badly, don't let me stop you. Get weaving!" This we considered the O.K. for action.

In looking around for a starting point for the tunnel the choice fell to my billet. It was the closest to the warning wire, a matter of only eight feet. Hence we would have to tunnel only thirty-five feet to break clear of all the wire and beyond the outside patrol.

The huts rested on posts with a clearance of one foot from the ground under the hut floors with a shallow banking of soil around the sides as a wind-break. This provided just enough clearance to wriggle about underneath yet remain unseen from the compound. Admittedly the exit from the tunnel would trespass into the German quarters, but as they were not enclosed by wire fences we didn't consider this a serious obstacle.

Mert "borrowed" a handy-sized lever from the cookhouse and we set to work. A scouting party went through every room in the compound including wash-houses, cook house, and latrines to make sure no ferrets or interpreters were on the premises, while a couple of stooges were posted to watch the entrance gates to give warning of a visit. On receipt of the O.K. signal, I levered up a section of the flooring in my room and dived below for a preliminary survey.

I found it rather dark owing to the soil wind-break around the outer edge but otherwise just as the doctor ordered. There was enough room to begin excavating but hardly room for anyone to crawl away with the excavated soil, so I got Bill to hand down the fire shovel and I dug a trench two feet wide and a foot deep to give the soil remover comfortable working space.

This extra space would assist a quick exit in the event of the Goons making a sudden search, and avoid bumps and bruises which might become difficult to explain if noticed.

With the service channel completed I moved over to the side nearest the warning wire and began digging downwards while Bill, Pave, and Robbie, dispersed the soil. Soon I found the shovel was too weak for the hard dry soil and I was unable to progress at the rate dictated by my restless spirits.

The shovel was ideal for removing the soil once the crust was loosened, so I sent up for my strong all-metal table knife so thoughtfully provided by our captors. This was a great improvement, and by the time we were obliged to pack up, I had sunk a shaft six feet deep by two feet square while my fellow conspirators had dispersed the soil around the sides underneath, using any old pieces of cloth they could find.

While working below I had noticed the hut was completely double floored. There were boards battened to the joists forming the flooring inside the huts, and another set of boards battened to the joists underneath the hut. A very convenient arrangement!

I removed a length of the underneath flooring, hacked it into suitable lengths, and covered the hole, sprinkling the boards with a bit of soil to match its surroundings. A start had been made, and I relished the prospects ahead. After a wash and brush-down to remove the evidence we were ready for tea.

The previous day we had been issued with our first Red Cross parcels, so this evening's meal took the form of a mild celebration. Our one-time palatial dining-hall had now become a permanent concert hall, and meals were taken in our rooms; taking it by weekly stretches, one man was responsible for collecting the daily rations for everybody in his own room.

But with the advent of Red Cross parcels, Lute, by unanimous consent, was appointed permanent housekeeper, and was now busy at the stove frying slices of meat loaf and chips. To celebrate the opening of the tunnel, the meal consisted of fried meat loaf and chips, biscuits, cheese, jam, and tea. Those possessing collars and ties were requested to wear them for the occasion.

The smell of frying chips is a challenge to anyone's patience at any time, but when the challenge comes only once in eight weeks, and you happen to be a disgustingly healthy young P.O.W. it requires considerable restraint to keep your fingers from reaching into the pan, and so it was on this occasion. Fingers were popping in and out from all angles until Lute gave up in despair.

Word soon went round that mice had been at work beneath the hut, and visitors rolled in to enquire how things were going and to wish us the best of luck. We had agreed not to work after lockup in the evenings as the risk of detection by the prowling dogs was very real, so we packed up until after next morning's roll-call.

As soon as everywhere was pronounced clear of Goons I popped below and opened up.

Starting from the bottom of the shaft I commenced to dig forward into the tunnel proper and after a few feet it became so dark I couldn't see a thing. I must have a light. We furnished a lamp from a small tin with a piece of wire suspending a bit of rag in some melted ration fat. We had a light right enough ... but oh, the smell and the smoke!

It was dreadful. The foul-smelling smoke both choked and blinded me, and often the lamp gave out for lack of oxygen, yet I made progress although often obliged to change direction and level owing to large stones and loose sand.

At the end of three weeks of hard work we reached the warning wire and I realised something would have to be done to increase the air supply and improve the lighting. Later in the evening my worries were increased by a torrential rainstorm which continued throughout the night.

Listening to the rain beating on the hut roof I lay awake in agonising suspense at the thought of what might be happening in my nice little hole down below. Once I heard Pave's voice below me, "Hey, Fancy, can you hear the ruddy rain? I expect the whole damn place will be flooded!" I miserably agreed, though hoping our fears would prove unwarranted.

But alas! After morning roll-call, I hurried to inspect the damage. My worst fears were realised. The water level was three feet up the shaft, and all operations would have to be suspended until the water drained away. It put a check on my optimism and acted as a timely warning for the future. Apparently tunnelling wasn't as simple as it looked.

I waited three clear days and saw that the water had drained away, but oh, the mud and slime. I crawled a short distance through the mud and found the whole thing blocked by falls from the roof. I felt heart-broken. No amount of shoring would prevent further falls; there was no alternative. I must harden my heart and abandon the project.

What with our sore knees and elbows from crawling about and our tired backs from the unaccustomed work it was a blow, but not a knockout. This disaster was soon overshadowed by the arrival of my first letters from home. I was delirious with joy. I must have read them through twenty times the first day. They couldn't have arrived at a more opportune moment. I lapped up the news of all the little intimate happenings at home like a thirsty desert traveller.

I kept taking them from my pocket and reading them over and over again in case there was some little thing I had missed in my first excitement. If only my folk at home could realise the pleasure they had given me! They made me all the keener to pursue the work in hand.

Then Red Cross parcels began coming in more regularly and in greater quantities providing a more ample and varied addition to our prison diet. And food becomes an obsession with P.O.W.s. Every thought begins and ends on the word food.

In consequence I was feeling on top of the world and resolved to review my mistakes and try again. I must pay more attention to lighting, depth, direction, and air supply. As the ferrets had not discovered our abandoned working we left it without troubling to fill it in.

CHAPTER EIGHT

We chose to renew operations below a small storeroom at the opposite end of the hut, in the hope that if we were suspected of tunnelling the Goons might find the old working and abandon further search. In the storeroom there was a stone resting on a concrete slab and we decided to tunnel beneath the slab, using it and the stove to camouflage our operations. Its removal and replacement would be a simple matter, and from the window which faced the compound gate we could post a watcher to give us ample warning whenever the Goons arrived; this would be a valuable contribution to our security.

With our own security staff at their posts, we removed the stove and the concrete slab and before the day ended I had dug another shaft six feet deep and two feet square, with room for a man to work and just deep enough for him to reach the edge of the floor above to haul himself out in case a speedy evacuation became necessary.

We figured that if only we had a length of wire we could borrow some electricity from the storeroom above and solve the question of light. A kriegie reported having seen a roll of electric cable in the guard-barracks.

That was enough. The same kriegie volunteered to clean the windows for a couple of cigarettes and arrived back with a hundred feet of lighting wire wrapped round his body under his clothing. Our troubles were over.

We connected up to the existing system and carried it below ground. I doubt whether the Electricity Board would have passed our fittings as safe, but they worked well enough for us, although I'm sure we were in danger of death by electrocution without realising it.

With a six-foot perpendicular shaft already sunk, I began the horizontal tunnel leaving the shaft eighteen inches lower than the tunnel, thus providing a drainage sump in the event of heavy rain. I then carved out a Norman Arch, eighteen inches wide at the base and two feet from base to apex, leaving thirty inches of surface soil above the apex as an insurance against a subsidence. I calculated my present tunnel to be considerably above the water level of my last effort and hoped thereby to avoid the snag of flooding.

It was now the end of October and approaching bad tunnelling weather so we worked overtime to beat the weather. The job went along with such deceptive smoothness from the very start that I felt as though a ferret was looking over my shoulder and laughing at me. We'd had a few scares and had to bundle out without sufficient time to get the stove back into position, but there was no large detailed search, but we had some rain and several times had to empty the sump, although the tunnel remained dry and stable. By hanging my poached electric light just below the apex of the Normal Arch at the entrance of the tunnel, and by keeping the light in view while I worked at the face, I was able to maintain a constant height and direction.

The soil dispersal squad kept pace with us so well that by the end of a fortnight we were beyond the warning wire and only three feet from the main wire … then it happened! A couple of Goons bounced in one afternoon with their prodding rods and began poking around on our bit of freehold!

Everybody had escaped from the working and the entrance was snugly covered in with the stove in position, while we anxiously watched from the hut window. But their persistence over the exact area of our tunnel was so prolonged, it betokened either clairvoyancy or prior knowledge of our activities.

I'd never seen such a concentrated effort. It was simply a matter of time for their search to be rewarded – and rewarded it was! For the third time Jerry held all the aces and I lost the game. The discovery precipitated a full-scale search while the searchers jeered at our discomfort. Although they caused us as much inconvenience as possible we found it amusing and tormented the life out of them.

As soon as the buzz went round that the Goons were abroad, the kriegies collected their most treasured possessions and furtively hid them away anywhere in the compound like dogs hiding their bones, because if they didn't the angry Goons would take their revenge on such articles.

Often the searches lasted for several hours, and anticipating this we left the huts carrying food, reading matter, and playing cards, prepared to make a day of it.

Eventually they became rather crafty and rang the changes on us by coming in as though for a routine roll-call, and as soon as we assembled on the sports pitch, suddenly switch their attentions to our rooms for a snap search, or enter as though for a search of the huts, but instead, lock us in the huts and search the compound for a change.

It all added to the spice of life and we usually managed to keep one step ahead of them, for we also had our own intelligence service; certain guards and even certain interpreters, were not above accepting a few English cigarettes, chocolate, or coffee, in exchange for services rendered.

In this particular case, the balloon went up in the late afternoon, so we weren't outside for long, as they would never risk having us loose in the compound after dark.

They found nothing very rewarding, except we lost our lighting equipment, or rather, they recovered their own property, but even this would be remedied as soon as a replacement became necessary. Of course, they destroyed the tunnel but, as no-one was caught red-handed and they knew how hopeless it was to question us, no-one was victimised. We were back just where we started.

As on previous occasions we had to put up with a lot of ill feeling from those whose sole interest was in pursuit of their own comfort, but their grumblings fell on deaf ears, and they received scant sympathy from the majority. When things quietened down a bit we would have another go; meanwhile we concentrated on football, concert rehearsals, and the circuits. The latter was a permanent feature of camp life, and consisted of ceaselessly tramping the interior circuit of the compound discussing our favourite topics: food, home, escape, women, and unemployment after the war, while the guards followed our movements from their own prison-like little observation boxes.

I often wondered who were the real prisoners, they or we. Hail, rain or snow, they were cooped up in their dovecotes in four-hourly stretches with never a chance in a lifetime of a pot-shot at an escaping kriegie.

You might be tempted to ask, what did we think about? I can only reply, it would be difficult to say. The idea of freedom certainly took precedence; no matter if we privately thought of home and our womenfolk, children and friends, parents, food, or ambitions in civil life, the whole gamut of our wishes and emotions would be swamped by the question, "When will it end?" – the end!

It included everything. Once a prisoner, life halted like a moment of inertia and would not regain momentum until those prison gates opened and we were free to return home. Then, and then only, would life move forward again. As each fresh batch of P.O.W.s arrived they had first to unburden themselves of the latest news, then face the inevitable question, "How long will it last?"

There was never any doubt of the final outcome in spite of the meagre news to assist one's private assessment of the present state of affairs. The only significant factor in our calculations was time – yet time was our greatest enemy and the only weapon we had to help our friends at home. We knew the Allies would emerge victorious ... but when? And the only way we could help was to embarrass the Germans and occupy as many of their troops as possible in the maintenance of discipline in the various P.O.W. camps.

To cheer us up, our thoughtful hosts began treating us to a weekly film show, similar to the British news reels. "*Die Wochenneues*" or weekly news, consisted mainly of brave German fighter pilots shooting down "*Die Engländer*", or their irresistible armoured columns crashing through France, Belgium, Holland, Denmark, Norway, or anywhere else their imagination could dream up, and depicting cheering crowds greeting their so-called liberators, with a subtle inference that England was next.

The kriegies cheered louder than the guards at anything and everything in an effort to convey our disbelief. Then one day an irrepressible P.O.W. stopped the whole show.

By now we had invented all kinds of apparently mad games, among which was the target-towing plane.

You first caught a healthy fly or blue-bottle, then attached a length of fine cotton to its rear legs, and at the other end attached a small paper cylinder such as a cigarette minus the tobacco to act as a drogue. You then launched the "flycraft" and checked how long it remained airborne. These endurance tests became all the more interesting with a cigarette as a side bet.

At one of these film shows the irrepressible had taken along his champion flycraft motored by a powerful blue-bottle, veteran of many competitions, and launched his pet just when a big air battle was in full cry on the screen.

Naturally, it flew straight into the light beam across the eye of the projector. You can imagine what happened. The flycraft became many times magnified onto the screen and joined in the air battle. And truly its capers created the most lifelike situations, while the kriegies let out wild yells and cheers as long as it remained in the light beam.

The German officers rose from their seats in the front row like one man and stamped out of the hall; their stormy expressions forewarned us of trouble ahead, and sure enough, at evening roll-call they informed us there would be no more film shows.

As a further reprisal, they set up amplifiers outside the main gates and treated us to half-hour doses of those delightful, crude perorations, interlaced with lots of martial music, invented for British ears by that evil genius Lord Haw-Haw. That soon ended, when they found we retired to the huts as soon as the mobile loud-speakers appeared at the gate.

Including the flycraft endurance tests we had several other crazy games; such as earwig races, baiting spiders with wingless flies, frog-jumping competitions – high and long jumps – beetle races, and many Goon-baiting games. The competitions were governed by the most stringent rules and supervised by committees, and well supported by many competitors.

There were eliminating rounds, quarter-finals, semi-finals, and finals, with a small prize for the winners. Our champion flies, frogs, beetles and earwigs, were guarded and fed like princes, and eventually buried with all the pomp and ceremony befitting the Gladiators of Rome. No wonder the Germans decided we were a race of madmen.

For stopping the film shows we engaged in every petty-fogging reprisal our mischievous minds could invent until, in desperation, they threatened the most heinous punishments if we failed to behave.

Down one side of the compound there was a road which led to the local recruit-training barracks, and along which squads of young German soldiers frequently marched during their training, led by instructors, and singing marching songs: the favourite as they passed the compound being, "We're marching away to England!"

It was our ill-mannered practice to crowd at the wire and sing as loud as possible any old tripe, dreadfully out of tune and time, as they went by, until they were all out of step and the song died a dismal death. The infuriated instructors screamed at us through the wire, and swung their revolvers about to our great delight, noisy jeers, and one final, big, father of them all, concentrated raspberry.

When our German-speaking P.O.W.s picked up the words of the song and substituted for the delights they were going to have in England, the foulest punishments possible, and we sang it to them in German accompanied by pantomime, official channels diverted them to a different route and our little game came to an end.

CHAPTER NINE

Winter arrived with such awful weather we declared tunnelling "out of season", so that Bill and I looked around for other interests. Which means escape interests. After long hours of discussion we came back to the wire. It looked most forbidding.

The summer had produced such a growth of weedy vegetation among the jungle of wire in the corridor that no amount of hand picking could possibly remove it, and while this had its drawbacks it offered certain advantages.

They hadn't thought of chemical weedkillers or flame guns in 1940; in any case they would win the war by Christmas, so why worry? This meant if only we could reach the wire unseen, the weeds would hide us while we hacked away, and if the job couldn't be done in one shift the weeds would again hide our handiwork for the time being. All we needed was the cutters and a really dirty night. As no-one had, as yet, attempted the wire, we hoped the Germans were lulled into a false sense of security, thinking the fences were impregnable.

Less than a mile away on the coast there was a small creek which harboured a fleet of small fishing vessels. With luck, we could swipe one of these and reach Falster, the nearest Danish island, about forty miles away, and be among friends by daylight.

"Shall we have a do, Bill?" I enquired as we ambled around the compound.

"Can't see anything else for it. At least, we stand a chance of being home for Christmas," he replied.

We set to work and produced a couple of peaked caps similar to those worn by most German civilians, and somehow, in spite of the many searches, I had managed to retain my small compass. But even now we had neither map nor wire-cutters. Then by a stroke of luck we found a chap who had secreted a silk-type miniature map covering the north German coast. With his permission I made an enlarged copy using contraband pen and marking ink, with which to set course for our friendly little island – matters like tides, prevalent winds, currents, and other navigational niceties had to take pot luck. If Captain Cook could circumnavigate the globe on a wonky compass, an astrolabe, and a mutinous crew, then surely we could make a land-fall over a distance of only forty miles.

There seemed no hope of acquiring a strong pair of wire-cutters until someone reported having seen a hefty pair of carpenters' pincers and suggested they be converted into cutters. We lay doggo for a full ten days before "collecting" these and a couple of files from a trusting carpenter's bag, and after much secret and laborious filing produced a most satisfactory pair of wire cutters.

All we needed now for the word "go" was a favourable night; in other words, a night that keeps policemen sheltering in shop door-ways. I love dogs, but it would be helpful if the guard dog could pick up a stinking cold and lose his scent just for one night.

Arrangements were settled to start a successful diversion as a cover up, so we just had to wait. Lock-up time for the huts was now four-thirty p.m. with roll-call taking place inside the huts at five o'clock. Hence with daylight at eight in the morning we had a maximum of fifteen hours' darkness to complete our task.

I spent an idle week until November did its very best by providing one of the dirtiest nights I'd ever known; all we could wish for breaking camp, but a bit unpromising for a forty-mile sea voyage in an open boat, a top-grade gale blowing, a thick curtain of rain, and the huntsmen on our shirt tails; although it would be as unhelpful for them as it would be helpful but uncomfortable for us.

For various reasons we chose to cut through the wire at a point on the side opposite our hut and forty yards from one of the guard boxes. Being a windy and wet night we agreed the inside patrol and his dog would patrol close to the huts for shelter, which gave us partial insurance against the guard spotting us, or the dog scenting us. Our main hope was in the guard finding a permanent shelter by the huts and remaining there until the weather improved.

To reach the seat of operations meant crawling under three huts, racing across a twenty yard open stretch and negotiating a further twenty yard patch of Brussels sprouts, before reaching the wire.

Had we chosen the alternative of only eight yards to reach the wire from our own hut and had to lie low while the guard made a circuit, the dog would most certainly smell us out, and the Goons would do the rest – and in the darkness, that means the guns would have spoken first.

Darkness descended early that evening; we were locked in at four-thirty and dutifully stood by our bunks to be counted in at five o'clock. We wasted no further time on vague fears of the unknown; we stuffed our bellies with food, gathered together our bits and pieces of escape equipment, donned Balaclava helmets, caps, gloves, and removed the floor boards. The boys wished us the best of luck, and we immediately scrambled below and waited. Sure enough, along came a pair of jackboots, and four canine paws past the underneath edge of the hut, and as soon as they were safely round the corner we heaved ourselves out and dashed for the shelter of number two hut and again waited, and again to number three.

So far, so good, but there was still the open stretch and then the sprout patch. I felt like a small mouse while crawling under the huts, but as soon as I got into the open I felt as big as an elephant. We made it across the open stretch without the searchlights blazing out, and I flung myself between the rows of sprouts for cover with Bill close on my heels, and waited, scarcely daring to breathe.

... No shouts ... no searchlights ... no guns blazing away ... nothing happened!

I breathed again and crawled forward between the rows feeling grateful to the tall sprouts for their friendly assistance ... but oh, the wet! I had no idea sprouts could hold so much rain, by the time we reached the warning wire we were both soaked to the skin.

I left Bill to stay put among the sprouts while I did a belly crawl forward to the main jungle of wire. The cold rain had numbed my fingers and I felt damned uncomfortable, but I soon had my cutters at work.

This was the moment I had so long anticipated and a warm thrill passed through my body. The snick, snick, of the cutters made pretty music in my ears as I merrily hacked my way through the wire. By the time I was half way through I was so concentrated on my job I became quite oblivious to my surroundings, and the pelting rain didn't mean a thing when ... crash!

There was an explosion that petrified me for a moment. It sounded right in my ear and I jumped like a startled rabbit. Great Scot! It was at my ear all right, for there, not more than four feet away was the business end of a rifle pointing directly at my head from the *outside* of the wire, and the gunman bawling his head off.

At the sound of the shot, which the guard had fortunately fired into the ground to scare us, all the searchlights came into action and finally settled on Bill and me. It was a ludicrous moment as the lights revealed Bill squatting in the sprouts like a surprised squirrel about to eat a nut.

I was lying half in and half out of the jungle of wire and we were both compelled to remain where we were until an officer and a reinforcement of guards arrived to escort us away. When Leut. Peeber, the officer, recognised the two culprits, he sneered, "Bad luck Mr. Fancy ... better luck next time," a sentiment with which I heartily agreed. "Sprouts to you, yer bastard," remarked the irrepressible Bill, sotto voce.

Next morning, following a severe reprimand, the Commandant awarded us another twenty-one days in the cooler with the added reminder, "Don't try it again, Mr. Fancy, or I'll probably be obliged by authority to have you shot. Think it over!"

While languishing in the cell we were visited by the guard who first spotted us and fired the shot. During the conversation he revealed that he had been sheltering exactly as we had anticipated (and having a smoke I've no doubt) when my movement in the wire scared the life out of him. What irony! My fourth attempt frustrated by a scared guard!

Towards the end of our period of meditation in the cells, I felt certain our jailers would break up our unholy partnership and send either one of us to another camp. It seemed to me a natural thing to do, and I spent quite a lot of anxious time cunningly quizzing every possible source of information, without, of course, putting any such ideas into their muddled heads.

I even went so far as to bait my hook with a couple of precious cigarettes – supposedly forbidden in the cells – when one day an interpreter visited my cell and jokingly remarked, "The Commandant is thinking of putting you in a straight jacket every night to put a stop to your wanderings, Mr. Fancy."

"Oh!" I thought "... I wonder how much more he knows," and parted with a cigarette, suggesting, "Perhaps he'll send me home if I make another bid, eh?"

But he didn't bite, so after further general conversation and another cigarette, I remarked, "He's threatened to have me shot. I think I'll ask for a transfer!"

That did it. "There's not much hope of that," he replied. "He calls you his pet Mole. You keep the guards from falling asleep!" That was all I wanted to hear.

I left the cooler with a clear conscience, yet there was plenty of open grumbling and grousing, and not a little sulky peevishness at my so-called selfishness.

On a major issue of Germans versus P.O.W., however wrong the P.O.W. might be, we stood together like one man and his trouble became everyone else's trouble. Nevertheless, fellows like Bill and I, deeply bitten by the escape bug, can become a confounded nuisance to their comrades and bring reprisals on innocent heads. Not that they would ever withhold their willing help or encouragement to an intending escapee; still nothing can alter the fact that, remaining behind, they have to face the interrogations, searches, and general upheaval caused by the suspicious ferrets, while such as Bill and I, get away and have fun! And to be hauled out for a roll-call and search on such a night as the one we chose for a break would strain the tolerance of an archangel.

So here we are again, and having failed, we accept the banter, friendly or otherwise, and join in with whatever is brewing.

At the moment, with Christmas so close at hand there is certainly some brewing going on. It's amazing what a little cheerfulness and ingenuity can achieve with limited resources in such circumstances.

Hidden away somewhere in our crowd the talent could be found for almost any undertaking; there were musicians, even an organ builder, book-binders, artists, writers, school masters, engineers, electricians, almost every trade was represented; in fact, you couldn't ask for someone to do some apparently impossible task but that an expert was there to do it.

Sandy, I remember, sat on his haunches deep in thought for scores of hours, like a broody hen, and no-one could drag from him the secret of his occupation, but on Christmas morning the neatest, and the most beautiful Christmas card you ever saw complete with a little verse fitting the character of each recipient, appeared at everyone's place at the breakfast table.

We all took a hand at chain and lantern making, and in the end we achieved a pleasing spectacle.

Outside working parties had been resumed and became a never-ending supply column for our interior requirements. There seemed no article or information they couldn't supply. Then again they received small payments in money, *Lager Geld*, or prison money. This led to the idea of starting a compound canteen. The idea was explained to the Commandant and he willingly gave his permission.

The idea was quite simple; the lazy-bones inside the compound sacrificed a portion of their rations for the hard-working outside party, who in return contributed an agreed part of their earnings to a central fund, to stock the canteen and provide a few coins for pocket money. And believe it or not, through the good offices of the German responsible for our canteen supplies we were able to obtain a supply of Christmas beer. It was a strange sight to see a brewer's cart pull into the compound with a load of barrels.

Young Ken Murray contributed a few drawings of his favourite nudes to the canteen decorations; women were always his favourite topic. Often when all was dead quiet in the room he would suddenly rear up on his bunk and scream in his high falsetto voice, "I want a woman, I want a woman!" and then subside with groaning noises. Then Chas, would dash over shouting, "Here you are Ken," and show him a picture of some wind-blown German Frau. Ken would take one look then pretend to be violently sick over the edge of his bunk.

Really and truly, the Christmas food preparations became an ordeal. There was nowhere to sit, you had to retire to the wash-house or latrine to write a letter, and unless you carried the whole of your belongings about with you they would never be seen again until they turned up in some concoction or other.

The lid of every tin you possessed became a cake-tin. Your biscuits, fruit, bits of cake, stale bread, milk powder, honey and what have you, returned in the form of a cake or Christmas pudding, and I'm not too sure my missing gym shoes weren't sacrificed to produce a pungent soup. I do know all my letters became paper chains.

Old Lute certainly knew his stuff. Once he produced his oven we hardly dared breathe. He pottered about grinding biscuits, bits of stale bread, mixing it with our milk powder, currants, sugar, and anything else we possessed, sent us off to find firewood, which he added to the fire like a chemist making up a dangerous prescription, adding "Ah! Just so!"

Then when the cake was rescued from its ordeal of fire and smoke he began spearing it with a splinter of wood, and after critically examining the splinter declared, "Ah, it's ready, lads!" We gathered round gazing proudly at the masterpiece, then yelled like one man, "When do we eat, Lute?"

"Pay up, the lot of you," exclaimed Lute, putting on his most aggressive frown.

"Before this cake is touched, I want some chocolate out of each one of you to ice it." So with the expression of a bunch of martyrs we each doled out a couple of squares for the tyrant.

"Are you sure the cake justifies this colossal sacrifice?" I enquired with mock solemnity.

"Now listen, Fance," replied Lute, "If you don't want any cake say so now, and you can have your chocolate back," offering me the already melted chocolate in the pan.

The finished article had the chocolate spread over it and, with a few kernels extracted from prune stones dotted here and there, it had quite the professional touch. Lute put it away in a Red Cross box and threatened everybody with sudden death if they so much as looked at it until the appointed day.

Meanwhile, Eastick, our brewer, filched from us the remainder of our fruit, dried or fresh, all the honey he could round up, and anything else likely to provide a kick. All the ingredients were steeping in an old earthenware crock – heaven only knows where that came from unless from under his bunk! – and floating on the surface of the brew was a raft of toast supporting some brewers' yeast, again from the Lord only knows where.

And Eastick watched over this concoction like a witch preparing a death brew – we could only express our fears of survival.

Not to be outdone, the Germans announced they were giving us a Christmas dinner consisting of *Schweinfleisch und Weihnachtskuchen*

– pork and Christmas cake – the cake was just ordinary slab cake, but this detracted nothing from their generous gesture.

My Christmas enjoyment was completed when, on December 23rd, I received the news that I was the father of a baby girl who would be three months old on Christmas day.

When the great day arrived, we all made a special effort to spruce ourselves up somewhat, and a German Pastor sent word he would be pleased to hold a communion service at six-thirty in the morning. He conducted the service in English and there were few absentees.

We then returned for breakfast: porridge, bacon and fried bread, toast and marmalade and coffee. After breakfast I did a few circuits with Bill discussing our ever-green subject of escape, and at ten-thirty we held a carol service in the concert hall, with almost every P.O.W. in attendance including some of the guards and interpreters. Herr Schreiber, I remember in particular, was there; he was always on hand with his lovely baritone voice when there was a spot of singing on the go.

Everything was now ready for dinner, with Lute, the High Priest, presiding at the stove. The table was set and our pork, stuffing, and Christmas cake collected from the German cook. Brewer Eastick served us with one of his cocktails, and really, I was astonished. Eastick certainly knew his onions.

We waded into pork and stuffing, mashed potatoes and peas, Christmas pudding and custard – Red Cross supplies – and finished off with cheese, biscuits, and coffee – the German cake would have to go into reserve. The feed so strained our unaccustomed stomachs that there was nothing else for it but to lie back and take things easy.

At tea, good old Lute hovered over us like a hen mothering her chicks, with *our* cake holding pride of place. As Lute ceremoniously cut and handed each one of us a piece of cake he eyed us as though defying anyone to say one wrong word.

Then he watched anxiously as we sampled it.

It looked very nice ... it tasted very nice ... it *was* nice! "Good old

Lute!" we yelled in chorus, "It's bloody good." And really, I've since tasted much worse shop cakes. Lute was all smiles as he reached under his mattress and fished out a hefty length of wood. "You can burn that now. I kept it ready to brain the first one to complain."

In the evening, our hosts co-operating to the extent of omitting roll-call, we tapped the barrels and settled down to make an evening of it.

We sang all the old squadron songs with more gusto than tune, often to words that would have been frowned upon in most drawing rooms at home, not forgetting a special adaptation for Adolf and his cronies. By "lights out" many of the younger ones had fallen by the wayside and had to be put to bed. By general agreement it had been a "Wizard do", but oh dear, next morning! The fancy brews must have contained delayed action bombs, for everybody wakened with a deathly pallor, and went about holding their heads. Nobody wanted any breakfast and by lunch time there wasn't an aspirin in the camp.

Christmas had come and gone and still our hosts hadn't won the war as they so often boasted they would. The interpreters and Goons, with whom we had most personal contact, suffered the tortures of the damned from our jeers and insults, and often expressed their annoyance in strong terms. We comforted them by saying, "Don't worry, when the Allies win you must stay with us, we'll guarantee you safe custody!"

Although Bill and I remained the two inseparables, we did everything possible to give the opposite impression, by creating the illusion that we blamed each other for our last failure, hoping the interpreters and ferrets would report back to the Commandant that we were no longer friends and thus be less likely to attract their attentions.

CHAPTER TEN

At this period, mid-January, we were completely snowed up, and from reading the German papers we discovered the Baltic sea was frozen solid and closed to all shipping. The idea of escape had never been absent from my mind, and one day I was sitting on Bill's bunk having a quiet natter when suddenly he came up with another bright idea:

"Eh, John, why not *walk* across the frozen sea?"

"That sounds O.K., Bill, but how do we get there? We haven't so far succeeded in getting beyond the wire!" I replied.

But the more I thought of it, the more I became impressed with his idea. Soon we settled down to the serious planning of ways and means, and it became clear to me we were regarded as being a bit mad even by our best friends.

"Forget it, you blokes, and settle down. You're going ga-ga. Why don't you see the M.O.?" seemed to be the general opinion.

Maybe we were a bit mad, maybe the others were mad and we the only sane ones. Maybe it would be helpful to be thought so, but if only we could get away, we wouldn't be thought mad any longer.

We decided to have a go, it now being early February. We had tried tunnelling and now dismissed the method as impracticable. We had tried cutting through the wire and failed only by a stroke of bad luck. We had no magic carpet but surely there was some way to get outside!

We settled down to analyse our failures. After all, we *had* trespassed beyond the dangerous warning wire once without being shot, and even cut half-way through the menacing jungle of wire, and were caught only because a guard was skulking in shelter instead of doing his duty, patrolling!

"Right!" I exclaimed to Bill, "We were caught by the *underneath* route, and again by the *through* route. What about going *over* the wire, Bill?"

Yes, it would mean another wire job, so we concentrated on means to go over the wire, and finally chose to go over the wire near the guard box at the corner opposite the main entrance to the camp.

Owing to the cold hard spell they had withdrawn the interior compound patrol and his dog and this should prove an advantage during darkness. We would have to time our departure with bad weather in the hope there would be no outside patrol close at hand. It was a bit nerve-wracking to think we should have to make our attempt right under the very noses of the two armed sentries in the elevated box, but even this had its advantages.

The plan was to scale the ten-foot high corridor fence using the sentry-box stilts themselves as hand grips, thus avoiding being hung up on the wire itself, then to cross the horrible corridor itself by hand over hand movements along the heavy underneath timbers carrying the flooring of the box. After that we should have to climb down the stilts on the outside, hoping our clothing would not become entangled on any loose wire that might be about.

Once beyond the warning wire and close up to the sentry-box we would be safely out of the sentries' angle of view, nor could the searchlights be deflected at this sharp angle; although we should still be visible to the occupants of its companion box but only provided they turned their lights on us.

Our preparations included a white camouflage to cover our dark clothing and help us to merge into the snow-covered area; this, including white hoods to cover our heads, we made from old vests discarded by the more affluent kriegies who received parcels from home. Seen in our going-away outfits, one of our gloomy kriegies, sceptical of our chances, thought they would make very nice shrouds. We each made a small haversack to strap across our backs so they would not catch on the barbed wire; I still had my compass, retrieved from among the sprouts where I had dropped it, which I intended to rely upon instead of doubtful maps.

Bill, the lucky blighter, received regular cigarette parcels from home, and with these purchased a couple of thick woollen pullovers and two pairs of warm gloves. After several time checks we discovered the searchlights came on roughly at five minute intervals and lasted about thirty seconds. The outside patrolling guard on our particular stretch of wire was more irregular in his patrols, depending on weather, and how much he had to talk about with the guards in the boxes. He was one of the risks we would have to accept as there was nothing we could do about it. I had doctored the window shutters so that they looked safe from outside yet could be opened and refastened from inside, so we were now ready for the off.

We chose a night of heavily driven snow, and clad in every stitch of clothing we possessed in addition to woollen socks over our boots, and wearing two pairs of gloves, we sallied forth ... this time through the window. It was bitterly cold with a howling gale driving the snow into our faces while we hid round a corner of the hut waiting for the most dangerous searchlight to switch off.

As soon as this happened we counted on having five minutes to act before it came our way again, but where was the patrol? I managed to spot him just passing the sentry-box on his way in the opposite direction to our approach, patrolling the wire. With luck we should reach the protection of the sentry-box without him seeing us.

The guards in the box were stamping up and down to keep themselves warm, little suspecting that two pairs of eyes were anxiously watching their movements through the glass upper frontage, so we sneaked across to the main wire. Here we parted for the climb, Bill to go over using one end of the box, and I the other.

A certain amount of loose wire lay around the base of the stilts no doubt in anticipation of such an attempt as this, and this had to be carefully trodden down to reach the upright supporting stilts before we could commence the climb. This accumulation of wire had escaped our notice and it was only the heap of snow gathered on top that warned me of its presence.

I couldn't see Bill although he was no more than twelve feet away and I wondered if he had met a similar obstacle.

The wire creaked alarmingly under my weight as I reached for the wooden stilt and would almost certainly be heard by our enemies above if they suddenly stopped stamping about; fortunately they kindly continued the racket until I reached the top of the stilts and could hear them talking inside the box. At this point the top of my head was within nine inches of the soles of their feet.

Muffled up as we were the climb was a laborious task and I was sweating freely. I waited a few moments to get my breath before making the dangerous crossing. Then grasping the heavy cross member and realising my head was only inches below the lookout level – in fact, they could have touched me and the least glance outside and below would have uncovered our escape – I edged my way across, my boots occasionally dragging on the jungle of wire below, and waited on the outside before descending the outer stilt.

I wondered just where the outside patrol might be at that moment, and remembered how near a bullet had been to my ear last time; I had no intention to provoke another windy shot which might send either of us to the burial yard. You would think I hung there for several hours if I related all the thoughts that passed through my mind as I clung to my precarious handhold in the perishing cold, whereas I hesitated only seconds.

I daren't wait any longer, and although I couldn't see the patrol, I could hear and almost smell the guards in the box above, and their near presence added urgency to the situation, so assuming the patrol was sheltering from the gale, I quietly climbed down the outer stilt to find Bill waiting for me.

This was probably the most dangerous moment in the whole undertaking.

Across the road was the main guardroom with the door immediately facing where we lay crouching in the snow trying to assess the patrol's present whereabouts; anyone opening that door could not possibly have failed to see us. We were between the devil and the deep blue sea. Stay where we were and we were safe until that door opened; move out of sight from the door without prior knowledge of the patrol's position and he sees us before we have time to surrender – then we are corpses. In the darkness, one cannot blame a guard for being trigger-happy.

Then came an ominous moment and everything went silent, the guards overhead suddenly stopped stamping. Had they heard something?

We crouched right down into the snow, and comforted by the knowledge of our white camouflage, we crawled silently away. We covered the first fifty yards with our faces so near the snow-covered earth I could scarcely breathe. Only fifty yards … but seemingly a lifetime, with every muscle tensed to receive the tearing, scaring, sting of a bullet that would leave me writhing and kicking in the snow until death intervened; feeling as large as a cow but straining to appear no larger than a beetle … and for a moment I wondered, was it worth it? We crept warily ahead for a further few hundred yards hoping the storm and the darkness had mercifully hidden our tracks beneath the snow.

I find it strange to recall that we had both hurried on for perhaps a further half mile completely unaware of each other's presence when we suddenly stopped and looked at each other as though we were total strangers … then laughed and grinned at each other like a couple of congenital idiots! Such is the effect of intense mental strain.

It was one moment in my life when I actually felt like shedding tears of joy.

We were free, and I found it hard to believe. Gripping Bill's hand and pumping away for dear life, I exclaimed, "Bill, we've made it. This calls for a celebration. What'll you have?"

"By hell, I know what I'd like right now, a pint of good dark ale. I'm sweating like a pig," he replied with his usual cackle.

So was I. We had hurried forward for half a mile overloaded with clothing and with our nerves at breaking point, quite heedless of approaching exhaustion. We were puffing and blowing like a couple of steam jets as we rested a few minutes to discuss the next move.

Already we noted how the falling snow was kindly obliterating our tracks, and I hoped would continue to do so until we reached the sea-ice. Taking advantage of nature's kindly help, and realising it would be dangerous to allow our overheated bodies to suddenly cool off, we pressed forward towards the creek.

It seemed fairly evident that no suspicions had as yet been aroused at the camp or all hell would be let loose by now, and therefore we would not be missed until morning roll-call, and not even then, if the chaps decided to cover our absence. Nevertheless we kept our ears attuned for sounds of alarm-sirens until we arrived at the creek in the record time of less than thirty minutes.

Before tackling the ice, we were obliged to remove the socks used as overshoes as they were clogged up with great balls of hard snow, and afterwards were surprised to find the going quite good. But on the approach to Zingst, the long neck of land on the seaward side of the creek, there was considerable drifting which made the going much more laborious.

Taking care to avoid the few isolated houses, we staggered across this neck of rough land and reached the vast expanse of the Baltic ice. We plotted the same course we intended by boat had we not been caught among the sprouts, and began our forty-mile tramp across the frozen sea – enough to deter any well-equipped experienced ice men.

By the time we had cleared the coast and were two miles out to sea the snow storm eased up. I felt the Gods were with us. The snow had fallen to cover our tracks right up to a point when it no longer mattered, and now it had stopped just when we could manage without its help. But with now only a thin layer of snow, we were obliged to replace our boot covers to enable us to make faster headway.

We were now very cheerful, thoroughly enjoying the sense of adventure attached to the walk, and chattered together like a couple of runaway school boys discussing the prospects ahead. We realised we'd never cover the whole distance before daybreak and that daylight might prove no friend to us.

"There's no stooks of corn here to offer us a friendly home," said Bill, thinking of other days.

"No, I'm afraid not, Bill. We'll just have to hope and keep moving if we want to live," I suggested, expressing only half my own personal fears.

At about midnight we rested for a hunk of bread and chocolate and a drink of cold coffee, and although we rested for only ten minutes after a few hours tramp over the slippery ice, we became so horribly stiff and cold it required a further hour's vigorous effort before our limbs became free and our bodies warm again.

Before setting out we had estimated that with ten hours of darkness ahead, combined with reasonable travelling conditions, we ought to cover thirty miles before the first light of dawn. It soon became clear we had been over optimistic in our assessment and instead would cover little more than twenty miles.

But why worry? So long as we could steer in the right direction and maintain a steady plod, we should eventually arrive. We preferred to arrive in darkness, as daylight might reveal us to unfriendly islanders who might hand us over to the enemy before friendly help could save us. It was a risk that began to nag at our very innards.

By four a.m. the cold had penetrated to the very marrow of our bones and we began to lag dangerously, so dangerously that we were incapable of the effort to combat the cold. I had the unspoken fear that if we were compelled to rest we would never recover our feet again.

Conversation, except for an occasional "Damn" or "Blast" when one of us slipped, had dried up completely. We decided to take turns setting the pace in Indian file hoping to bring warmth to our numbed feet and put more distance between us and Germany.

We'd been walking for at least a week, or so it seemed, but it was actually six a.m. when dawn revealed a pair of puny, yet hopeful, humans surrounded by an unbroken expanse of ice with many weary miles yet to travel. We felt small indeed as we penetrated the early mist, trying to distinguish the least break on the distant horizon that might betoken a landfall; but no, we were forced to conclude we hadn't made the distance we had fondly hoped.

We were so tired we were compelled to rest, and feeling that food might help us to get along a little faster we ate more bread and chocolate than we should have done. We both groaned with stomach pains.

The decision to rest during the early daylight hours was a sad mistake; nevertheless we plodded on for several more miles when I remarked on the utter silence. It was a bad omen, for in the next moment we heard the faint drone of an aircraft engine.

We flopped down on the ice hoping our white clothing would hide us from watching eyes, feeling the size of a couple of ice-locked battleships. Soon the engine noise materialised into a spotter-plane flying at low level. It circled around us twice then headed east followed by the worst possible wishes one airman could ever wish another.

The cursed occupants couldn't have failed to see us, and it looked as though the hunt was over and we'd soon be back in the cooler. We increased our pace, cursing them with every step; at least we'd give the swine a run for their money! We kept going for a further three hours and even congratulated ourselves that possibly they hadn't seen us after all.

The next time we looked behind we broke into a string of horrible oaths...

We had no further doubts. There on the horizon, travelling in our direction, was a dark object. In a matter of minutes it came within hailing distance and we could hear familiar German voices yelling, "*Halt!*" There was nothing more we could do ... we halted. The dark object became a motor-sleigh with a crew of four, all armed with Tommy-guns. They ordered us aboard and with a wide turn headed back to land.

If words could kill, those four Germans would have died in a thousand different ways, each one far worse than any endured by their victims at Belsen.

To think of all the risks we had taken, all the cruel foot-slogging in the perishing cold and wind without sleep during the past twenty-six hours, the destruction of our great hopes when within three hours of safe protection, and now, in a matter of less time than it takes to tell, we will be back just where we started, to face another period of soul-rotting solitude back in the cooler. Damn ... Blast! ... and curse everything that ever came out of the womb of German womanhood!

If they could have understood one half of the things we said about them they would have dug a hole in the ice and pushed us under, head first. In two hours we were back at Barth where four grinning guards and an interpreter received us and marched us back to camp ... how are the mighty fallen. I dreaded meeting my own friends again.

"Well, well! If it isn't our old friends, Mr. Fancy and Mr. Street, back again," said the Commandant, with a meaning leer. "You don't seem to like my nice camp, Mr. Fancy? Do let me know next time you want to sleep out in the cold snow, and I will arrange it for you!"

"Nuts!" muttered Bill, hiding his disgust with a loud cough.

Knowing Bill, I always went in fear of these interviews, expecting some time he would go haywire and really get it in the neck. Even now I could see he only just managed to restrain himself in time. You must remember the Commandant was always protected by a couple of guards with fixed bayonets at the ready during interviews and the guards wouldn't wait for an order; one move from Bill and those bayonets would have gone through him in an instant, and the questions come later.

The Commandant was very keen to know just how we managed to escape, but we had already arranged what lies to tell him, for our little secret was far too good to reveal just like that. In the end the Commandant sent us to the cooler for four weeks.

"One week extra to rest your poor tired feet, eh?" he sneered.

So here we are back again in the cooler, and now regarded as thoroughly bad eggs, with the threat of a very short life ahead if we persisted in this anti-social conduct.

When the Commandant mentioned his concern for our "poor tired feet" Bill cheekily thanked him as a parting shot. "You are being premature, Mr. Street. Please reserve your thanks. The war is not yet over," warned the Commandant; for the first time he spoke with his mask off, and I didn't like the look on his face.

It transpired we had not been missed from camp until the plane reported two bods on the ice, when a quick check revealed our absence. Again a piece of bad luck had worked against us.

All things come to an end: in spite of the snow and one night's exposure followed by four weeks on cooler diet we duly returned to our billets feeling little the worse, and immediately began making up for lost time on the grub stakes.

Spring was now in the air, and brought with it a new bunch of P.O.W.s bringing better news from home to cheer us after our sad disappointment. Our guards ceased mentioning dates to end the war owing to our horrible ragging, but maintained it was unthinkable to end otherwise than in their favour. The increasing number of P.O.W.s was a sure sign of our ever-growing strength in the air, and each one had something good to report. How we tormented the guards on their fearful air losses in the Battle of Britain! Of course, they never believed us so we checked up their losses in every conceivable place as a constant reminder. It really got under their skin in time and made them visibly sore.

CHAPTER ELEVEN

The lengthening days and health-giving sunshine brought out our gardening experts with spades and seed packets to work on their plots, under the maddening advice of the knowalls who took care to avoid working themselves. Sports and games were in full swing and we could spend more time outside until later in the evening.

By now we had a corps of entertainment experts, and regular concerts were the order of the day.

And with this being also the escape season we got some extra entertainment watching the antics of the ferrets, or Goons, on their periodic searches, and though they thought they were having the fun, we thought we had the best of it watching them sweating and swearing in their ponderous German way, as they dug here and there seeking evidence of our shameful activities. We never missed a chance to raise a chorus of tormenting laughs at each of their failures.

Another source of entertainment was a game called "Looting the Pawnshop". During their searches they would retrieve certain *verboten* articles and deposit them in the stores. During the "off season" the number of these confiscated items became considerable, and in due course whenever a kriegie, or party of them, were sent to work in the stores, cleaning or unloading wagon loads of newly arrived goods, nearly every *verboten* article would trickle back into circulation plus any useful tool or piece of equipment carelessly left unguarded.

In fact, it would make an amusing book in itself if all the monkey tricks and schemes to rob our jailers were put together between covers. Many would seem quite unbelievable.

By the system of barter and promise, mostly promise, fluent German-speakers of whom we now had many among the P.O.W.s would work on the guards. A steady flow of vital necessities such as maps; various coloured inks; information on travel and work permits, for use in Germany and the occupied countries and in some cases the actual documents, borrowed for the making of copies; radio valves; and civilian clothing, was now accumulating in great quantity. By this means, and others not so obvious, we gathered a useful miscellaneous stock, and a real escape organisation was taking shape, ready for the moment to make a tilt at a mass escape.

In fact we were already thinking in terms of tunnelling under the dining hall at the other end of the compound. It meant a greater distance to tunnel and would pass under the roadway used by the lorries bringing supplies to the camp, and great quantities of timber would be required to box-in the road section to avoid a subsidence.

There was an advantage in starting under the dining hall because of a three foot clearance under the floor, thereby offering a greater working space for the tunnelling crew. This greater clearance naturally offered a clearer view underneath by way of the open sides. Nevertheless, by keeping well to the centre it would be fairly safe.

I listened with interest to all the pow-wow on ways and means, knowing full well from experience how necessary it was to learn something from our failures. It must not be overlooked that while we gained knowledge from experience in methods of tunnelling, the Germans were also gaining experience in methods of detection: by now they could almost predict the manner in which we were likely to camouflage our entrance. I therefore pointed out that, more than ever at this stage, it was necessary to reduce the margin of error to absolute zero.

Six weeks had passed since Bill and I left the cooler, and it was already the end of April; I was itching to be up and doing. Despite this restlessness I was determined to eliminate every predictable risk. I hadn't forgotten the look on the Commandant's face when he, for the third time, warned me I was heading fast for the firing squad.

He was a quizzical sort of bloke whose expression seemed to infer that he rather enjoyed my escapes for the fun of fetching me back again; rather like a cat pretending to allow a poor little mouse every chance of escape, several times, before the final kill.

His merry wink seemed to say, "This is fun, Mr. Fancy, keep trying. But one of these days I'll have you wiped out just at the moment when you feel safest!" – and this effort could be just that moment!

And if I knew anything of the German mind, that is characteristically how it works.

It would be the simplest thing in the world to turn a blind eye on my preliminary preparations, and then at the moment of the attempt, while we concentrated on watching normal and expected guards and patrols, to have a duplicate squad sitting pretty at a distance from the exit ready to shoot us down just when we gained our freedom.

Oh, yes, Mr. Commandant. I will be extra careful next time. I could justifiably have been killed during the road-mending attempt, and again in the sprout patch. There must never be a third opportunity. I preferred to remain a living kriegie rather than a dead hero.

The escape committee at last agreed upon the plan and we got down to work. On account of my previous tunnelling experience, I was appointed "ground engineer". It was now a matter for the committee. I was the ground engineer, true, but I hadn't the last word; however, I assured them I would wipe my hands of the job if there appeared the least relaxation in concentrated watchfulness.

There were no hard words and never likely to be any. It was simply that previously I had gone to work under my own individual supervision without asking anyone's permission, except the help of a few willing and faithful friends. But this time I reckoned with my enemies, the Germans, whereas previously I had relied rather too much on myself, and thought too little of my enemies. There was no room for blunders this time!

Because our working site was isolated from the billets, wash-house, and latrines, we organised an elaborate stooging system to give us ample warning to get clear in the event of a sudden flap. We'd just had a full scale search and hoped for at least a fortnight's peace before another major upheaval, so we decided on a blitz effort to push the job through within the next fortnight.

Following this decision, four of us casually strolled across to the dining hall and at the agreed signal dived underneath and immediately started digging out the shaft; I was the digger, Bill dragged the soil away to enable me to work freely, while the other two made a cover to place over the entrance to the shaft.

By lunchtime my six foot shaft was completed and enough of the tunnel for Bill to join me below in the afternoon. We worked like beavers and by the end of the day eight feet of tunnel had been excavated. As speed was the watchword, we dispersed the soil under the floor where there was ample room without appreciably raising its level. We forged ahead at terrific speed; I hacked out the soil, Bill kept my feet clear by hauling it to the bottom of the shaft, Neil Prendergast raised it to surface level, Paddy Flynn, Bill Garriock, and Harry Leggett spread it about under the floor. Others prepared lengths of boarding to shore up the roadway for when we reached there.

The estimated length of tunnel to enable us to surface clear of the outside patrol was sixty feet, and at the end of the first week we were more than half way there and almost across the roadway. Everything was going just as the doctor ordered complete with torches and spare batteries, and I was ready to push up several obscure airholes to keep a regular air flow. With an anticipated week yet to go I was at least two days ahead of schedule.

One morning we were hard at work when the signal went up from our stooges that the food supply lorry was entering camp and would soon be on its way to the cookhouse attached to the dining hall. This was a daily occurrence and, as the lorry was accompanied by the driver and one guard who never bothered much about anything except guarding the lorry, we usually carried on below while it was unloaded and took its departure, those below taking care not to be under the roadway when it passed overhead. As this had been a routine procedure for more than a week we saw no reason to change the order of things in the present case.

The lorry pulled up in the usual way and out jumped ... four Goons! They nipped round the building before anyone could warn us and dived underneath. Paddy Flynn and Harry Leggett made a dash for the huts and got away, the remainder were caught red-handed.

Bill crawled out from the tunnel claiming he was the last one below, while I lay doggo at the face, without quite knowing what was happening above.

But the Goons reasoned – quite correctly – that if Bill was involved, I must be somewhere around. Three of the Goons each collected a prisoner and crawled out of the tunnel, while the fourth waited patiently by the entrance to the shaft, unknown to me, like a cat waiting for a mouse.

I kept still for a few minutes, and with everything seemingly so quiet, I crawled cautiously back to the bottom of the shaft. I then waited breathlessly with my ears tuned for the least sound, and not hearing a thing, I slowly raised myself to ground level and peered out from the entrance ... The sitting Goon just grinned down at me and said, "Come, Mr. Fancy!"

Of course ... I went, and soon found myself again in the cooler facing another three weeks' stretch with an added veiled threat from the Commandant. "You seem to like tunnelling, Mr. Fancy. I'll see if I can get you a job in the mines. Which would you prefer, salt or coal?"

I didn't reply. He was hardly the type to understand a joke in spite of his sadistic humour. I considered him the sort of German to kick a man to death if he had him down, but scream for mercy if you had him down.

Even the interpreter who conducted me to the cell was copying the Commandant and trying to be funny as he opened the cell door. "What time would you like dinner, Mr. Fancy?" he jeered.

"Stick it up your waistcoat!" I replied.

I thought of the spring sunshine I was going to miss, and for the first time in the cooler felt rather despondent. Bill and I had better reserve a couple of cells, I thought; we were certainly entitled to this consideration, every attempt had landed us back here. I was furious, but consoled myself that I was learning … learning the hard way.

In those days, when I left the cooler and joined my pals, it ceased to be a question of, "How long were you *in* for?" the normal greeting. But the greeting now accorded me by facetious friends was, "How long are you *out* for this time?" The jokes and each successive incarceration merely strengthened my resolve to get away.

CHAPTER TWELVE

It was the summer of nineteen-forty-one and our compound was full to overcrowding when the Germans apparently decided it was time to have a wholesale sort out among the old lags, so one day following a roll-call they read out a list of prisoners' names and announced they were being transferred to another camp. Naturally they did not name the camp.

Bill's name was listed but not mine. Here was another example of the splitting up process of groups of recorded bad hats. The Goons evidently thought it was time Bill and I were parted. I knew it must come to this sooner or later and I was most surprised it hadn't happened sooner.

The deportees collected their kit together, and next day marched away amid tantalising shouts of, "See you in England, soon!", "Save one for me at the Rose and Crown", "Take care of the guards when our troops invade". Those remaining behind struck up with "It's a long way to Tipperary", and off they went, as gay a party as though they were embarking for England and home.

As the gate closed behind them I watched the Commandant shaking his head as he strutted towards his office. "Yes," I thought, "… those English are a problem for you. I've no doubt you think we are all quite mad."

I certainly felt mad … mad enough to knock his block off. Bill had gone, and there would have to be a regular re-shuffle among us until one levelled up or levelled down to find comparable intimates.

The empty bunks were soon re-filled by succeeding batches of new kriegies who were now rolling in faster than ever. It was pleasant music to hear from them how the air-war was being stepped up over Germany. What a kick we got out of any bit of home news! Our main current question was "When are we going to invade?"

Security measures were now being so tightened up that we found it increasingly difficult to put any particular line of escape technique in motion. No matter what plan we cooked up it presented such insurmountable difficulties that we were obliged to abandon it almost as soon as it was mooted. This was a most discouraging state of affairs particularly as I found so many anxious co-conspirators among the fresh newcomers.

So few were the probabilities that we even started a tunnel from underneath the latrines. A rather unsavoury choice of site but it offered a short direct route to the outside, and meant negotiating a ditch within the main wire fences.

The ditch proved our undoing.

It was deeper than we estimated and however much deeper we went to pass underneath the continuous seepage of water made working conditions so boggy, and made such a full time job of baling, that we had to abandon the attempt. Later on another party had a go from the same site but at a slightly different angle and met with the same obstacle. I thought I knew the layout of this compound like the palm of my hand but I hand it to the Goons for thinking up the ditch and diverting waste water into it.

Another winter came and went during which we occupied ourselves with concerts and indoor games of the craziest invention, and ice hockey, in preparation for which we had already flooded the compound – the sticks and skates we obtained through the good offices of the Swedish Red Cross, a commission from which had recently visited the camp and noted our requirements.

We formed a league composed of huts, gunners, navigators, radio types, and played some of the toughest and keenest games under the tutelage of our Canadian fellow-prisoners that brought every German from miles around to witness, with explosions of, "*Sie sind übergeschnappt!*" (They are crazy mad!). How on earth we survived the games without serious casualties no one will ever know.

When spring (1942) arrived our hopes ran high that the war would soon end. The camp was so impregnable that every avenue of escape seemed effectively blocked. There was nothing else for it. I would have to make myself such a nuisance they would be glad to send me to another camp. I even prayed for a move to a new and virgin spot where I could begin afresh. Little did I guess at the time that the Germans were thinking on similar lines and would soon grant my earnest supplication.

For some time rumours were heard through the grapevine that there was to be a move, and one morning at roll-call an announcement was made that the whole population of the compound would soon be leaving for new pastures – but when? Was this just a trick to keep us in a good mood and deter any wild spirits from attempting to break out? We were soon to know. Two days later came orders to pack our belongings ready to leave.

When only a few P.O.W.s are detailed for evacuation, packing is a simple matter as any suspicious pieces of contraband can be conveniently bequeathed to those remaining behind, but when a complete compound is evacuated it is a problem to know what to do with any unwanted evidence which may later reveal our sinful activities and bring retribution at the new camp. This retribution could be subtly fitted to forestall the possible uses of such stuff as we had left behind, or a direct restriction, without any given reason, of former liberties.

In the present instance we found ourselves overburdened with an accumulated assortment of personal belongings during our long stay, which we hated to jettison. We knew we should have to hump everything ourselves and if the march were a long one something would have to go, but whether short or long we were never told beforehand – hence the problem.

We found it too painful to bury our hard-won unauthorised stores so some careless blighter crated them up with Red Cross Stores which the Germans kindly transported for us. By some mischance three old lags also got themselves crated up and moved on as "heavy stores". Two of them successfully broke out of their crates which were loaded on trucks while waiting overnight in the Goods Yard, ready to move on next morning. What happened to one of them we never knew, but the other actually succeeded in getting aboard a ship at Stralsund bound for Sweden before he was caught. The third chap failed to break open his prison because of the other cases stacked around and on top of him. We found him in a pitiable condition, still in his crate, three days later when we unpacked our belongings on arrival at our destination.

To return to the main body of evacuees. We moved out, each looking like a rather overloaded Christmas tree, with tied-up bundles hanging from every angle of our bodies. I should have said more like scarecrows when you consider our patched and torn uniforms! We were a very gay party as we sang every inch of the march to the station.

I found it interesting to watch the civilian faces on the way; anyone would have thought they were the prisoners from the stony way they gazed at us. I could only wonder what they were thinking to see these mad English prisoners of war singing along the roads, looking as happy and undefeated as though they were victorious troops returning to their homelands. I felt proud of my race.

On arrival at the station we were informed the journey would take a full couple of days to reach Sagan in Silesia, south-east of Berlin. Under the curious and malignant stares of the not-too-prosperous-looking bystanders, we piled into covered railway trucks and made ourselves as comfortable as possible in the space available.

The train pulled out from the mean little station into the sun-splashed countryside at about eleven in the morning and as soon as we got nicely going the conversation turned to means of escape. It was certainly the right kind of weather for a long hike into the blue and, judging by the mood of the moment, I had visions of a mass escape being attempted.

"Wait a minute, boys," said our top roughneck, "no mass escapes for me. The machine-guns'll mow you down like ripe corn!" And then the fellow produced a brand new pick-axe from his kitbag.

"Where the hell did you get that from?" we exclaimed.

"Jus' found it," he replied laconically, "Didn't you see them on the platform, there were fifty of them! I stuffed the head up my jacket and the handle down a trouser's leg, limped into the crowd and shoved 'em into my bag. They were on a luggage bogie just behind me!"

Well, it shook me. I thought I had a quick eye for anything useful seeking a good home, but I hadn't seen them.

"And what are you going to do with it now you've got it?" I enquired.

"Hook it on a moonbeam and do a gliding stunt back home to the Missus," he replied with a rare twinkle in his eye. "Move your feet and I'll show you."

Immediately he began hacking the floor boards out of the wagon until he had a fair sized gap. "Now look at that and use your thinking box," he went on.

I looked and caught on to the idea instantly.

Usually on these long journeys the trucks were shunted overnight into a siding where we slept the night, but tonight we hoped to slip through this gap and creep silently away during the quiet hours. Too bad! The guards on this route must have been caught this way before. The train had no sooner halted than we were ordered out of the trucks, checked by name and then counted, while other guards closely examined the wagons and the gap was discovered. Naturally, it caused quite a stir, and in the end we were transferred to another wagon and locked in for the night.

The second day's journey passed without incident except that a few pettifogging restrictions were placed on our liberty to repay for the damaged truck. We were counted and recounted at every stop to the accompaniment of our ribald remarks which usually reflected on the parentage of all Germans; we were locked in the trucks without a streak of daylight, making it impossible to tell night from day until we arrived at Sagan early one evening. The march from the station was so short I hardly had time to check my surroundings before we were locked in the billets.

These we found very different from our last. They lacked the comfort of our small cosy rooms and stoves, and we found ourselves in barn-like wooden huts composed of two-tier bunks with only one stove in the centre of each hut. But as you move around a bit you develop an aptitude for settling in with your belongings in a matter of a few minutes.

Next morning they unlocked the hut doors and I was glad of the opportunity to stretch my legs while pounding around the interior perimeter while at the same time inspecting the layout of the camp.

CHAPTER THIRTEEN

The new compound was much larger than the old one, with similar defence precautions except that the warning wire was roughly thirty feet inside the compound away from the main barbed-wire fences, and would mean a longer tunnel to dig from whichever point we chose to make a start.

Our inspection revealed that in the recent past the whole area must have been a huge forest. An area had been cleared of trees, the stumps of which were clearly visible in the compound, and the camp made within the clearance. The stumps would have to be dug out from the compound before we could play any games or sports.

The forest of pines surrounding the compound offered dark and forbidding prospects to the would-be escaper. Nevertheless, I reflected, no camp is stronger than its weakest loophole, so I must search diligently until I found it.

We had been here only three weeks when I saw a new batch of kriegies arriving, or rather I thought they were new until I saw the amount of kit each was carrying. Newly captured air types usually have very few possessions following a forced landing, and only the old lags can accumulate such quantities. I searched their faces for old friends, and when the gates opened and they marched in, there was Bill and all the old gang grinning like a school of monkeys!

I was delighted to see Bill again, but at the same time I wondered what could be behind such a move. I knew the German mind well enough to realise they would not bring old friends together from sentimental reasons. There was a snag somewhere. Either they thought the compound was impregnable and it would be a good idea to collect all the bad eggs into one basket, or they had something worse in pickle. It was something we should have to find out.

As soon as the newcomers were dispersed to billets Bill and I had a good old natter on our experiences since last we parted. He laughed his head off as I related the unprintable incidents concerning the latrine tunnel.

He told me he had been down at Stalag 8.B., the army camp in which we had spent an uncomfortable three weeks in August 1940. Apparently it had developed enormously and was now used as a base camp from which large working parties were selected for the mines, factories, and farms in the surrounding district.

Bill had tried one break from a farm working-party, but had been given away by civilians the following day as he was heading into Czechoslovakia.

Merton and Pavey had both made a break but were caught by the Germans in Czechoslovakia after three weeks on the run. Bill found conditions at 8.B. much worse than he had previously known and was very glad to leave it.

Since my arrival we had been mainly occupied digging up the tree stumps to clear the compound in readiness for gardening operations – with an eye to our main theme. The newcomers had missed this sweating job but immediately set to levelling the land. Within a week, plots were staked out and gardening was again in full swing, while Bill and I discussed the future possibilities of testing the camp's impregnability. The compound was composed largely of sandy soil, which offered easy digging and gave us ideas. We decided to stake out a plot and have a go at gardening … I confess, not without ulterior motives.

Our manner of starting must have seemed most peculiar to our watching guards. We picked a site for our garden, way out in the open as close to the warning wire as we dared without arousing undue suspicions. It was in full view of two guard boxes as if to say, "Now here's two bad hats, and to prove we have no evil intentions we're going to work right where you can watch us all day long."

And here, one afternoon immediately after lunch, looking as innocent as a party of doves, a circle of chaps squatted down to an afternoon's game of cards with a large blanket stretched over their knees in place of a table. There was nothing unusual in this except that I was underneath the blanket busy with my tunnelling knife cutting a nice shapely hole in the ground. As I dug and pushed out the soil, the quarrelling card players shuffled about spreading the stuff around.

The guards showed their interest in this game by watching the players through their binoculars, and I thought, if they were enjoying themselves then everyone else was quite happy. By the time the call went out for tea I had excavated six feet of tunnel – enough room to work and hide the worker.

The innocent-looking boards I had earlier smuggled out and which were used by the players to sit on now fulfilled their intended purpose as a covering for the hole. So far, so good. I felt satisfied.

To sustain the guards' interest in our pose of innocent gardeners, we thought it about time to demonstrate, for their particular distraction, a more flamboyant and active attitude towards bringing our garden into being; obviously, a card school couldn't sit in exactly the same spot day after day without exciting their curiosity ... nay, even suspicion, nor could sitting players successfully dispose of an ever-increasing quantity of soil with the same ease.

So after the dispersal for tea along came two other chaps who, pompously and with a great display of measuring from every possible angle, finally staked out a pretentiously large garden.

The next morning we began gardening in earnest, vigorously digging and raking but all the time taking care to bring any surplus of soil so as to form a large patch of broken soil around my initial opening – but we did no actual tunnelling. The following morning Bill and a pal went out with rakes and started to work carefully uncovering the tunnel entrance, although to all intent seemingly to level the surrounding area.

A little later I casually trickled out and began a conversation with them, pointing here and there as if making suggestions. Then at a given signal when both guards were otherwise engaged I dropped straight down and inside the hole while Bill went on raking a spot between the hole and the guards' line of vision. In the event of any suspicious move by the guards, Bill carried a small ball of paper in his hand which he would drop into the hole as a signal for me to pop out with all speed. I allowed a few moments to pass and as nothing happened I began digging and pushing the excavated soil towards the entrance.

The entrance took the form of a shallow slope, like a rabbit bolt-hole; naturally, facing away from the guard boxes. I would push the soil to the edge of the hole while Bill casually raked it away and distributed it over the garden, taking care not to spend too much time in the area of the entrance. For obvious reasons I had to work with the minimum of equipment, and in those circumstances I chose a line of treestumps to give me direction, using the stumps and their roots to hold up the roof while I maintained a depth of a little more than two feet between my roof and the garden surface.

At this depth, by using a thin rod I was able to drill small holes at suitable intervals through the roof, to obtain a sufficient supply of fresh air; and further, by fixing a small mirror in a wire bracket hanging at an angle of 45° under each hole as I progressed deeper into the tunnel, I cast a shaft of sunlight directly on to the tunnel face, which simplified my task considerably.

By the aid of this little lighting invention I was able to make rapid progress, and at the end of a couple of days I found it necessary for Bill to join me in the tunnel. For both of us to enter the tunnel we carried out the same procedure as for one, with a slight modification. First Bill and another chap would be working on top when I sauntered along and at the appropriate moment disappeared below, then another chap would appear on the scene and Bill would make sure the guard saw him return to the hut. Soon after, Bill would reappear and when all was clear, he too would vanish below. It worked like a well-oiled machine, right up to the last day.

With two of us working below (one full-time removing the soil to the surface) we progressed at an amazing pace, so fast, as to cause our surface crew a spot of bother, they considered the garden was growing suspiciously higher and higher above the adjoining land and would soon become palpably noticeable. As I viewed it later I could see it was all too horribly true. We decided to take in more land.

By the tenth day we were well beyond the warning wire and by evening had reached the main wire fences so we planned to dig right through during the next day, and after the evening roll-call take down our kits with us and break through the remaining crust to the surface and freedom – this last bit of soil we would leave behind us in the tunnel.

We had just begun this final spurt when we received a flash warning which meant that something most unusual was afoot. Such a warning would brook no delay so we scrambled out with all speed and dashed to the wash-house to remove all trace of our unofficial enterprise.

We made cover only just in time! Entering the compound at that very moment were a squad of Goons armed with long spikes. They went directly to the warning wire and began methodically probing the ground as they went along.

Bill and I watched them for what seemed an eternity of agonised suspense as they approached the danger area. It was too much to hope that our hard-won tunnel would escape those prying spikes. Poor Bill was on the point of exploding as they closed in to our patch.

"God blast the swines!" he moaned, "if I had a ruddy grenade I'd let 'em have it. It's all over, Johnny, the bastards have stopped right over it!" He looked really dangerous.

In a few minutes they were all congregated above the spot with their spikes deep in our tunnel, spades were sent for and soon our hole was laid bare. It was time for us to sneak into our billets before they found us. Our secret had been so well kept that the discovery was a genuine revelation to the majority of chaps in camp, and would have remained a secret had not another tunnel on very similar lines just been revealed in the next door compound and this discovery had brought the Goons on the mission which led to our undoing. Just think, in a few more hours we would have been free!

I felt the failure of this effort like a physical blow in the face.

"Either the Gods are reserving us for some special fantastic break-away, or they are protecting us against death from our own rashness," I told Bill. We soon saw the funny side of it all and promised ourselves a "next time."

I'm afraid we lost all interest in gardening after this setback and our garden became sadly neglected. I could only think of it as the grave of all hope. Bill and I were now definitely marked men and viewed with open suspicion whenever we met the Goons.

No matter how tight the Commandant and his satellites put the screw on during investigation of these subversive activities the culprit could rest assured that no P.O.W. would give him away. Both mass and individual interrogations were conducted; and often, thinking they'd found a real softie who would soon break down and tell, they took him aside and bribed him with cigs and other scarce luxuries, subtly and gradually mind you (all of which he slyly accepted, of course). Then when the "softie" had bled them white and no further luxuries seemed to be forthcoming he would "confess" he'd seen a "luscious blonde trying to sneak *into* the compound!"

The Germans seemed to us utterly void of the least intuition or judgement of human character in all their dealings with British or

Empire P.O.W.s. How could they imagine so-called "softies" being members of bomber or fighter crews engaged over enemy territory? We answered their questions by telling them the most impossible imaginative rot, while their blood pressure rose to boiling point. I do believe they'd seriously interrogate the Great Sphinx!

A certain Canadian pilot had a stock answer to all their direct questions – "I'll write to Mother and ask her!" and he had a permanent smirking smile that nothing could wipe from his face. He wasn't alone in this respect, nearly everyone had a repertoire of the daftest replies – we really did everything possible to cultivate the prevalent German conception that the British race were quite mad. No matter whether we behaved naturally or unnaturally they still thought us mad.

And although Bill and I sometimes acted innocent and sometimes deliberately acted like deep-eyed conspirators to draw their attention to something purposely to make them feel fools, they had no doubt that we were the tunnelling culprits. They became more than ever nervously interested in our behaviour. If we were seen about together they watched us like a cat watching a mouse, if we were not seen about together for a few days (and this we did deliberately to test their interest in us) they grew frantically uneasy and the interpreters would rush around seeking us from hut to hut while our chaps directed them always in the wrong direction as we dodged them, until finally we allowed them to find us innocently playing "noughts and crosses" under a hut, in the latrine, or any other such crazy place.

This unhealthy interest in our welfare decided our *modus operandi* for the future. We began by taking a pack of cards and sitting down outside so that the Commandant and his snoopers could see us. We played the time-honoured game of "banker" with cigarettes for stakes. In a few minutes we indulged in a mild argument which, as soon as we were certain the snoopers were watching, became wilder and more violent, until we both jumped up and started a beautiful fight. By arrangement a couple of blokes rushed in to separate us whom we pushed left and right to get at each other, until more came to their help and we were finally subdued under the satisfied gaze of the Chief Ferret who now stood watching from the doorstep of his office.

The crowd then started to argue, taking sides, and making ostentatious efforts to persuade us to shake hands. This we refused to do and slunk off in different directions threatening each other all the time. We were no longer friends, or at least we hoped our guardians were thinking so.

We further promoted this idea by never being seen together again, so that we could work on separate shifts with either one of us always in circulation to be seen about the compound.

CHAPTER FOURTEEN

We had settled down for a while in the hope that our artificial atmosphere of unfriendliness would become firmly established in the minds of the snoopers, when the activities of our repertory company gave us an idea.

We had obtained permission from the authorities to use an empty billet in the centre of the compound for a theatre and, most surprisingly, permission was also granted to excavate a large pit below floor level (part of the floor being retained for a stage) to build seats and a pit for the orchestra.

This meant excavating large quantities of soil which was dumped at the end of the building right opposite our billet. The thing that caused our ears to flap and our eyes to bulge was an old rustic German and his bullock cart. I could scarcely believe my eyes as I watched him loading the cart with this surplus soil and carting it away from the compound accompanied by a guard.

My heart missed a beat or two to see so much soil being carted away free of charge. The same bell was ringing in both our minds; such an opportunity should not be missed. We must start at once from under our own billet and dump our surplus soil on our neighbour's heap. It remained simply a question of which direction to tunnel.

It was too great a distance to tunnel to the outer perimeter wire fences, but we were quite close to the *Vorlager* (German compound)

103

containing the sick-bay, stores, and administrative offices, and although this meant trespassing on a harmless neighbour it would amount to an unthinkable display of ingratitude to decline the invitation. So through the *Vorlager* we planned to go. In effect we planned to dig a tunnel across our own compound and then across the enemy's compound, a total distance of roughly a hundred and sixty yards.

I removed the floor boards from under my bunk and we got down to the real thing. I sank a shaft eight feet deep, filling any available receptacle with the soil, then as soon as the old man went off with a load a squad of chaps rushed out of the hut and dumped their loads ready for his return. It was the craziest thing you ever saw. The two excavating points were so close together that none could tell whether the haulage squad were working for the theatre or me.

I had no idea how long we could rely on help from the bullock cart, so I called the chaps together for a blitz, and by this means I excavated an underground room eight feet square and six feet high leaving two feet of soil above the ceiling to shore up with timber. This room, which I later called the "dispersal chamber", I intended as an insurance against a sudden stoppage of work on the theatre when our means of dispersal by bullock wagon would be severely curtailed.

But fortunately the work on the theatre continued so I opened out on a grand scale. Using a "borrowed" shovel I now dug the tunnel deep enough for me to work standing upright, and planned to continue on this scale for the length of the billet, then reduce to a smaller scale until I reached the German *Vorlager*, when I would break and surface under a large store shed. The distance to this point as accurately as I could estimate, was about a hundred and eight yards – no mean task.

But once there I visualised endless possibilities. From underneath the stores I could range around in undisturbed peace and without fear of interference from the Goons, to say nothing of the chance to loot the stores for any useful pieces of equipment and clothing.

I was eagerly anticipating the joy of ransacking those stores, but mainly I could crawl under the full length of the stores without digging an inch and then start another tunnel at the far end to carry me outside the German compound with very little risk of detection – a distance of about fifty yards that the Goons would never suspect.

I'm afraid my anticipation of the pleasures ahead is carrying me along too fast. I must return to my present task. Our present rate of progress was governed only by the speed at which my helpers could remove the excavated soil. The soil being mostly sand it made easy digging, so much so, that I was digging merrily away at about half-way under the billet when the lot caved in on me – both walls and a large section of the roof. Had I been bending down I would certainly have been suffocated, but fortunately I was standing upright having a breather, and there I stood completely trapped and unable to move even my arms.

It was a desperate moment as I could neither breathe nor shout for help, and the weight of soil held me motionless. I was just beginning to think what a lousy way to die when I felt someone scraping the soil from my face and head.

It was Bill. He had just arrived to see how things were going and finding me missing guessed what had happened and got to work. Except that I swallowed quite a bit of soil with my first few gasps of air so far no damage was done.

He then freed my arms and we both scuttled back expecting another fall any moment. Fortunately the roof held but I didn't breathe freely until we were back in the "dispersal chamber".

We congratulated ourselves that the roof hadn't collapsed outside the hut in the open. It would have taken several tons of soil to fill it in and would never have been safe. As it happened the hole was under the middle of the billet and not likely to be seen from outside, so we decided to leave it as it was.

But such a disaster offered no easy solution; we must first find the cause before attempting any remedy.

So we held a council of war and concluded there was no remedy if we pursued our present course. We would have to start all over again at a new angle from inside our disposal chamber and, to prevent a recurrence, reduce the tunnel to a smaller scale. We could use the abandoned workings to disperse the soil from our new tunnel as and when the bullock transport dried up – and there was every indication that that would not be long.

So away we started on our new and smaller tunnel which we intended should take a course outside the hut. Here again we ran into lighting troubles and reverted to our neat little trick of the airhole and mirror. For some reason we could not fathom, the Goons became very active and were popping in and out at more frequent intervals, thus slowing down the work and becoming a general nuisance. There were more panic scrambles than I thought good for our safety. Nevertheless, we made some progress and three weeks found us about two-thirds of the way to the wire – approximately thirty yards of completed tunnel.

This new course took us alongside one of the brick incinerators, built at intervals around the compound for the disposal of our rubbish. The same old German and his bullock cart, with the ubiquitous guard in attendance, had the job of clearing the residue from these incinerators and on one of his periodic visits set about cleaning this particular one. The guard, with nothing better to do was doodling with a long stick, just idly poking it in the ground.

Suddenly, and to his great surprise, it disappeared straight down one of my ready-made airholes, the one I'd made close to the incinerator.

What a fuss he made. I thought he must, at least, have broken his leg, until I saw his damned stick protruding into my tunnel. Of course, he didn't know I was there although I was working actually right underneath him at the time. For a moment I felt tempted to pull him down and choke the life out of him, but there was the old man to consider and I would have to choke him as well, and that was unthinkable. So realising the balloon would soon go up I decided to vanish, and Bill and I scrambled out with all speed.

We then carefully refitted the lid over the entrance and replaced the floorboards under my bunk with a careful dusting, and by the

ROYAL AIR FORCE STATION,

WYTON,

HUNTINGDON.

25th May, 1940.

Dear Mrs Fancy,

        I very much regret that I have not written to you previously concerning your husband who was posted as missing from my Squadron some time ago.   In the first instance I deferred writing, hoping that he and the remainder of the crew might have landed in France and returned to the Unit. This unfortunately did not happen, and in the meanwhile I was transferred to another Command, and have in consequence been somewhat occupied.

        Your husband was an air observer in one of a number of aircraft which were engaged recently in operations to hold up the German advance into France. We do not know precisely what happened to his aircraft, but the formation encountered extremely heavy anti-aircraft fire and was also engaged by enemy fighters.   It is known that your husband's aircraft completed its mission and made an effective bombing attack on the target. During the withdrawal from the target area, the aeroplanes were subjected to very severe fire from the ground, and it seems certain that his aircraft was disabled by this.

        There must therefore, be some hope that the aircraft landed safely and so there is some possibility that he and the rest of the crew are prisoners of war.

        Your husband had done very well as an observer in this Squadron, and I am extremely sorry that he failed to return on this occasion. I can only hope that he and his companions have been fortunate enough to have been taken prisoners of war. In the meanwhile, please accept my sincerest sympathy in these anxious times.

           Yours sincerely,

           R.17.Foster.

           (Group Captain)

The letter sent to John Fancy's wife, Elsie, by RAF Group Captain John Foster on 25th May1940, confirming that he was missing and expressing the hope that he had been captured as a POW. She had recently discovered she was pregnant with their first child.

Prisoners in the canteen of the hospital to which John Fancy was taken to recover from his wounds after being shot down. He is at the back on the right, looking quite gaunt.

Dulag Luft at Oberursel near Frankfurt was the initial reception and interrogation centre for all captured airmen.

John Fancy (front, far right) and his fellow prisoners at Stalag Luft I, in a photograph taken early in his stay there.

Christmas Day 1940, in Stalag Luft I. John Fancy is not shown in this photograph but he was in the camp at this time.

A photograph taken at Stalag Luft I in 1942 showing POWs who had been recaptured after an escape attempt. Being one of the main protagonists on the escape committee, John Fancy was involved in planning many of the breakouts.

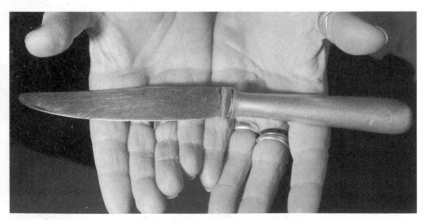

The German-issue butter knife with which John Fancy dug eight tunnels from three POW camps between 1940 and the end of the war in 1945. The strains and stresses to which the knife was subjected eventually caused the metal to split. He used the knife to tunnel instead of a spade because the Germans had a seismograph, which detected digging.

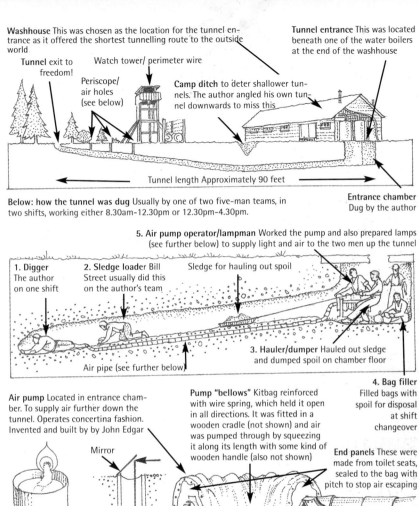

The tunnel dug at Stalag Luft VI (in occupied Lithuania) by John Fancy and his friends. Illustrations by Eric P. Budge.

Kriegies at Stalag Luft 1 in 1942. John Fancy is seated, far right. The prisoners managed to persuade the Germans to convert their canteen into a theatre, which made it easier for them to disguise their tunnelling exploits.

John Fancy on stage at one of the camps during a Christmas production.

KRIEGIE EDITION

YORKSHIRE POST

VOL 1 No 3   HOUSE JOURNAL OF THE WHITE ROSE CLUB   MAY 1944

UNITY IN DIVERSITY

In the cause of war it has been our misfortune to enter upon this phase of restricted existence. Fate decreed it thus, and no matter how unpalatable we find the conditions and elements of this life; how cruel the jest of fate, one fact remains unpleasantly clear and pointed....

On the face of things we are serving Prisoners-of-War for the duration, and with this fact in mind, it is vital we realise the moral and mental dangers offered by this 'Negative' mode of life... As most of the old and seasoned Kriegies are aware, the only way to offset this undesirable state of "Gefangen-ism" is by individual and concerted endeavour towards mind stimulation over a wide field.

In our creditably organised camp one is forcibly struck by the amazing assortment of type - of personalities, and the many representatives of different lands — appropriately lending itself to the phrase .... "Unity in Diversity".

In this united camp therefore, made up of so much diversified humanity, inclusive of so many branches of thought and talent, one is brought to abrupt realisation of the amazing possibilities which are revealed for mental stimulus and mind promotion.

Quite so you agree, but what bearing has the above on our private effort, 'The White Rose Club? .... Exactly the same valuable possibility as hitherto mentioned, but naturally in lesser degree....

Our club is a small private and personal unit of fellowship within the greater atmosphere of Stalag camaraderie...... The following remark by Gilbert White, is truly consonant of the existence and aim of The White Rose Club'...... vide :– "My little intelligence is confined to the narrow sphere of my own observations at home".

The club unites us by virtue of our common ties to a native county. Our roots are deep in the soil of Yorkshire, and we are closely interested and identified with the pattern of Yorkshire life .....All that smacks of county flavour — stimulates our interest.....In short "A dog biting the Mayor of Pudsey is of more direct interest to us than a Mayor biting a dog in Peru"

The need and value of the club is, therefore obvious to us. Under its auspices many idle hours will be profitably filled by learning more of the industrial, social historical and human pattern of the county. The spotlight will focus on scores of interesting topics and subjects through the medium of print and discussion.

Remember that our membership is quite formidable...... amazingly diversified, covering as it does many schools of thought. Artist to Artisan; Textile Expert to Farmer, Doctor to Surveyor, Newspaper-men to Mathematician .... In truth we have a wealth of talent on tap.....

Not forgetting too that in organised strength we are better able to keep abreast of local and topical affairs. More advantageously positioned to approach necessary depts. at home, via Red X.channels. Conversely, 'The White Rose Club' facilitates the efforts of bodies and groups at home who desire to approach and contact Yorkshiremen here.

To-day, the name of 'The White Rose Club' rings familiarly not only within the confines of Stalag Luft VI, but also within the boundaries of our home county. The progress, interests & activities of the club are closely followed by Yorkshire Folk. This fact is truly evidenced by the acclamatory letters which our secretary has had the pleasure to receive.....

For we Prisoners in Germany — is it not a pleasant thought to realise that some measure of the pride we invest in the club, is also shared by others of the county......

R. B. Pape.
Editor.

The Yorkshire Post, Kriegie's edition, produced at Stalag Luft VI in May 1944 by the POWs and distributed to all Yorkshiremen at the camp – all of whom are listed at the back of the *Post*.

John Fancy at the age of 85, photographed in 1998 in his beloved garden in Slapton, Devon.

time the Goons finally traced the tunnel back to the billet I was laid out on my bunk peacefully snoring.

They carefully examined the flooring under my bunk but failed to find an entry from there. They eyed me very suspiciously, and if ever looks could kill I was a dead man there and then. The Chief Goon was especially suspicious, a brutish type of lout and one I disliked intensely – and I don't think he loved me a great deal. He waggled his fist in my face and muttered a string of horrible German threats accompanied each time by a shower of spittle and ending in the German for "Do you understand?" But I found it always most convenient not to understand any German on such delicate occasions.

What he was going to do to me next time didn't sound too encouraging to attempt a next time. He stamped out and banged the door to make his point clear – a quite unnecessary emphasis as I was well acquainted with his brutal methods.

Finally, they co-opted the fire engine to fill in the tunnel, leaving a fair sized duck pond under our billet floor. They ruined some prize lettuces which subsided with the garden over the length of the tunnel, for which the heartbroken owner severed diplomatic relations with me and refused to renew speaking terms until some time after my next spell in the cooler – I've no doubt he thought it a just, though long-deferred punishment, for the crime against his lettuces. Another example of the sort of people it takes to make up a world of P.O.W.s.

Although I was obliged to add our latest effort to the ever increasing list of failures it was some consolation to escape the cooler. Of course, the Goons and interpreters left me in no doubt as to their private opinions on who was the culprit, but officially it was another matter. No form of interrogation would reveal the real instigators hence no individual would be punished, although they often slyly punished the whole camp or compound. What they wrote in their records, only they know.

Probably our No. 1 roughneck's reply at his interrogations best fits the records – "I think it was fairies," or as our Scottish wit replied,

"Ah think maybe it was the Loch Ness monster."

When they tried to trap Bill, that an alleged confession had included him in the party and of course he couldn't tunnel without Mr. Fancy, Bill roared, "If you offered to fly us back home together in the same 'plane I'd refuse to travel in his company. Besides I was hibernating at the time!"

It just didn't seem fair the way the luck ran against us. I recalled the days when my schoolteacher gave me something to draw. He would tear up a dozen efforts and still send me back, "to try again!" I felt by now I had served a fair apprenticeship at tunnelling, yet each new underground venture taught me some new angle, all of which I hoped to use more successfully at some future date.

Despite our many disappointments neither Bill nor myself ever thought of giving up, but perhaps we were too dense to recognise the truth when others so often told us we were wasting our time.

Our repertory company had completed their transformation of the spare billet into a theatre and were now producing some really first class shows, despite the German periodic closures as reprisals whenever some misdemeanour called for corrective treatment.

Since our arrival at Sagan in May 1942, our underground activities had occupied us throughout the spring and summer months and into September. After two and a half years as P.O.W.s we were no nearer home than when we started; in fact, geographically speaking, we were farther away than ever.

Although the news brought in by new kriegies was very heartening we could only conclude we had still a long road ahead of us as P.O.W.s unless we could get home by our own unaided efforts.

One of the gang who worked with us on the garden tunnel, had gone out with a party to collect Red Cross parcels at the local station and vanished, and several months later we learned from new kriegies who had met him in England, that he had arrived home safely via Sweden. It was encouraging to know that not every effort ended in failure.

CHAPTER FIFTEEN

The monotonous sequence of disasters which ended our spring and summer efforts brought with it a period of doldrums during which we were completely devoid of ideas, and in consequence, I can only think, we became rather desperate – and desperation breeds carelessness. After long and frequent examination of our failures and the close approach of winter we reviewed the autumn possibilities for another attempt.

But how, and where?

We found it impossible to renounce the idea of escape and resign ourselves to the long period of stagnation before next spring.

"I'd rather take a chance of being killed than muck around doing nothing for another six months," said Bill. And I could only agree.

We then decided to have another go. This time from one of the latrines which backed up close to the warning wire, a similar unsavoury site to the one at Barth, and so abominably odorous that we had to spend long periods under the cold showers after each spell below ground before being fit for human company. Everything went well until we were about a third of the way across no man's land when we were obliged to stop work owing to a three-day spell of heavy rain. On resumption of work we were faced by such conditions as to be quite unmentionable here.

Nevertheless, with handkerchiefs tied over our noses and mouths we set to and cleared away the awful accumulation of sludge and filth until we reached the face again. Then, one afternoon, I was down below shoring up before proceeding to dig further in towards the wire, when suddenly the whole roof and face caved in. It didn't just collapse, it ran like a never-ending stream of lava. I made a short effort to stop the rush of muddy soil until it gradually drove me back along the tunnel almost to the starting point.

I thought the subsidence might eventually reach to the wire itself, and so it had, only I didn't know it at the time. But the guard outside the wire had seen it and reported it to the Goons, and when I eventually emerged from the latrine there was the Chief Goon waiting angrily to welcome me. Angrily hardly fits the case, he was howling mad, not only for the trouble I had caused him in the past but chiefly because of my filthy unsavoury condition. Without a word he swiped me across the side of my face with his revolver (leaving a scar which I still carry) calling me a "bastard English sewer rat", and all the foul oaths in the German language. Bill escaped scot-free, but I was marched to the cells and, after being hosed down, awarded a month's "solitary".

Our efforts at this camp certainly weren't bringing us much success in the escape line, although I was becoming well acquainted with the topography of the cooler.

It was a pleasant surprise to find a letter from my wife awaiting me on my release. These letters, though distressingly infrequent, due to the German restrictions, were a very bright spot in every kriegie's life, and I was glad to hear the little everyday doings of friends (as it seemed to me now) from an existence of long ago; they helped to keep the flame of hope still burning steadily. My daughter (two years old) was now prattling around the place, and I wondered what our respective reactions would be when first we were introduced.

Out of the many personal parcels of clothing, chocolate, and cigarettes dispatched to me by my family and friends I received very few, but those few were always most welcome. Bill, on the other hand, was snowed under with parcels (or so it seemed compared with my lot) and I used to tell him he would smoke himself to death. Being his pal, I helped him out so that we could both die together.

My first job on leaving the cooler was a spot of laundry work as after a month in close company with latrine odours impregnated into my clothing, I could stand it no longer.

I searched the compound for any avenue of escape that I might previously have missed, but decided the place and the ever-watchful Goons, together with the experience they had gained from my own revealing failures, had just about sealed every pot-hole.

I began to dream of eagles carrying me off or myself transformed into a wriggling worm. My brain was obsessed by one idea, and some of the chaps even warned me to give it up before I went crackers and did something rash.

It was no use, the urge was too strong. I would keep on trying as long as I kept my sanity. I could but hope for removal to a fresh camp where possibly new loopholes existed and my bad reputation would be unknown. I hung on to this hope all through the winter little knowing that the German mind was thinking also along similar lines.

CHAPTER SIXTEEN

It was in the late spring of 1943 when rumours of another move began buzzing around the camp. My flagging spirits revived to the extent that I renewed my interest in the German language through our interpreters, one of whom eventually tipped me off, strictly on the Q.T., that official orders had come through for a move. It was now late in June and two days after my private tip we were ordered to pack our kit, and after being checked and counter-checked, searched, and generally messed about, we marched to the station looking more than ever like a bunch of tramps. This time, much to our surprise, we entrained in passenger coaches with upholstered seats. It was a corridor train to enable the guards to form a roving patrol along the carriages, with two special lookout vans mounting machine guns covering both sides of the train.

As we were told to take three days' supply of food it looked as if we were off on a long journey, so it was some consolation to travel in comfort. We soon moved off and there was much speculation on our probable destination. It soon became evident we were heading north for Berlin, and there we spent the night in a marshalling yard.

Next morning as we moved off at first light through the city, we glued our noses to the windows greedily seeking signs of damage, and what I saw cheered me immensely. I reckoned the damage in terms of payment for my long spells in the cooler.

Whether by accident or design, Bill and I were separated on this trip, he in the forward part of the train and I in the rear, without any means of communication. I was fairly well acquainted with most of the fellows in my compartment although none of them had ever part-nered me in my escape bids and I began to wonder whether one of them felt prepared to take a chance if the opportunity came.

I sat in my corner enjoying the passing scenery. It seemed to me a cruel shame that I couldn't be out there instead of locked up in this small confined space. The green fields and trees seemed to beckon me in some irresistible way, and I began to examine the situation in a hazy sort of fashion without any definite intention to bolt. "Surely, with three days ahead some opportunity will crop up!" I thought.

I looked around at the other fellows trying to figure out a likely partner to join me in a bid for freedom, and my eye settled on a young boy whom I thought looked the type.

"No," I told myself. "He is too young! I'd never forgive myself if he got killed."

He was a young lad called Kernow. I think he must have read something of my intentions from my looks because I'd no sooner dismissed him from my mind than he remarked, "This ought to be a good opportunity for a break, Fancy. What about it?"

I looked him over with a critical eye. He'd certainly never been a party to my previous efforts. I began to wonder, "Has he been planted on me by the Jerries? Is that why Bill isn't with me?"

I had no justification for this suspicious attitude regarding Kernow personally, but it cannot be denied that many of my former ventures had ended in a cloud of suspicious coincidences.

When all is said and done, any chap, after several years under P.O.W. conditions, may break down under cunning German pressure or promises, and no one is in a position to blame him if he does. Only those who have spent five or six years under these conditions can speak with authority. It is all very well sitting at home in comfort and telling yourself what you would do and what you wouldn't do. It is usually the big talker who is first to break down. And we, who were there, know all too well the cunning insinuating ways of P.O.W. Camp Commandants.

They are not appointed for their kindly humane natures. Most of them had held civil prison commands and some of them had been hardened criminals themselves. They knew all the tricks of intimidation and subtle suggestion.

Some were trained psychologists as well as having practical experience in prison work. They were even more subtly dangerous than the others, and could select unerringly the right material to nurse and prepare for further implantation of ideas. The victim himself would never be aware of this exploitation.

I hated myself for doubting the integrity of my fellow P.O.W.s, especially one I didn't know too well. The accusation could just as well apply to me as to anyone else. I hated also to insult Kernow by turning him down without a satisfactory explanation.

His "What about it?" suggested he was willing to join me and it was a generally accepted principle that one or even both of a pair had a better chance of success than a lone escaper. His offer made it very difficult for me to choose someone else, so I went carefully to work on Kernow before I agreed. Unknown to him I quizzed how long he'd been a P.O.W., what trouble, as such, he'd been in, his air station at home, what mission he'd been on and by the time I'd finished I knew my man.

By careful manoeuvring I had him sitting next to me. We then decided that when we reached a suitable point farther north we would try our luck. The plan was to doctor the windows ready to make a dive at the first suitable place.

The windows were all tightly screwed up, but by working on the screws with a conveniently broken knife we finally managed to remove them and fill up the holes with bits of well-chewed bread as a temporary stopper to hide the holes. We then sat back with everything in readiness to await the right moment. Our opportunity came on the afternoon of the second day when we were well north of Berlin and still heading in a north-easterly direction toward the Baltic coast – of unpleasant memory!

The train was struggling up a long incline and had appreciably slowed down along a stretch of line that had been built up with an embankment falling steeply away on both sides. We agreed this looked a good time and place to make the dive, so waiting until the guard had passed our compartment on his patrol, we pushed down the window.

Kernow leapt out first and, landing safely, began to roll down the embankment; I followed immediately, but caught my heel on the window-frame as I dived out and landed on my head on the hard track before rolling down the embankment. For a few minutes I lost all interest in the venture and knew nothing of what was happening.

I awoke to find a couple of guards shaking the life out of me, and the train at a stand-still, while a line of guards were moving across the fields like a party out for a day's partridge shooting and letting off occasional rifle shots left and right of me. But friend Kernow had managed to evade them and the guards abandoned the chase.

They hiked me back to the train and escorted me to my seat, having in the meantime well and truly screwed up the window. I suffered a thick head for a few hours which soon passed off leaving me none the worse for my carelessness.

The third day out saw us still heading north and across the long neck of land reaching up from the old Poland to the Baltic port of Danzig, and formerly known as the Polish Corridor. We were now in East Prussia and finally came to a halt at a small place called Hydekrüge not far from the Lithuanian border. The swine made us march the two miles to the camp non-stop and, with the load of kit we carried, we arrived there just about on our knees.

We were the first intake to arrive, and were placed in a compound bordered on two sides by other compounds – as yet vacant – and on a third side by the German Staff Headquarters, with only the fourth side having any access to the great big world beyond. The compound had its warning wire even farther from the main wire than at Sagan – about 45 feet – plus a wide ditch and a cleared area beyond the main wire fences for another thirty yards.

It was evident they liked our company and intended us to stay at home. Four oblong brick-built billets, each with an annexe of two smaller wooden ones, a cookhouse, ablution shed, and the large latrines – again of painful memory – abutting on to the warning wire at the open side of the compound, made up our new home.

What with *brick* billets, an extra long distance to the warning wire, a ditch, thirty yards of outside clearing with every inch of it covered by machine guns, and bordered by other compounds, I thought the place really formidable. Not content with these safe-guards I was placed in one of the smaller wooden huts together with nineteen other bad eggs where, according to an interpreter, they wanted us together to keep a special eye on us. As Bill had not been included with the bad eggs I wondered how he had managed to whitewash himself. When he later peered in at a window while we were sorting ourselves out, I motioned to him to join us. "Oh, no!" he teased. "I'm not coming in there among you wicked lot. I might get contaminated." All the same, he spent most of his time with us.

I had been there only a couple of days when the gate opened and in marched Kernow closely escorted by a guard at each elbow, and looking very much the worse for wear. I was immediately located and conducted to the office to join Kernow, where we were ordered 21 days in the cooler. As we were its first tenants, while the doors were being unlocked we conducted a short ceremony declaring it now offi-cially open. It was never to lack customers when later the camp once got properly going.

As soon as the guard was out of earshot we discussed how Kernow became recaptured. Kernow reported that after his roll down the embankment, he had picked himself up and dashed along the side of a cornfield away from the railway line.

As soon as he heard the train halt and the guards shouting and firing he kept belting along as hard as he could go for half a mile, and then dropped exhausted into a ditch grown over with weeds, and remained there listening. No one came his way, and eventually he heard the engine start off again, so he came out from his hiding place to find all was quiet! Then taking a rough direction from the sun he headed north.

He did not know his position except that he was somewhere in north-east Germany between Berlin and the Baltic coast, so avoiding all built-up areas, he plodded along until nightfall when he went to ground in a haystack.

Early the following morning, feeling hungry and thirsty he approached an isolated farmhouse and asked for food. He was given some bread and a drink of milk, but thought the farm people eyed him curiously. However he carried on and about an hour later he was ambling along a country road when he noticed following him a village constable on a bike. The game was up. He was taken to the local lockup and later handed over to a military escort and returned to Hydekrüge.

CHAPTER SEVENTEEN

During my period of meditation in the cooler, Bill had been scouting around getting the layout of things, but had nothing very promising to report when later I returned to circulation. However, as nothing is ever so bad as it seems at first sight, we did not readily give up the ghost. We settled down to sports and games hoping for an inspiration in the near future.

My particular billet containing all the bad eggs became a veritable hotbed of intrigue, a cabinet of plotters with no other topic but discussions on ways and means of escape. By the time I'd heard everyone's story I calculated, in the total, that we twenty bad eggs had tied down at least 400 German troops in a full-time job for a period of two years.

Take one chap who was free for five weeks. The troops in an area of 100 square miles were alerted day and night before he was captured. He broke into places and stole food, money, and clothing to keep himself on the run. The whole district had panicked. Cafes, bus stations, rail stations, cinemas, and what have you, all had guards looking for him.

Our billet assumed the air of a labour exchange with the constant comings and goings of the cloak and dagger boys as the escape committee were called. They did sterling work in this capacity, and at Hydekrüge, the organisation reached such a stage of efficiency and

self-support it became their proud boast that they could supply a
P.O.W. with food, money and clothing, and equip him with a
complete set of papers permitting him to travel, and even obtain
work, in any part of the Continent. We also had our own daily n'ews
bulletin conveying accurate information ahead of German news
releases. At a pinch we could have duplicated a "pass" complete with
the Commandant's signature, but I doubt whether, without a
complete German military uniform, we could have satisfied the
guard's at the gate.

There still remained the big stumbling block of how to vanish
from "A", inside the compound, and arrive with a whole skin at "B",
outside the main wire fences. For any chap who was not a fluent
German speaker, to whom forged papers would be useless, and who
was prepared to travel with only a supply of food and protective
clothing, tunnelling was undoubtedly the best means for the
vanishing trick.

As a result of my experience at the tunnelling game, I had now
fully earned my exalted title of "the Mole" and it was unanimously
agreed that I be immediately commissioned as sole executive to find
ways and means to push one through.

I promptly co-opted Bill on the board of management and
together we carefully surveyed every possible loophole; we had no
intention this time of being rushed into the first scheme to offer itself,
so as soon as a loophole revealed itself we both became Goons and
guards in an attempt to find the snags. We surprised ourselves at the
scores of ways in which we could be caught. We even decided that all
helpers should be changed daily and the parties mixed every two days
and to mask our joint activities, Bill and I to work together only when
absolutely necessary.

Search as we liked, we could find no loophole absolutely invul-
nerable against the snoopers' sudden and determined investigations
so, realising no matter which site we chose we would have to accept
risks, our interest finally centred inside the two wash-houses.

Here the difficulties were greater than most other possible sites, but offered greater security to counterbalance those difficulties. The wash-house offered the shortest distance to the wire, and good cover for our comings and goings – people were constantly using these places hence our visitations there would not be suspect. But the question remained, from which point should one make a beginning? The floor was solid concrete and once we had broken through for the initial opening it would be difficult to fit a foolproof trapdoor of wood.

One day we were busy washing our smalls, while at the same time considering our problem, when Bill suddenly exclaimed, "I've got it! Under the boiler!" I quite thought he had been touched by the sun until he started to explain.

"Why not shift one of the boilers, and break through the cement underneath, and replace it at the end of the day's work?"

I stared at him as though he'd just told me the war was over. With the boiler back in position, we had perfect cover when not engaged digging below, or for that matter, while a party remained below. The idea was good!

The three large cast-iron boilers used for heating washing-water, for showers and laundry-work, stood along one side of the wash-house, and one great-hearted chap had the self-imposed task of looking after them to maintain a constant supply of hot water.

We immediately placed our plans before the escape committee as a necessary preliminary, in order to avoid a clash of interests with any other scheme which might be afoot at the same time. We received their blessings and the all clear to go ahead, with a promise of the committee's resources behind us. This would be a great help as they organised all stooging and the preparation of escape kit.

With the help of our boiler-attendant we set about dismantling and removing the end boiler to see if the idea was practicable. In case the Goons should suddenly pounce before we had time to re-assemble it, we could rely on the attendant to explain, so long as we had it back in position covering the hole, that he had taken it to bits to clean out the accumulation of soot. Such an explanation would be quite feasible even if one or two of us were found there helping him, as no one man could handle the component parts alone.

We first removed the inner lining, then the outer casing, and finally the base-plate including the fire-box. Before breaking through the concrete we re-assembled the whole job.

This operation we timed, and repeated the whole thing several times until each helper knew his drill and the job was completed within a certain time-limit. This we hoped to reduce, that is the re-assembling only, to sixty seconds. These boilers were of the old field-kitchen type, in other words similar to the housewife's copper still to be seen in many farm-houses.

All we had to do now was augment the crew we had been drilling as a surface crew, as Bill and I would be required below, and recruit our underground workers. With our crews completed, we started from scratch to time the dismantling before attacking the concrete. With very little practice they could replace the whole boiler, place a few shovelfuls of fire in the firebox from one of the other boilers, and refill with hot water in a matter of forty-five seconds. This was purely an emergency drill in the event of the Goons making a sudden pounce. The forty-five seconds taken for the replacing and assembly of the boiler gave us a forty-five seconds margin of safety, as we had proved it required ninety seconds at normal walking pace to cover the distance from the compound gate to the wash-houses.

We now had our outside stooges posted who gave the signal for other stooges to start a chorus of shouts and banging as a diversion, while we attacked the concrete, and we soon had a nice eighteen-inch opening broken through and a six foot hole ready for tunnelling tomorrow. I considered it a satisfactory start, and returned to the billet.

Until there was enough working space below to get a team down and the hole covered, the next two days would be a critical period as the hole would have to remain open. So I dug like a slave, while an endless stream of chaps carted away the sandy soil and dumped it in the next door latrine.

By working frantically for a couple of days I managed to excavate enough room for three men to work below, and while I dug they filled the soil into bags and buckets and handed it up to the surface squad for disposal. At the end of a week we had carved out a subterranean chamber six by eight feet by six feet deep under the wash-house floor without disturbing that portion supporting the weight of the other two boilers.

We now had enough space for a team of four men to work, with a room large enough to store the excavated soil they might be expected to dig in one shift.

Hence we could now permit the boiler to be replaced over the opening while a team below worked a shift in comparative security … or so we hoped! Although things were running smoothly at this stage, and we could be forgiven for a little premature rejoicing, there was much yet to be done before breaking cover to freedom.

I estimated a total distance of one hundred and forty feet of tunnelling to complete the job including the formidable hurdles to negotiate en route. These latter obstacles presented real difficulties; at every alternate post carrying the surrounding wire, the technically minded Boche had set up a seismograph; now if your mother never told you about these crafty little machines, it's just this.

Suppose a small earthquake or tremor occurs in Tokyo, it can be recorded in graph-writing on one of these contraptions at the opposite side of the Earth eight thousand miles away! And we had to dig a tunnel one hundred and forty feet long and actually pass between two of these at not more than six feet without the damn thing giving us away. They are almost sensitive enough to record one's heartbeats!

The second obstacle was the ditch; we had no way of even guessing its depth although we must pass underneath it, and pass deep enough underneath to avoid subsidence or even a steady drip of water which would soon become a column and flood the working. You will recall the ditch that ended one of my previous attempts!

We had a fellow-P.O.W. called Beaver but he disclaimed any relationship with this animal, and the job would need the experience of one of these clever little chaps.

We had now reached a stage when we could work to a set programme. I divided my helpers into two working parties; Bill and I leading one; and a couple of diehards, Prendergast and Leggett, leading the other. The two parties would work below in alternate periods between 8.30 a.m. to 12.30 p.m. and 12.30 to 4.30 p.m. while a surface gang remained on the lookout for Goons and be ready to replace the boiler at the first sign of danger.

I started off by leaving a thickness of soil between the tunnel ceiling and the outside surface measuring three feet, and planned a gradual downwards slope aiming to increase this head cover of soil from three feet to six feet, without increasing the dimensions of the tunnel, by the time I reached the ditch.

The section underneath the ditch I intended to support by encasing the tunnel in a wooden box, with whatever timber I could find, then once beyond this Achilles' heel, to rise again to my original levels at the main wire fence and continue until we reached the point to break surface outside the compound.

With each party taking down with them several lengths of bedboarding the programme worked so well that, by the time we reached the ditch, we had enough planks to completely box in the six-foot ditch section and provide a lighting system – a much improved model on my former efforts, I must add.

Having progressed to twenty feet of tunnel the air was becoming dangerously thin, and to add to this problem we had to consider that light in any form would consume air at a disproportionate rate, so an air pump had to be constructed.

John Edgar, the inventor, produced a marvellously simple contraption in the form of a concertina and on the same principle. Using a kit-bag opened at both ends for the bellows, he tacked a lavatory seat cover to each end, and to make it airtight sealed the edges with pitch – scraped from the walls and roof of a wooden hut. To prevent the bag collapsing he sewed a spiral of wire around it strong enough to stand the pressure of the hand pump and act as a return spring. In the wooden ends of the bag he drilled suitable holes fitted with leather clapper valves – cut from old boots – to open and close as required to draw in air at one end and force it out at the other end, with a wooden handle to operate.

For an air line he found that two certain types of tin which arrived in Red Cross parcels would fit nicely into each other and with a smear of pitch, were quite airtight, and when holes were made in the bottoms would carry a column of air to the face of the tunnel. Naturally it required a great number of these tins and more would be needed as we progressed further into the tunnel, so every billet was warned to conserve them for our use – and we never ran short of them. He then made a cradle to hold the thing rigid during pumping operations.

Finally the components were smuggled below and assembled together. The intake pipeline led up to the fire-box above when the boiler was covering the hole, and the air supply line lay along the tunnel to the face ready for an extension as required.

When first tested, it was such a success it blew out all the lights, and when operated too energetically it thumped and made a noise like a water ram working at high pressure. It certainly did the job and was a credit to its inventor and constructor. It was the kind of thing that filled the need so effectively that without it we were stumped, and in other circumstances would have earned him a decoration.

We now required the type of operator who would use it intelligently. Here again we were lucky, we recruited two chaps, one for each shift, who proved themselves most adaptable.

We also constructed a sledge for hauling the soil from the face to the storing chamber, composed of a shallow wooden box on runners with a hook at each end attached to lines made from plaited parcel twine; one line led to a chap in the disposal chamber at the tunnel entrance who, on receiving a jerk from the face hauled in the sledge and dumped the soil, then those at the face would haul it back empty.

This unique dodge saved us an awful lot of sheer muscle graft. Without it every ounce of soil would have had to be dragged the length of the tunnel by someone crawling backward on his belly and returning on his knees.

The underground team worked as follows: – I sliced out the soil with my knife and pushed it behind me; Bill loaded it on the sledge – both of us lying on our bellies – and signalled by a tug on the line to the chap in the disposal chamber, number three, who hauled the sledge through the tunnel and dumped the soil in the storing chamber; number four loaded it into small sandbags ready for disposal above ground during the shift change-over and acted as storekeeper to send up planks and additional tins to extend the air-line as required on the empty sledge; number five was the pump operator who also prepared a supply of lamps for our use up at the face.

Even when the Goons were snooping around the compound we carried on the work below as there was less risk staying there than trying to scramble out and clean our clothes without being seen.

In spite of all our careful precautions we had many dizzy moments to add to the spice of life. Several times we received the Buzz just when we were in the act of changing over, and that meant ten men – five leaving and five taking over – had suddenly to disappear after returning the boiler into position and sluicing away the soil from our boots and the wash-house floor.

They were moments when one's heart stopped beating. Some chaps would dive below, others replace the boiler and sluice down and then dash under the showers, while a couple would whip off their shirts and carrying them over their arms, calmly walk out towards their billets as if they'd just finished a spot of laundry work, or walk out pretending to button up their trousers.

It wouldn't be unusual to see a couple of chaps fighting over a shirt and accusing each other of pinching it. When all is said and done ten men congregating at the same moment in a wash-house is suspicious enough in itself and would give the Goons sufficient grounds to start tearing the compound to bits until they found something amiss – and all these cover-up movements had to be thought up and carried out in the ninety seconds it took them to walk from the gates to their preselected site for investigation.

The moment they entered the gates they shot off in all directions, dashing here and there like a bunch of lunatics. Sometimes we got the laugh but often the Goons had the joke!

The only concession the crew below made to the Goons' presence above was to cease operating the pump while they were actually in the wash-house, as the soft hiss of the intake pipe under the boiler could be distinctly heard. As they often came into the wash-house for a chat and a cigarette with the boiler-man while our lungs were bursting for air below and the lamps were flickering for oxygen, we used to curse him afterwards for not getting rid of them sooner.

Bad weather held us up for six days just when we were only a few feet from the ditch, and resulted in rather bad flooding. But after the flood had subsided we found the only damage was a blocking of the air line which had to be dismantled and cleaned out. However, we soon had things moving again and reached the ditch.

Here I was obliged to take every precaution and prepare for disaster. I had no idea what to expect, not knowing its depth, and I figured I could just as easily dig into the waterline and flood the tunnel in a few seconds, as find myself low enough to dig into good sound soil. It felt to me like returning from a raid with a bust radio and compass and no stars or moon on a pitch black night, with all the sky to roam in without sense of direction.

It was no use kneeling there looking at the job, so I began with gentle stabs of the knife waiting breathlessly for the inrush of water. Inch by inch I cut my way forward and every six inches (the width of a plank) fitted a box in the section with the bottom board a few inches below floor level to allow free passage for the sledge. In this way I unhurriedly and safely negotiated the section with the ditch above me and began to move upward.

Here I had to recruit another member to my team, as the direct haul from face to chamber had become too long and the haulage line kept breaking. I placed him at the ditch where the tunnel changed course as a half-way haul to lessen the strain on the line and to negotiate the altered direction. It worked!

The longer haul was now slowing down our progress to a snail's pace, and, coupled with the extra work due to the flood period, the fifth week had now passed before we neared the main wire. At this point, and judging we were almost back to our original level, I pushed up a small hole to ground level, with the idea of trying to locate the seismograph point. We had already designed and manufactured a long periscope for this purpose and with its aid I now hoped to avoid serious trouble.

I poked it gently above the surface and cautiously peered around, and after examining the wire in both directions for a time I at last spotted a thin wire running down a post to the earth about six feet to the left of my present course. There did not appear to be anything on the post at the same distance to the right so I decided to alter course in that direction to give me a wider margin of safety.

Incidentally, the infinite possibilities of the periscope occurred to me only at this moment. Why hadn't I thought of it before! I could see everything going on around me in the compound without the slightest risk of detection; for instance, I watched the guard's boots as he marched up and down on his beat outside the wire – but little did he know it! I also amused Bill with a running commentary on a game of football being played in the compound behind us until he told me to shut up before he collapsed.

Next morning on my arrival below I went straight up the tunnel to start digging, and had just reached the ditch when I heard an ominous crump and rumbling behind me.

I manoeuvred my body round as quickly as possible in the

confined space and began to crawl back again. At about halfway to the entrance I was confronted by a complete blockage. A tremendous fall had occurred. "Good Lord, how far did it extend?" was my first thought. "Was Bill underneath?" I visualised the most shocking possibilities as I frantically clawed away the soil to squeeze through, then I heard Bill's voice from the other end yelling to me to come back. He was filled with the same idea as myself and was clawing away expecting to find me underneath.

We cleared a narrow passage-way and then looked upwards to find the daylight filtering through the cracks of a lightly-held, thin crust of surface extending over an area of two square feet, with only a few grass roots holding it together – I wondered how long it would hold! There was no time to lose; the thin grass crust must be saved from falling in at all costs otherwise the Goons would spot the hole, so I sent out an S.O.S. for sandbags and boards while Bill and I cleared the area to give us working space.

To raise that drooping grass patch without it falling in was going to be a delicate job and I felt scared of touching it and more scared that some Goon above might walk right into it, situated as it was between warning wire and main wire. My God, the thought made me sweat!

It would be madness to tackle it from outside and what's more it would have to be a permanent job. I had to take myself in hand to ward off a growing sense of panic. While waiting for the bags we determined to board up a section much longer than the affected area; this would leave an empty space above to be carefully filled in and gradually raise the grass area – any idea of cutting sods and filling in from outside was quite unthinkable. At last we were able to get cracking.

While Bill filled the bags I boxed in a large section leaving a gap for the centre board to be fitted last. Through this gap I carefully pushed up the bags, building up the edges of the weak area first; then I laid some bags to fill in the middle. Then so as not to break through the crust I forced other bags of soil underneath the first layer until finally the frayed surface grass was resting firmly on the bags and no longer in danger of falling.

To prevent a hollow appearing above from a subsequent settling down of the soil I finished off by lying on my back and heaving the bags up with my feet while Bill packed more and more bags underneath to make a solid top, then we finally heaved the missing centre plank up into position and called it a day!

It had been a difficult job working in a tunnel in which our bodies fitted like a lady's leg in a silk stocking, but a job well done … I hoped! A surface inspection later, through the wash-house windows, revealed no sign of subsidence.

Despite several intensive searches and the almost daily perambulations of the Goons around the compound under our watchful observation, they seemed to have no suspicions that we were again engaged in our pet hobby.

By now we were actually beyond the main wire defences with only a few feet to go before surfacing into the open and freedom, a matter of a few hours' work.

I now reported to the committee that everything was set for the final act. My original intention had been that only a bare half dozen chaps would make the bid, but the committee took the view that it was a shame after all the work that had been put into the tunnel to allow only a few to get away, and now embarked on a really ambitious scheme. In effect, to get ONE HUNDRED chaps away in two batches of fifty.

The scheme required very careful and exactly timed preparations. The idea was that the first party would enter the tunnel fully equipped between the last rollcall of the day and before the lock-up hour of seven-thirty p.m. They would wait there until zero hour, nine p.m., and then bolt. This meant that they would be absent at next morning's rollcall and this absence would have to be covered in some way to deceive the camp guards. So the cover plan was tried out first.

The twice daily roll-calls were held as a parade on the sports' pitch. We formed up into twenty squares each made up of fifty men. And to test the scheme fifty men were to be absent themselves and hide in all sorts of odd corners until the rollcall was over. Rather than choose a few men from each of the twenty squares to play truant it was thought safest for a whole square of fifty men to go absent leaving only nineteen complete squares on parade, the absent square being the one usually counted last.

Then as each separate square was counted the men would immediately but casually, fall out of line and wander in all directions until the parade ground presented a disorderly rabble. As more and more squares were counted the rabble got denser and more scattered, while the requisite number of fifty worked their way to the rear and re-formed into the missing fifty-man square. The Germans methodically worked their way from square to square and finally arrived with an all-correct count. They were happy and so were we. But, in fact, they were fifty men short!

To make sure the scheme would hold up on the appointed day we rehearsed the trick on several occasions and it never failed. So that with fifty men away and accounted for on next day's rollcall, the second party of fifty would disappear that evening and their absence on the following morning would have to look after itself. The first party away would then be covered for thirty-six hours and the second party for one night only unless the scheme went wrong in the meantime. In any case we could never hope to cover the absence of one hundred men!

With the assurance that the doctored rollcall was working, a huge amount of kit began to be turned out. The first batch of fifty would be really well equipped, but the second would have to take pot luck in the matter of clothing and certain faked papers. It was agreed that only those with a passable knowledge of German could make use of papers in the event of their being questioned, so the others would have to travel as best they could. All those making the bid had previously consented to this arrangement.

A week had passed since the main wire had been passed and by this time many of the hopefuls were becoming restlessly anxious; with such large numbers involved and the amount of kit about, something was almost bound to leak out, and then a snap search would blow the place sky high. The committee began to feel worried over the situation and several members favoured an immediate break.

Considering the tunnel reached only a third of the way across no man's land and that one hundred men would be crossing twenty yards of this no man's land in full view of the sentry boxes equipped with deadly machine guns as well as a patrolling guard, I felt it was asking too much of Lady Luck. I appealed for time to complete the tunnel right across no man's land as far as the bushes. At lunch time a full meeting was held with all interested parties present and I stated the position.

In the end a vote was taken and I was defeated – an immediate break was now on.

During the afternoon, Bill, Prendergast, and I went below to complete the preparations; this meant continuing the tunnel for a few feet and then pushing a shaft up to within a few inches below surface level. We then had to make a lid to fit the opening, and fix four supporting corner posts to carry the lid, so that all it would finally need was to run a knife through the upper crust of soil around the edge of the lid, and lift soil and lid outwards like a manhole cover.

We crawled back feeling highly satisfied with our work – and not a little excited at the prospect ahead. After a good wash and a meal I carefully checked the items of kit I would take with me and distributed the remainder among my pals. I then rested until evening roll-call. Rest is relative and I suddenly felt overwhelmed by an awful burden of responsibility.

Here were one hundred men risking their lives as the direct result of my own restless urge to escape. Would some of them be killed before the night was over? Would the tunnel collapse while fifty men lay head to feet for two and a half hours without room to turn inside it? Would the air system fail and suffocate them? Or would they emerge dazed and too stupid to use discretion at the vital moment? Would someone panic in no man's land and cause those death-dealing guns to snuff out the lives of his companions?

I determined that each one should be acquainted with these horrors as he rolled up for his kit. Not one withdrew.

It was now time for the evening rollcall.

Except for the leisurely fall out of each square the parade was more orderly than usual and an air of suppressed excitement pervaded the compound. Soon the first fifty would be on their way out. Tomorrow's rollcall would decide the fate of the second party.

Lock-up was at seven-thirty p.m. The first party of fifty German-speaking chaps had already collected their kit, strolled casually over to the wash-house in twos and threes, and dropped below to the disposal chamber, where they donned gloves and balaclavas and took up their position in the tunnel with myself in the lead.

By six-thirty p.m. the whole fifty were down below plus one extra-stout fellow! He had volunteered to replace the lid on the exit after the last man had gone and then stay below all night, because firstly he would not be able to remove the boiler to get out, and secondly his billet would be locked and he could not return to it. This was a job requiring an iron discipline. Just think of him staying in that tunnel for at least twelve hours at night without a light and both ends of the tunnel sealed up, and with the chance of freedom within his grasp. In my opinion he was a hero to undertake such a job for the benefit of his pals.

We were timed to break at nine p.m. and watches had been synchronised with various diversions which had been planned to take place inside the huts to hold the attention of the guards while we broke out. Each man had been warned not to leave the exit until he was certain the outside patrol was well out of sight no matter how long he had to wait. One false move and the whole thing would go up in smoke – and possibly death! We settled down to our two-and-a-half-hour vigil in the pitch blackness.

The total length of the tunnel was roughly ninety feet, so with fifty men below (less than two feet each) there was very little room, if any, to spare. The chaps were doubled up nose to tail and the chamber packed tight. One chap kept the pump gently working but even then the air soon became a serious problem especially for those in the section below the ditch (the lowest point) and was likely to become worse until I raised the exit lid to release the concentration of foul air.

To make matters worse many of the chaps had never before been underground and the present conditions were likely to test the stoutest heart. Soon a situation very near to panic developed as the clock ... oh, so slowly ... crept round towards nine o'clock. It did not help to steady one's nerves to crouch there in the darkness for several hours listening to the sound of the guard's boots as he tramped forward and back, forward and back, just above our heads, while we anticipated the earth above to give way under him.

Oh, how the seconds dragged on! Soon the tunnel became as hot as a Turkish bath and everyone began whispering about the heat. I was sweating like the proverbial pig so I knew how the others felt and I began to wonder who would panic first. Fortunately everyone behaved magnificently and I tried to cheer them by passing along the time.

It was now eight-fifty-five p.m. and we had managed to hold out. I sliced all round the manhole lid until I could feel that it was free to lift. Five more minutes to go!

I found it tiresome watching the luminous hands of my watch move slowly round. At last the minute hand was racing to zero hour when suddenly all Hell was let loose and pandemonium broke out in the compound. The guard's footsteps halted and I hoped the attention of the box sentries had been similarly attracted. Bill counted off the last thirty seconds and dead on the second of nine o'clock I cautiously raised the lid and peered out.

Oh, the lovely fresh air! I could positively taste the difference.

CHAPTER EIGHTEEN

I could see the patrol about twenty yards away to my left discussing with one of the box sentries the unholy commotion in the compound. I moved the lid to one side, lifted out my haversack and then heaved myself through the opening.

Although I crawled away to cover as swiftly as possible it seemed like a day's march before I reached the friendly shelter of the bushes. I knew Bill would be watching for my disappearance before starting to follow me, as everybody had been previously warned that only one at a time was to be seen in the open. I moved on a little farther and waited for him to catch up with me, and as soon as he arrived we crept off through the trees without making the least sound.

We had gone perhaps only two hundred yards when we were startled by a shot, and then it seemed like a general blitz; rifles and machine guns were blazing away, guards shouting, all the search-lights swinging round in our direction. Finally the sirens started their fearful wailing.

This was too real, we waited no longer but took to our heels as fast as we could run until the sound of the sirens faded into the distance. Heaven knows how many, or few, had managed to get away behind us and, horrible thought, how many had been wounded or even killed! At the moment we were alone and it sickened me as I tried to visualise what could have happened.

I had memorised the first part of our map which showed that our shortest route to the Lithuanian border, a distance of twelve miles away, was to ford a tributary of the river Memel. This lay across our path about a mile ahead so we made for it in a non-stop rapid gallop. I think it was the fastest long distance sprint either of us is ever likely to make. Anyhow, gasping for breath, we had just reached the bank of the river and were wading in, when along the bank dashed what looked like a guard followed by his massive guard dog.

We hesitated, not wishing to draw his fire, and then we were joined by number three instead. It was Paddy Flynn with an Alsatian right on his heels. Paddy was a tall, gangling Irishman with no noticeably soft spot for either Germans or their dogs; he immediately jumped into the water, still followed by the dog, until he turned round and grabbed the brute by its hind legs and held it under the water. When it ceased to struggle he let it float away down stream.

Meanwhile Bill and I had floundered across to the far bank, where we spent a few precious minutes ridding ourselves of surplus moisture until Paddy joined us.

I wasn't feeling at all happy over the situation at the camp behind us and I tried to quiz Paddy.

"Let's get on a bit," he replied, so we set off for the border taking care to steer away from all buildings. We were now feeling the perishing cold from our uncomfortably wet clothes following our sprint to the river, so we set off at a brisk walking pace to return some heat to our shivering bodies. The sirens and guns had ceased their nerve-tingling racket but we could still see the brilliantly lit camp area in the distance, growing dimmer and dimmer as we put more miles behind us.

I knew the guards would throw a wide cordon around the camp, possibly as far as the river, hoping to trap us within the area, and should they locate our tracks at the river bank or the dogs hold our scent, they would extend the cordon beyond the far bank. So we halted periodically listening intently for sounds of our pursuers. We heard nothing; only our whispers and heavy breathing broke the silence around us.

By midnight we estimated we must be close to the Lithuanian frontier where we would have to proceed more carefully and keep our eyes skinned for any possible border patrols. Up to now we had hurried along in a bunch and consequently offered a better target to watching eyes; now we changed our tactics and mooched along in Indian file, fifty yards apart, keeping one another in sight, and varying the lead by changing positions about every half-mile. We were getting tired, and realised how easily the leading man, remaining there for several miles, could gradually become less and less keen in his lookout. A change-over would maintain a more constant watchfulness.

Bill happened to be in the lead and we were following along a track through woodland country when we saw him stop and beckon us to close up. Paddy and I crept softly forward in readiness for the worst. Bill pointed to a clearing in the wood ahead of us.

It was fifty yards wide and stretched away to the left and right of us as far as the eye could see, with a line of white-painted posts running down the centre in both directions, obviously the border line of Lithuania!

Dare we cross? A fifty yard dash and Germany would be behind us. Just fifty yards, and not a soul in sight.

But how were we to know whether or not every inch of that narrow strip might be covered by machine guns? It was still dark and ominously silent. I felt certain there were keen eyes watching those posts and anyone attempting to cross would either be questioned or shot down without questioning.

Paddy threw a hunk of rotted wood to tempt the guns. Nothing happened. One by one we crawled across on our bellies.

We were over, and hidden by the woods on the opposite side. We often had a good laugh about this incident because we later heard there were no guards or inhabitants within miles of the place. Nevertheless, better safe than sorry.

Although Lithuania was technically neutral, we knew it was classed as occupied territory, but now we were there we felt comparatively safe from the Germans. The night was still young and although our clothing remained wet and cold we felt in good spirits. It was wonderful to feel that at last we were free. I could have enjoyed a rest at this moment were it not for my wet clothes. I knew the danger so we kept on the move until dawn began to break.

The country was now mainly open heathland broken by patches of scrub and isolated farms, so we searched and found a nice thick patch of scrub, collected a huge pile of leaves, buried ourselves in them and went to sleep.

Daylight revealed our hiding place at not more than two hundred yards from a farm, close enough to have set every dog in the place barking. Already the farmer and his dogs were on the way to round up the cows for milking, and as we lay doggo we could hear transport wagons rumbling along the road only a short distance away. We wasted no time at the first opportunity to remove ourselves to a safer spot away from both road and farm.

As soon as we were settled I reopened the question of the disastrous breakaway with Paddy. He could tell me very little except that as soon as he reached the trees a bullet smashed into the earth close by him and when he took cover behind a large tree with the searchlights on him another two bullets smacked into the tree. He dropped to the ground and the searchlights veered away from him, no doubt thinking he was dead. He then bolted deeper into the woods and when he stopped for a breather there was a huge dog making straight for him.

He just had time to grab a thick branch, and as the dog leapt he crashed him with it, but, being rotten, it shattered in a thousand pieces. Fortunately the soil and mould got into the dog's eyes and he had to keep stopping to rub them with his paws while Paddy made all speed for the river. He thought that no more than twenty could possibly have got away.

It was still barely six o'clock in the morning and extremely cold, yet we dared not light a fire, so we did a spot of P.T. to get our blood circulating. Once more we buried ourselves beneath the leaves and, protected by the thick bushes, tried to sleep away the daylight.

It was our plan to continue moving east for a couple of nights which ought to keep us away from towns and take us deep into the country, then to turn north and gradually west to complete a semi-circular course which we hoped would bring us out on the Baltic coast well clear of the German and Lithuanian border area.

It was a wearisome business trying to sleep through the hours of daylight; what with barking dogs, yelling farm workers, and passing traffic on the nearby road, to say nothing of my fears that some straying dog would bring about our discovery, I was glad to be up and doing. Darkness was now closing in so we tucked into some of our rations; a little chocolate, some Horlicks tablets, and half a bar of specially prepared escape compound consisting of Bemax, condensed milk, sugar, and raisins. Then we shouldered our kit ready for the road.

It was a really dark night as we set off in a light drizzle to cross the road where, the night before, we had heard so much traffic, and as we stumbled over the obstacles in our path to the chorus of barking dogs, I expected any minute to meet an armed farmer. It seemed to be a country of dogs. So far we had evaded the Germans but this was the third time we'd had cause to curse the dogs.

Anyhow we got safely away and had been on the move for a couple of hours when we ran into a bog. Thinking it might be only a small patch we explored left and right of it seeking for firmer ground. It was no use, we were wasting precious time, so we plunged right ahead.

The farther we pushed forward the deeper became the bog. Plunging through this terrifying stuff in the darkness seemed like a horrible nightmare.

By midnight we were exhausted and considering whether to turn back, when a screeching owl drew our attention to a tree whose roots formed a small island above the surrounding morass; like shipwrecked mariners we struggled ashore and flopped down with our backs to the tree, content to rest and await the dawn to reveal our surroundings.

The chill of the bog had reached the very marrow of our bones, and with our soaking wet clothes I think it was the coldest night we ever spent in all our wanderings.

It was a great relief when the first streaks of daylight penetrated the surrounding blackness and we were able to take stock of our miserable situation.

The vision before us was enough to deter the stoutest heart, for stretching ahead in every direction as far as the eye could see was the same vast watery landscape broken here and there by clumps of trees forming small islands. Not a patch of dry land or a building could be seen anywhere, no evidence of moving traffic to indicate a roadway, only black muddy water!

Despair was written on each of our faces. Any choice of direction was no more than a guess. Would it become deeper? was the obvious question; no-one could say. It was no more than six inches at this point with a black spongy bottom that offered no foothold.

There were the tree islands ahead so we decided to hop from one to the other, and keep straight ahead. So, as plunging had now become the operative word we again plunged, intending to maintain our original course until we ran into the impossible. And what then? We'd have to trust in Providence to help us out.

Uncertain of our absolute direction, and none too sure of our fate, with our feet void of any sensation except weariness, we stumbled forward in this manner for several hours until the line of trees ahead became more and more continuous, and at eleven a.m. we dragged our feet on to dry land. We were in a bad condition as our feet would not hold us upright on the solid ground and we stumbled about like three drunks. My feet were so cold that my ankles kept turning over and I couldn't tell whether I was standing on the bottom of my feet, or on my turned-over ankles.

It was a nice sunny morning so we removed our socks, and after vigorously rubbing our feet, changed into a spare pair from our rucksacks, then after a snack, and a shave in a bog pool, we set off feeling warmer and much refreshed. We had emerged from an experience that we determined never again to repeat. Bogs – never again! Night marches in this country were taboo; in future we would sleep at night and travel during the day unless traversing populous areas when night travel would be safest. Even in daylight the countryside was so primitive that during two days' travel we hadn't met a soul, and in that time crossed only one road, so the possibilities of a large scale search seemed very remote.

We were now travelling through deep pine forests and found it easy going and made much better headway. We came out of the forest on to a road which I calculated headed directly on our course, and feeling very bold we marched along for several miles without meeting any locals. Then as we turned a bend we spotted a horse and cart coming towards us. We didn't feel quite so bold at this moment but, thinking it would look less suspicious to carry straight on instead of trying to dive out of sight, we sauntered by giving the driver a cheery, if mumbled, greeting in passing.

He returned our greeting quite cheerily, and in equally indecipherable language, so we were all happy.

We glanced back occasionally but he appeared to be taking no further interest in us, and we considered his disinterest as a fair test of our appearance. We now felt part of the landscape and wondered how far we could cash in on the prospects.

"It's not the people you've got to worry about in this country," exclaimed Paddy, "… it's the dogs. If we can make ourselves smell like Lithuanians we'll get through O.K."

I thought it a pretty true statement and asked him if that was how it was in Ireland. This was about the longest conversation we'd had since leaving Hydekrüge and it led to further banter as we marched gaily along. We were relaxing and Bill brought us up with a

141

jerk. "Save the laughs until we're eating steak and chips in Sweden," he remarked.

I couldn't have agreed more with Bill's sentiments but the manner of his delivery reduced me to sullen silence. I began to wonder if we were getting on top of each other. The bog incident was enough to strain the best of relationships so I chose this moment to clear the air.

"Look chaps, I know we're all damned tired and I think a rest and a good chat will do us good, and if there's any misunderstandings let's straighten them out," I suggested.

Both Paddy and Bill spoke together and made it clear there was nothing to straighten out, but Bill went on to explain that he thought we were all inclined to take our luck for granted. There was the fellow in the horse and cart. Suppose he was playing clever and after all had his suspicions of us.

"These people would sell us to the Jerries for an extra loaf of bread, and while we're having our jokes a bunch of armed motor-cycle guards could be this minute on their way to collect us. We ought to have been in a position to spot that horse and cart before he spotted us. He could just as easily have been an armed German, and even now we're taking no precautions should a patrol be on its way seeking us. I still say, let's save the laughs until we can afford them."

I told Bill he was right and suggested we used better scouting tactics while marching on any highway.

At the next bend in the road we decided to check our position, and were finally able to pinpoint ourselves on our rough map. We had penetrated far enough into the interior and it was now time to alter course to the north.

We struck off across country and were soon travelling through more open scrub which offered frequent hideouts on the way.

After several hours, the scrub gave way to cultivated but unfenced fields, and soon there were houses ahead, perhaps a dozen or so, perched on either side of the grass-covered road or track along which we were walking. Usually the inhabitants of such small communities are well known to each other and we three strangers would certainly call for comment as we came into view. The situation called for a bold face, so not wishing to create suspicion by separating and taking to the fields we marched boldly ahead.

Although there wasn't a soul to be seen as we passed between the houses we felt the watching eyes at every window, and walked on for quite a mile without once looking behind us. We then suddenly dived behind some bushes and waited to see if we were being followed. As no one appeared during a twenty-minute wait we continued our march.

In the late afternoon we came to a rocky stream crossed by a small suspension foot bridge which we identified on our maps as a tributary of the river Jura and as we were feeling sticky after our day's hike we disrobed and hopped in for a bathe. The water was deliciously cool and simply teeming with small fish. After chasing about for some time we managed to capture four which we wrapped in a handkerchief and put in a rucksack. We then dressed once more and pushed forward.

At this point, after travelling several miles, we found ourselves back again in a thick forest of high trees, where we were obliged, owing to fallen trees and thick undergrowth, to abandon our compass course and follow the well-trodden tracks. We were now very footsore and weary, and as darkness was quickly surrounding us, we kept our eyes skinned for a likely camp site to pass the night.

Here we were luckier than we could have anticipated for ahead among the thick trees we spotted a trim little shack. On closer examination it turned out to be a roughly built stable of hurdles, thatched with heather, with a sturdy false roof inside covered with a deep pile of heather. We hauled ourselves aloft and sank down on the warm springy pile. It was sheer bliss and we could have fallen asleep immediately, only we were so hungry.

After resting our aching limbs for a few minutes we decided to light a fire down below and make a hot drink.

I had earlier on made the fatal mistake of wearing a new pair of boots and consequently my feet were terribly swollen and sore; so swollen, in fact, that I had the greatest difficulty in removing the boots. I had struggled on in this condition for several hours without complaining to my companions, and I now realised I was in a rather distressed condition, whereupon Bill made me lie still while he and Paddy busied themselves with the fire.

For a kettle they propped our metal water-bottle over the flames and as soon as the water heated, they dropped in a few Horlicks tablets. I assure you I've never before nor since tasted anything so delicious as that hot and nourishing drink – it was ambrosia indeed.

For a second course the four little fishes were grilled on sticks, and were very tasty, but unfortunately there was no meat and veg. course to follow; nevertheless, although our stomachs demanded more and more we managed to limit demands to resources. After a second boil up of water, which I poured on a pair of old socks, hurriedly drawing them over my sore feet, we settled down on our springy and surprisingly warm bed in more contentment than we had experienced since our breakaway.

We had passed a very refreshing night, and were awakened by an unusual grunting noise. On carefully glancing outside, to our amazement, we saw a couple of wild boars rooting about among the trees. Wild boars were a new phenomenon and we hardly knew quite how to tackle the situation; anyhow, Paddy decided to handle the matter and the sound of him jumping down from the loft scared them away.

We had a conservative snack from our escape rations and prepared to move on. The overnight idea of cooking my feet in hot socks had proved most beneficial but I still had the utmost difficulty in getting into my boots again, and when at last I did eventually squeeze my feet into them, I could only just hobble along.

Although we were all feeling wretchedly stiff from our strenuous exercise we started out in Indian file with Paddy leading the way. His long legs left me continually lagging behind until I managed to work up some sort of rhythm which enabled me to keep him in sight.

My chief worry during my isolation was the wild boars; I wondered how I should deal with them if they suddenly attacked me, for I recalled some of the horrible tales of their vicious nature.

I had covered about five miles, dreading all the time a sudden attack in my rear, when we reached the fringe of a rough clearing and saw some peculiar buildings. They were a group of one-storeyed wooden shacks built on stilts about four feet above the ground. We immediately remembered the wild boars and wondered if we had blundered into an infested area. We side-tracked the clearing and its small community of shacks and pushed forward on a northerly course, and at midday came out on the edge of another horrifying bog.

We searched left and right for more solid land, but it seemed that straight ahead through the bog lay the shortest route. We could see a forest about a mile ahead, and as trees indicated land, we divested ourselves of our outer garments and with everything draped around our necks we plunged into the mire.

In the deepest places the mud reached to our waists, but fortunately we had taken the precaution to arm ourselves with sounding sticks and we managed to feel our way across without our clothing or gear getting wet.

On reaching the far bank and solid ground, we found a small pool of clear water and washed away the mud, dressed ourselves, had a snack, and then plodded on through the forest.

By now the skin on my feet had broken in several large patches and walking had become a very painful business; a halt of anything more than a few minutes made re-starting all the more painful and difficult, and I began to welcome the idea of capture and even suggested that Bill and Paddy continued on together without me. Of course, they wouldn't hear of it.

In the late afternoon we reached another bog; the country seemed riddled with them. There was nothing we could do about it so we adopted the same procedure and got across without accident. I dreaded the moment when I was obliged to get into my boots again, and almost wept with pain as I stood up and began to hobble along.

We had scarcely left the bog and travelled a short distance when we entered an open stretch of country and saw an isolated farmhouse. I felt that I could just make it, but no further. So I told Bill and Paddy, "I'm going there. If it's all right I'll give you a signal, and if not you two must carry on," but again they wouldn't hear of it. "If you're going, so are we. We'll stick together as long as it's possible."

It was only a very small farm and looked quite poverty stricken. Paddy went first, he marched boldly up and knocked at the door while Bill and I waited a few yards away.

Close by the door were a couple of beehives, and Paddy no sooner knocked than the bees, scenting a stranger, attacked him in full strength. Poor Paddy was covered in bees from head to foot and as he was fighting them off from all directions the door was suddenly snatched open and a woman grabbed him by the arm and hauled him inside. We followed, naturally.

Without a word, the woman dashed outside and returned with a pot of ointment to doctor Paddy's stings; she then turned to us. Bill had only one sting, and as I had waited some distance in the rear I escaped the lot.

We now had a moment to take stock of our surroundings; the floor was of hard rammed earth with a plain deal table in the centre of the room, two wooden forms in front of an open fireplace, and a bed in one of the corners, yet the place was tidy and spotlessly clean.

So far, not a word had been spoken, and I felt anxious to assure the woman that we meant no harm to her. She didn't seem to need our assurances as she stood there smiling at us, yet obviously wondering who we could be.

I tried to explain in German and English, then Bill took a turn in French, and finally Paddy tried her in Polish, a language he spoke quite fluently, but she just waved her hands and laughed. She understood none of us. It seemed quite obvious to us that out here in these backwoods the local populace had had little, if any, contact with the occupying powers.

Without knowing who we were she must have sized up our most urgent needs and immediately began preparing a meal. She placed home-made bread and cheese, a honeycomb, and pots of milk on the table and motioned us to draw up a form to eat. She was plainly delighted with the way in which we attacked the spread and beamed on us all the time we were eating. I had taken off my boots and showed her my heels; she raised her hands in shocked horror and then brought out the ointment once more, evidently a family "cure-all". It was certainly very soothing and brought instant relief.

Soon afterwards, the husband came in followed by a little girl of about eleven years; the whole family seemed to be equally friendly towards us and with the aid of our maps and the help of the little girl, who had had some schooling, we managed to convey to them who we were and where we had come from.

With the aid of our little interpreter who spoke some German, we carried on a conversation and related our experiences as flying men and prisoners which seemed to amaze them more and more. We in our turn learned that they had never seen the Germans and that so far as they knew there had never been any in the area, which we found most reassuring. Eventually the husband escorted us to the hayloft where we spent a very peaceful night.

In the morning the farmer came in to waken us and showed us the well in the yard where we hauled up a bucket of water and had a good civilised wash. We were then taken in for breakfast.

While warming ourselves before the fire, I spotted in a corner of the room a pair of old boots, very down at heel but with beautifully soft uppers, so I offered my new ones in exchange. The farmer was delighted with the arrangement and so was I. They were rather big, but with a padding of hay my feet nestled snugly inside and I could walk in comfort. I doubt if he ever wore his new acquisition as the family usually went barefoot, so I expect he kept them as a souvenir.

After breakfast we made them a few little gifts from our kit; a bit of chocolate, two handkerchiefs, and two spoons; these latter especially seemed to give them great pleasure. They in their turn gave us a large loaf, about a pound of cheese, and three eggs. We set out in high spirits. Paddy's stings were cured, my heels were comfortable, our stomachs were full, and everything was lovely. We kept turning round to wave to our hosts until we disappeared among the trees – they were grand folk.

This sort of kindness and help was the last thing we expected. I would willingly have given them my service for a few days in exchange for food and a bed in the hayloft to enable my feet to recover. I now often find myself regretting I had omitted to take their name and address so that I could have written to thank them and return their kindness in some way.

There must have been many Continental families who helped escapees in this way yet will never be known to the Allies or recognised for the on-the-spot services they rendered – just simple, kindly folk.

Feeling recovered in health and spirits we pushed ahead on a north-westerly course which, according to our maps, should take us across a main road running from East Prussia to one of the few towns in this area. We had covered only a few miles when we were obliged to renew our bog-trotting act. Although we were becoming used to these bogs, they lost none of their terrors, but fortunately we found they shortened the route and were much quicker than trying to find a way round them.

About midday we were walking along a grass track by the side of a young pine wood when we heard voices and saw smoke rising above the trees. When we arrived near the source of the sounds we got a real surprise, for there, about twenty yards in among the trees, were eight men all sitting in a circle around a wood fire which was blazing merrily under a large boiler.

Leading away from the lid of this boiler was a long length of copper piping; this piping described various bends and twists with the open end suspended over a small tub from which a strong smell of raw spirits emanated. "The Illicit Brewery!" They did not seem at all concerned by our sudden appearance and their airy wavings invited us to join the party.

There were among them one or two German speakers and we learned that rather than hand over a quota of their grain to the Germans they hid it; then as the opportunity arose they brought it out to the woods and distilled the spirit.

We were persuaded to try some but a very little was enough, as it just about took the lining from our unaccustomed throats. We stayed chatting for a while and received much back slapping and handshaking when they discovered who we were. I would hesitate to say they were drunk but they were certainly merry.

Eventually one of the party volunteered to guide us on our way and stayed with us for a couple of hours pointing out on our maps (when he could get them the right way up) the places to avoid, and areas where there were German troops. He seemed to possess a wide knowledge of the country unless it was the schnapps that stretched his imagination. Finally he left us with more handshakes and good wishes.

We continued our charted course and after an hour's steady walk through the wood we came upon more open scrub land, and sure enough in the distance ahead was the road marked on our map. But we not only saw the road but a lorry travelling on it, and a power-driven one at that, and since anything mechanically driven in this country suggested Germans to us, we waited until the coast was clear before moving northwards along the side of the road.

We had gone a couple of miles, ready at any moment to dive for cover should any more vehicles come along, when we came to a group of peasant cottages. Consulting our map we were able to pinpoint our position as being south-east of the town of Plungyani.

Here we made another mistake. Instead of by-passing the houses we marched straight between them to reach the outlying woods behind.

Why we should have done this surprised the three of us, unless our late friendly experiences at the farm and the illicit "stillers" had made us think that everyone in the neighbourhood were our friends. Anyhow, as we passed an opening between two of the cottages we spotted a fellow closely watching us and carrying a pretty useful cudgel; we decided things didn't look too bright and prepared ourselves for trouble. And glancing behind us just as we entered the wood we saw five men, equally armed with heavy coshes, unmistakably following us.

It was a dizzy moment, and as soon as we reached the shelter of the trees we took to our heels fully aware of the sounds of pursuit behind us, until they gradually died away and at last there was silence. We then slackened our pace for a few miles and finding a thick patch of undergrowth, sat down for a rest and some food.

After this short spell we footed it painfully for several miles, and having crossed our second bog of the day, at seven in the evening we began seeking a place to spend the night. Although we were disagreeably tired and footsore we were in no way oppressed by our experiences through the bog and the task ahead.

Still having some food with us, we decided to camp outdoors instead of seeking what might turn out to be dangerous undercover quarters – we were still only a few miles from the five suspicious trackers – and seeing a small haystack in the distance we ambled along and burrowed our way inside and were soon fast asleep.

Early next morning, following a meagre snack, we set out again, and apart from our regulation one bog before lunch, the morning proved uneventful.

We were now in more open country and came across another good road. We followed this for perhaps a mile or so until a signpost informed us we were thirty-seven kilometres from Telshi; this of course meant little to us except we were able to pinpoint our position on the map, which directed us to strike across country again – and we associated "across country" with bogs and more bogs.

We hadn't gone far when a curious figure dashed out from a poor-looking cottage by the side of the track, shouting wildly for us to halt; he was barefoot in a ragged old shirt, and wore a baggy pair of pantaloons, his head crowned by the queerest helmet I'd ever seen. He blundered up to us striking his chest and shouting "*Polizei! Polizei!*" I never expect to see a funnier-looking policeman off the stage. He was most insistent that we should not proceed further along the track and motioned us back to the road and kept repeating the word "Papier" which we took to mean that he wanted to see our papers.

We adopted a blustering attitude in return, and flourished our passports which informed the world that we were Swedish seamen, and shouted back at him, pointing to ourselves, "*Deutsche Polizei Gestapo!*"

He obviously could not read and in any case did not try, for our mention of the word "Gestapo" reduced him to a state of abject terror. We were reasonably well-dressed apart from my old boots and I suppose this fact also impressed him. We pointed ahead and mentioned "Telshi", the name of the town we had seen on the signpost. He humbly nodded his head so we left him gazing despondently after us.

After about one hour's walking we discovered the reason for his attitude.

We had been following a forest track for some time, Indian file, and in complete silence, when suddenly we came out in a small clearing about thirty yards across. We stopped and watched for about a couple of minutes. Here was another distillery similar to the one we had met before only on a larger scale.

About twelve men were seated on logs all round the fire all wearing wooden pattens. One chap sat on a log facing us across the fire busy with a knife whittling on a piece of wood; he just glanced up from his comrades and spotted us standing there. The expression on his face was really comical; he gave a startled yell, leapt from his log and disappeared into the wood.

Within seconds the others had joined him in the wood and we could hear them crashing through the undergrowth in their mad rush. Everyone had left his pattens behind. We hung around for a few minutes in case anyone should pluck up the courage to return and attend to the brew – it seemed such a shame that it might be spoiled – but no one showed up, so throwing a few more logs on the fire we continued our journey.

A few minutes later we came out on the bank of a large bog and there half way across the bog and heading for a village on the far side were the illicit brewers, they were all on tall stilts and were making a cracking pace.

We just sat down and howled, it was the funniest thing we had witnessed. I imagine our so-called policeman friend (really the look-out man) would be in trouble when next his pals saw him.

We deemed it imprudent to follow the same course in case the whole village, thinking we really were Gestapo, be evacuated, so we ambled along the bank for some distance until we came to a place where the bog narrowed down to roughly two hundred yards wide and a rough road ran down to the water's edge on both sides. This was obviously a fording place and would have a solid bottom; we rolled up our trousers, removed our boots and socks, and waded across.

About six miles farther along, the forest gave way to open culti-vated land, where we passed through a small village and shortly after-wards crossed a single-track railway. This was shown on our map as running from Telshi down to Memel and was useful as a further check-point on our course.

We followed the rail-track for several miles, and then, as dark-ness was fast overtaking us, we decided to seek shelter for the night. We could see a patch of trees away to our right so we moved in that direction hoping to find a suitable camping place. Night clamped suddenly down on us the moment we entered the wood.

In these latitudes a comfortably warm day will turn to bitter coldness the moment the last rays of the sun disappear, and we began to regret leaving it to the last moment before seeking shelter.

We recalled passing a well-made shelter of bales of straw about a mile behind us and considered retracing our steps but feared becoming lost in the pitch blackness. Night in these parts means total blackness, and to become lost without shelter might bring death from exposure.

A cool wind started up and seemed to penetrate our thin clothing so that it landed direct on our naked bodies. To keep ourselves active we began to collect a few sticks and started a fire. From the firelight we discovered a thick patch of scrub which we covered with more and more pine branches and armfuls of dead leaves and to which we transferred our fire. Inside the scrub we felt some protection from the cold wind so after a light meal from our fast-diminishing stores we settled down for the night.

After about three hours' sleep we were awakened by a howling wind, and hissing rain pouring down on us through the branches and dripping from the leaves of our shelter like water through a colander. We were so thoroughly wet and cold we decided if we stayed there any longer we would become too stiff to move; there was nothing else for it but to get moving and keep moving or our scrub shelter would become a grave. To turn back in the hope of finding the straw shelter was out of the question, we would push forward.

We staggered on in the fearful darkness, with an eye to the metal rails as a guide, feeling miserably cold and wet, struggling against the cold wind, and continually falling, first one and then another, stumbling over fallen branches, knocking our shins and tearing our hands as we tried to save ourselves, until we glimpsed a dark shape on our right. We were travelling head down to avoid wind and rain and the fallen logs, and it was a miracle we saw the dark shape at all. It turned out to be a small cottage.

It was beyond midnight and not a light to be seen in the cottage, and we hesitated over the ethics of waking and possibly frightening the inhabitants to death if we knocked on the door. The point was soon settled when the sounds of our approach aroused a dog somewhere in the rear of the building. We knocked on the door. The dog heard us and went almost mad in his fury to get at us, but there was no response to our knock. We cautiously circled the cottage hoping to find a hayloft, and discovered that, fortunately for us, the dog was fastened in a small outbuilding.

Thinking the cottage might be empty we searched for a ready means of entry at the back but everywhere was securely fastened. Surely, we considered, the presence of a dog meant somebody lived there so we tried the front door again.

After a considerable time standing there knocking and listening for footsteps, and getting more and more wet through, we heard a movement inside, and then a voice obviously enquiring who we were in a language we could not understand. We shouted in our best German that we were escaping English prisoners seeking shelter from the rain. And after further discussion we heard the bolts being removed, and the door opened to reveal a very old man, and standing a little behind him holding a lighted candle, an elderly lady.

They both looked very frightened and we did everything we could by mime to assure them we meant no harm, hoping our bedraggled condition would help in our appeal that we were relatively harmless. Suddenly Paddy had a brain-wave and made the sign of the cross to them a couple of times and raised his hands in pious prayer. The couple then beckoned us inside.

At least we were under cover although conversation to express our needs and remove their false fears remained still quite impossible as they understood no English, French, German or Polish. We could do no more than point to our wet clothing and our bloodless hands in a mute appeal to their understanding.

In the end our gesticulations together with our appearance seemed to suggest our needs, so that they both set to and, bringing out a number of coats and rugs, motioned us to remove our wet clothes and make ourselves comfortable where we were. We felt rather surprised to see them collect our wet things into bundles and carry them away, and we wondered if this was a scheme to prevent our escape while they informed some local authority.

Anyhow, we had reached a state of mind when we didn't care much whether we were recaptured or not, so we let it pass without worrying ourselves; our main concern was to get some sleep ready for the next day, so we got down on the hard earth floor covered by our coats and rugs and remembered no more until the old woman came in next morning to wake us.

She took us into the only other room where we were greeted by a lovely glowing peat fire and saw our clothes all spread out and beautifully dry. While we were dressing our hostess was busy mashing a huge bowl of steaming hot potatoes on the table, and when these were ready she made a hollow in the centre of the mash and filled it in with sour milk in which floated a large number of small dried cubes of fat bacon. She then handed each of us a large wooden spoon and demonstrated how to dig the spoon into the mash to secure a quantity of potato then dip it into the fluid and capture a few cubes of bacon and swallow it; we drew up a form and waded into the hot food with a relish.

It was hardly a breakfast to tempt a jaded palate but to our ravenous appetites it tasted delicious. Not wishing to appear ungrateful or fastidious we did our best to empty the bowl, but even with our capacity for good hot food we were still straining at our girths while the mound of food remained only half demolished. While the dear old soul was urging us to greater effort we could do no more than pat our full stomachs and make deep explosions of air from our mouths to indicate our repleted appetites.

Our failure to demolish the lot certainly disappointed our kind hostess; she smiled and spread her hands in dumb appeals for us to clean up the bowl, but it was no use, we were whacked.

We staggered from the table bowing and thanking the good lady as best we could to make her understand our gratitude, and then searching the meagre contents of our rucksacks we unearthed a few pieces of chocolate, a handkerchief, and our last metal spoon which seemed to give her great pleasure. We then tried with the aid of our maps to explain where we came from and who we were, but I'm sure she never understood; she just nodded and smiled and seemed content to accept us on trust.

When she gave us a huge home-made flat loaf of bread and a piece of raw bacon I hardly knew how to express my thanks. At first, I felt I would like to kiss the old dear, thinking she might understand it as gratitude from the son of an English mother to a foster-mother in a strange land; but I was afraid she might think I was impertinent, and we did no more than shake her hand and express our gratitude in our eyes. Of the old man we had seen the night before there was no trace, so we presumed he had gone out in the early hours to his work.

It would appear we were all three thinking the same kind of thoughts. I said to Paddy, "Fancy the old man leaving the house and the old lady at the tender mercy of three unkempt strange young men, and foreigners to boot!" They all agreed.

It was Paddy's opinion that they knew, or guessed, who we were, but that it would be safer for them not to acknowledge their suspicions in case they were questioned by authority.

Said Bill, "She was just a kind old mother and mothers are like that the world over. I've no doubt the old man would have handed us in so the old dear sent him out of the way." It became a subject of conversation for many a long mile as we trudged along.

The rain had ceased but the ground remained very wet and soon our boots and socks were soaked. My poor old boots were showing the effects of their hard and continuous usage and I was obliged to tie the soles on with a piece of string. Nevertheless they were still very comfortable and my heels were gradually improving.

Our full stomachs made walking a very uncomfortable business for the first couple of hours, and consequently we did not make much progress; we had to keep stopping for a rest. However, the weather improved with every hour and so did we.

We seemed to be reaching higher and more open country; farms were more numerous, and more prosperous looking, and in passing one we witnessed a threshing scene, the motive power for which was provided by two horses harnessed to the long arms of a roundabout (similar to the old horse pumps one used to see at home) and connected by a system of cogwheels to a long driving shaft leading to the flywheel of the threshing machine.

Only a few miles farther along we saw an even more primitive form of threshing. In a small barn by the side of the road a man was busy with a flail; the floor of the barn was covered with a layer of sheaves and by spreading out the head of each one in turn he was beating out the grain with his flail. We stood and watched for a few minutes but he ignored us and continued with his work without once looking up.

A feature of this area through which we were now travelling was the number of roadside shrines we saw; some of them were really beautiful pieces of carving depicting the Nativity, and at many of them reverent hands had placed small posies of wild flowers to commemorate the Divine Birth.

During the afternoon we crossed a fairly wide stream and as we were feeling hot and sticky we indulged in a luxurious wash and swim, taking the opportunity to wash our socks and a vest before changing into our spares. We had no reason to keep to any particular timetable on the march, so we just plodded along until we were tired and then rested for half an hour or so; sometimes taking a snack from our small stock of food, or a drink, and then pushing forward again.

During the day we were careful to eat as little as possible for we had found from experience that a stomach full of food does not agree too well with heavy footslogging carrying even a small load; it often produces severe pain from a kind of internal cramp, so we saved our best feed – if such it could be called – until we pitched camp at nightfall. So far we had been very lucky for food and fared moderately well, but our own stock of ration food had now been used up, and all we had left was a small supply of Horlicks tablets which we sucked at rare intervals as we marched along. From now on we would have to rely on local charity or by living on the land – a wartime supply term meaning plain theft.

We were now in the sixth day of our originally estimated ten days that should bring us to the coast. According to our maps we were keeping well up to schedule; therefore, some time tomorrow we should reach the Latvian border.

In the late evening as we ambled along we kept our eyes open for a likely place to spend the night.

We had decided that as the weather was still rather unsettled and the evening was coming in cold, we would pick on an isolated farm rather than risk another soaking. We had followed a cart track through a stretch of woodland and when we came out on the far side we saw some men busy harvesting. We approached them.

I gave them a greeting in German and one young fellow replied. I asked if he was a German, a suggestion which he seemed to think was in very bad taste judging by his indignant reply, and as it looked as if we had struck lucky I chanced telling him who we were and what we were doing, hoping for his sympathetic co-operation.

He just could not believe it at first, and talked the matter over with his companions in the local lingo. They all gathered round to gaze at us, and finally they reached some kind of a decision and our German-speaking acquaintance told us to go along with him.

Closely questioning us all the way, he led us to a large farm a couple of miles away. Although the fellow seemed straightforward enough we were filled with suspicion, and each few hundred yards or so we became more and more alarmed that he might be leading us into a trap. Bill first broke the spell. He had always been the one to sniff danger, and now he stopped suddenly.

"Look here, you chaps, I'm not liking the look of things. This bloke's German is too bloody good for me. Up to now we haven't met a soul who could speak a word of any language except the local lingo. How come a farm worker speaks German, unless he's in some way connected with them? How much have you told him about us already, Fancy?"

Bill's logic raised a whole mountain of suspicion in both Paddy and myself. Said Paddy:

"You're right Bill. It's time *we* did a bit of questioning, and if he doesn't sound too good, I'll give him one bloody smack that'll put him out for a couple of hours. Go ahead, John, ask him where he learnt his German!"

As soon as I turned to question the chap he seemed to have sensed the gist of our conversation. "Me have English, good fren he have me learn. Me O.K. You frens think bad. Me no bad. Come!"

"To hell with that talk. Go ahead, John," insisted Bill.

I went ahead in German. He told me his family were very rich, had plenty of land, and that he had been educated in Germany. His sister was educated in America, was a doctor and married to an American doctor in Baltimore, and everyone in this district hated the Germans. I told Bill and Paddy and suggested we take a chance. Paddy suggested that Bill and I wait ten minutes while he went ahead and, at the end of that time, bolt without him.

In the end we all three agreed to go together and waited outside the farm while the young fellow went in. Before we could complete our plan of action in case things went wrong, he returned with a middle-aged lady, who rushed towards us and clasped our hands as though we were her returning lost sons.

"Come in, come in!" she kept saying in perfect German. "My son has told me." And all the time the son was excitedly repeating to her all that we had told him. Even Bill was satisfied, and without more ado we were ushered inside to a large well-furnished room, obviously the home of people of some consequence.

The lady drew us to the fire while the son brought a pair of wool-lined slippers for each of us, and eagerly questioned us on our escape, as we removed our crippled boots. We were then escorted upstairs to a bedroom containing a double bed and a single bed; wash bowls, soap, and three lovely soft towels were provided, and we were told to rest ourselves until we were called down for a meal. We then stripped down for a good wash and shave, and lay on the beds enjoying the unaccustomed luxury of civilised comforts while we speculated on what sort of place we had stumbled on. We could scarcely believe our luck, and began to wonder how it would all end.

We had passed through such a rough period that we were reduced to a pretty low condition and thought of offering our services for a week to enable us to recover a little more strength before pushing ahead. We had not arrived at a unanimous agreement on this point when an hour later the lady called us down stairs and led us into a magnificent room, typical of an English manorial room, where we found a large dining table beautifully laid out with linen tablecloth, glass, and silver, and set for at least a dozen people.

She handed each of us a glass of schnapps to start the proceedings and while we were drinking and chatting other people began to arrive.

When the last to arrive was introduced to us as the local Resistance Leader, all our fears and doubts evaporated and we settled down to enjoy ourselves. He spoke English with a strong American accent, and informed us he had spent eight years studying at Pittsburgh; he also told us the welcome news that the Italians had capitulated and were now fighting the Germans alongside the British and Americans.

Suddenly he broke off the conversation, looked at his watch, lifted the seat of an easy chair to reveal a forbidden radio, and with earphones listened to the news. This titbit gave us an extra kick, and added confidence in our extraordinary friends. He was listening to the B.B.C. and he explained how he distributed the latest news around the district to trusted friends.

The meal now commenced, with servants to wait upon us, and we waded into a feast fit for a king. Throughout the meal we were incessantly questioned from every direction, especially by our Yankee friend, as we called him, and we had to answer endless questions about England and recount all our experiences as airmen and prisoners of war under the Germans.

With the latest news of the Italian collapse and the Russian change of fortune together with British and American advances on the Continent, our friends expressed their anxiety as to who would be their "Liberators"; British, American, or Russian? They had experienced Russian domination and they liked it even less than the German type. I'm afraid our many assurances on this point went sadly astray at a later date so that we owe our kind friends an apology.

We gleaned much valuable information concerning our journey ahead and about German dispositions on the border about twelve miles away. We were also given a detailed route to the border and told of the fallen tree by which to cross, as at this point a wide stream formed the boundary line.

Our party continued into the small hours of the morning and we consumed a considerable quantity of schnapps, not the type we had already tasted but a well-matured variety. By the time leave takings were conducted all round we had to be helped up to bed, and there we lay dead to the world until lunch time when we arose little the worse.

We were pressed to stay a few days but we felt our presence might endanger their lives, and told them so, and begged them to let us depart. They were loathe to agree, and after a lengthy explanation of the British way of looking at things our Yankee friend exclaimed, "I see, truly English, always the gentleman!" He interpreted our principles to his people and the matter was settled, we would move on after lunch.

We made a good meal, and with full stomachs and three rucksacks bulging to capacity with good food, we bade farewell to our kind and tearful hostess and her family and friends, and set our faces for the border.

CHAPTER NINETEEN

As we passed out of sight of their waving handkerchiefs I couldn't avoid the reflection that the war was revealing many heroes and heroines other than those who manned the aeroplanes and guns and ships.

These were brave people, who risked their lives harbouring us escapers and helping us on our way with food and information. We would never know whether they suffered for their kindness to us at the hands of their beastly German masters, nor in more peaceful days will we ever be able to thank them. We can do no more than carry our gratitude in our hearts unknown to them, and hope they were spared German reprisals.

We planned to cross the border stream at dusk, and as we had ample time, with five hours of daylight before us to travel a mere twelve miles, we ambled leisurely along. The route we were given by our friends proved absolutely accurate, and we arrived at the border area at eight in the evening.

At this point we exercised extreme caution as we had been informed that armed Germans occasionally patrolled the river bank; we spotted our fallen tree trunk, forming a bridge, without the least trouble and, realising such a convenience would qualify for special patrol attention, we reconnoitred the area in both directions.

As soon as we considered it dark enough, Paddy left his rucksack and boots in my care and he then crawled on his stomach towards the log, and still on his stomach with his feet in the water, made his way to the opposite bank. He remained flat on the ground for several minutes and surveyed the surrounding area before motioning us to cross. I then walked boldly across with my own and Paddy's rucksacks and waited for Bill to follow. We were now in Latvia.

We had just one more river to cross, but a mighty big one – called the "Baltic" and we were not yet there. Our point, at crossing the border stream, was roughly fifteen kilometres south of the little border town of Sckudi. On the Latvian side we found ourselves hemmed in by deep and close forests so we pressed on for half an hour to become well clear of the border and deeply hidden among the trees.

It had been pretty hard going for that half hour stumbling over rotted branches in the darkness, so we set to and built a wigwam of fir branches and got a small fire going, over which Bill half fried and half smoked several pieces of our gift bacon.

Between slices of bread it didn't taste too bad. It was a trifle tough perhaps, but small liberties may be taken with the digestion when one's appetite is sharpened by an outdoor life and a limited choice of supplies.

We spent a comfortable night in our wigwam, sleeping on a bed of rotted pine needles, and after a good breakfast, we were early on the move. As a precautionary measure we dismantled our shelter and scattered the ashes from our fire before heading west.

As we piloted our course through the trees it became clearly evident that we were travelling in another country; here the forest was managed on commercial lines with fire-breaks and open rides at well spaced intervals – a marked difference from the higgledy-piggledy primitive forest land we had encountered in Lithuania. The farms, too, that we sighted during the daylight hours were larger, and on a more prosperous scale.

We had an uneventful hike until late in the afternoon when we came out on a road which we identified as leading to the Latvian port of Libau. It didn't appear to be a particularly well-used road so we marched along it as it led in the direction we wished to go. We hadn't been walking for long when we heard the sound of a motor engine away in the distance behind us, and thinking discretion the better part of valour, we dived for cover into a ditch by the side of the road and lay low.

In a few minutes along came a German truck followed by two more, and peering after them from our cover we saw they were loaded with German troops. This happened twice more within the hour – we had defied lady luck "third time pays for all" – so we decided to give the road a miss and strike off across country.

It was quite dark when we came upon a small village, which we had approached from the fields. Having arrived at the back of the houses, and chosen a house with a number of outbuildings and a large barn, we walked quietly across the yard and knocked on the back door.

The house was in darkness and securely shuttered, but after several knocks a middle-aged man opened the door, whom we made to understand that we were British P.O.W.s seeking shelter for the night. As soon as he fully grasped the situation he just stared open-mouthed for a few seconds and then quickly ushered us inside and bolted the door.

He then examined his windows more carefully and lit a small lamp. Without saying a word, he walked to a corner of the room and opening a cupboard door switched on a radio just in time for us to hear the B.B.C. announcer saying, "This is the nine o'clock news."

We listened spellbound to every word; it was the first time Bill and I had heard it since the 13th May, 1940, three and a half years before. What a thrill we had to hear of the large scale air raids and all the activities in the Middle East. When it was over he switched off and turning to us with a grin said one word – "*verboten*" (forbidden).

He told us he was very worried at our presence in his house as there were a lot of Germans in the district. After giving us a feed of bread, butter, and cheese, with a drink of the inevitable sour milk, he led us out to the barn where he set up a ladder against the side of the hayrick and told us to climb up and stay there. It made a nice comfortable bed so we were content to follow his advice and were soon sound asleep.

Early in the following morning, our farmer friend arrived via the ladder with a basket containing bread, butter, and a dozen salted herrings. He told us to stay on the hayrick, and not to move outside at all until he told us it was safe to do so. We found it very tiresome up there during the morning as there were certain matters we were obliged to attend to and which we had to manage in a very primitive fashion.

Lunch arrived, again via the ladder, consisting of more salted herrings! We managed to get them into our stomachs, but during the afternoon our barn became like an oven. And oh, what a thirst! We lay sweltering on the hay with our tongues hanging out. We resisted the temptation to stretch our legs as we had no wish to cause any trouble for the farmer.

It was some relief when the cool evening at last arrived and with it came the farmer and his basket. We glanced apprehensively inside and felt quite relieved to find cheese for a change, but unfortunately, with the cheese he brought the doleful news that a party of Germans were billeted in the village on manoeuvres, and he dare not allow us to leave.

Having safely reached this far we deemed it best not to stick our necks into a ready-made noose by being rash at this stage. So we settled down for our second night in the barn.

Morning brought the same procedure and, so help me, more perishing herrings! The baleful look in their glassy eyes completely put me off. We buried them in the hay intending to dispose of them when we moved off in the evening, for we had definitely decided not to remain another night.

Paddy was feeling rough, I think the drinking of tainted water as we travelled up country had taken effect on him and this, coupled with the salt herrings, was really doubling him up. The day was not quite so hot, and we managed a little better, but we all felt fed up with our enforced idleness. When the farmer arrived in the evening he found us booted and spurred ready for the off.

He was very apprehensive about our going but we insisted that we must, and finally, when it was quite dark he led us out at the back and took us across the first field away from the houses. Then pointing out the direction to the coast he bade us goodbye.

We plodded straight ahead for perhaps two hours until we came up against a canal with very steep banks. We must have gone about three miles along the bank before we found a bridge by which to cross, and by this time Paddy was about all in. So we entered a cornfield in stook, and we each built a little house of sheaves and crawled inside.

We intended to rest until daylight but the number of harvest bugs allowed us no rest; we were continually being bitten. I could hear Paddy dashing out at frequent intervals and at about three a.m., he came over and said that he could not stand it any longer.

He felt that in his present condition the only thing for him to do was make a quick dash for Libau, about twenty kilometres away, and try to board a boat bound for Sweden; if there was no boat he would have to give himself up. Since for all three of us to attempt the same course together would lessen everyone's chance we divided our stores, and Paddy took leave of us.

Bill and I feeling that any more sleep was now out of the question, we set out for the coast and after stumbling along for a couple of hours, entered heath land with scattered pine trees, just as dawn was breaking. We could now smell the sea air, and about an hour later, topping some sand dunes, we had our first glimpse of the Baltic.

CHAPTER TWENTY

It looked glorious with the rising sun glinting on the wave crests. Finding a sheltered spot among the dunes we had a meal and then lazed about soaking in the sunshine and gazing out across the water, dreaming of Sweden on the other side.

All we needed now was to find a boat and either sail or row the eighty odd miles to freedom, but as this was no part of the coast to be looking for spare boats in broad daylight we just took our ease until evening should arrive.

The coastline was very low, comprising a sloping shingly beach backed by low sand dunes with patches of scrub, and behind these the pines.

Eleven days had now passed since our departure from Hydekrüge, including two days enforced idleness in the barn and we had covered about two hundred and fifty miles. Although we had not been actually without food for any length of time, it was only on rare occasions that we had been able to eat our fill. In consequence of food shortages, rough sleeping, living on our nerves following long periods of tunnelling on a restricted diet, and to a large extent our struggles through the bogs, we were now dog-tired and in very low physical condition.

As we were down to rock bottom, we realised we would have to replenish our food supplies at the earliest moment even if it meant stealing.

We wanted most to find a boat so that when we had collected some food we could go straight to it and put to sea. We set off immediately to work along the coast in the hope of spotting a suitable boat that would be accessible at night and not too heavy for us to launch. After a four hours' tramp in one direction we found none available, so we returned to our starting point and as the evening shadows lengthened we set off along the beach northward towards Libau.

We had been walking for about an hour when we came to a cart-track leading across the dunes, which we followed for half a mile, ending up at a small farmhouse. After a couple of knocks an old lady opened the door and we asked her for food and water. She could not understand my German and went off to fetch the farmer – presumably her husband – and he wanted to know who we were. I told him we were British P.O.W.s and that we had escaped from East Prussia.

He turned very surly and gave us an oddly searching scrutiny without a word of comment. He then spoke in his own language to his wife, who disappeared inside and returned with a loaf of bread, a piece of cheese, and a hunk of raw bacon. He indicated the pump, still without a word, where we refilled our water bottles. We never could decide whether it was the word "British" or "Prussia" that made him so surly. In my view our story sounded so fantastic he just didn't believe us and was glad to see the back of us at the price of some food. We thanked him, saluted, and wished him goodnight, then ambled back along the track towards the coast keeping a lookout for a place to pass the night.

It was quite dark by this time and after stumbling about for twenty minutes or so among the dunes, we found a small wooden shack with half a roof and no door.

I struck a match and to our surprise found it contained a couple of wooden bunks, and in one corner an old rusty stove. Breaking away a few more pieces of the hut we lit a fire and frizzled a piece of our bacon.

After supper we stumbled across the dunes and returned with a pile of pine branches and laid them on the bunks, climbed aboard, and slept.

We were awake early next morning and I slipped out for a preliminary scout round. At one side of the cart track, just behind the dunes I came upon a potato patch. Here was a nice supplement to our breakfast rasher. I got down on my hands and knees and was busily scratching out some nice roasters when I was suddenly pounced upon from behind. I was scared stiff, and staggered to my feet to find myself surrounded by four hefty young men, all in civilian clothes but wearing green armbands.

I assumed a most indignant attitude and asked who they were. They ignored my question and began questioning me instead.

"*Wer sind Sie?*"

I replied, "*Ich bin Englander!*" and then the fun started, and like a sustained volley at tennis the conversation continued.

"*Nein, Sie sind nicht Englander.*"

"*Aber, ich bin Englander.*"

Then in chorus, "*Nein, Sie sind nicht Englander. Sie sind Russe!*"

"*Nein, ich bin ein Englander!*"

Chorus: "*Nein! Nein! Nein! Sic sind Russisch saboteur.*"

None of us was perfect in our German and the conversation seemed to be getting into a groove so they marched me away and to my surprise, returned me to the farm we had visited the previous evening, and here the fellow who seemed in charge of the party began to cross-question me in earnest.

Apparently there had been a lot of sabotage carried out by Russians dropped by parachute into the country near port installations and other useful targets. These locals had been recruited into a sort of Home Guard unit by the Germans to fight the menace.

In our case, I have no doubt the old farmer had considered us Russian parachutists and passed on the tip that there were suspicious characters in the neighbourhood. I pointed out that if we were

Russian parachutists we wouldn't have begged food; we would have knocked the old man out and taken what we wanted. They seemed to agree.

I then told them about the Italian collapse and the British and American advances up the Rhine, and that soon, possibly, they would be liberated by us and the Americans. And in the end, with the help of my faked Swedish papers, I was able to convince them I was not a Russian but really an Englishman escaping from a German prison camp.

When this point was finally established and I was assured of their satisfaction the atmosphere completely changed, and we were shaking hands, when in walked Bill escorted by two more of the Home Guards. He told me he had been having a dip in the Baltic when "that couple of Goons" – pointing to his escort – just stood on the beach waiting for him to come out.

I had been watching the antics of the old lady, who seemed to dominate the "asides" conversation, and I feel sure it was due to her understanding and influence that we eventually secured our release. By now we had become a very convivial party, and the old lady supplied us with bowls of thick vegetable soup and great hunks of fresh bread.

We had thought to raise the question of a boat but abandoned . the idea as Bill thought it wisest not to alert them on this score and further, they might feel too much involved, should we be caught and questioned. We did make them understand that we were heading up the coast for Finland, and they made it clear they thought we were quite mad.

The leader said we were to understand they had not seen us, and this we took as the "all clear" to proceed on our way.

After handshakes all round and many gestures of thanks on our part, we tramped back to our hut where we had a shave and brush up and, considering our appearance quite passable, we decided to walk boldly along the coast into Libau.

As we approached the town we came to the bathing beach with the usual huts, swings, seesaws, and other seaside amenities, but not a person to be seen, so making the most of our luck we plucked up courage and walked along the road leading from the beach into the town itself.

Nobody seemed to take the least notice of us as we ambled along the streets, and as there was nothing peculiar in our dress to make us appear outstanding in a crowd, we became quite bold and did a spot of sightseeing. We mooched around the shops and casually set out to locate the docks, both to test our appearances in the dock area and to pin-point any specially guarded approaches to the ships.

A river ran through the town, spanned, as far as we could see, by one main bridge. On the seaward side of the bridge were the main wharves where we naturally expected to find the ships. All this area was apparently taken over by the German navy and looked well guarded. We could see several naval patrol boats moored alongside, and farther out a couple of destroyers, but no sign of merchant ships.

It was a very distressing outlook, and we began to wonder what might have happened to poor Paddy.

As all the small fishing vessels were moored farther upstream from the bridge we wandered along the side of the jetty to take a looksee, and managed to make conversation with an old fisherman. We asked if any boats from here went over to Sweden, whereupon he looked at us very suspiciously and shook his head. We then asked what were the fishing limits and he told us fifteen kilometres (roughly ten miles). We tried to probe him on the amount of fuel they were allowed to carry, but at this he closed up like a clam and began hurrying away. Things didn't look at all bright so we decided to leave, too.

We wanted to cross the bridge but it was guarded by sentries at both ends, so we waited to see what happened to the locals as they crossed. They crossed without interference. We waited until a party came along and we joined them and crossed over. I felt an almost irresistible impulse to thumb my nose at the sentries and Bill chortled away, "Look at the silly so-and-so's. What the hell are they there for?"

We didn't bother to stop and ask them, but subdued our impulses and passed safely over heading into the northern suburbs.

Passing through a shopping centre we were attracted by the lovely smell of freshly baked bread. We found it irresistible so we entered the shop and asked for a loaf of bread and a drink of water. The baker said he had none and pointed to a public pump a few yards farther up the street. We were bitterly disappointed and I felt sorely tempted to grab a couple of loaves and make a bolt for it.

That momentary craving for fresh bread could easily have ended our travels. I did the most stupid thing.

On the spur of the moment I told him who we were. My statement made him gape and stare, then suddenly he disappeared to the rear of the shop and returned with two glasses of milk, and while we drank he planted two large fresh loaves on the counter. I brought out some money but he refused to accept anything, and ushered us out of the shop with all speed. We were bewildered but doing fine.

There can be no doubt that Hitler or the local representatives of his mob would have handsomely rewarded in cash, or in amelioration of their slavery, any one of these kind people had they turned us in to the authorities. Our benefactors were not selected individuals, the escape committee at Hydekrüge were unable to supply us with any information on organised parties of underground workers in these countries to help us forward. We struck at random depending on luck, and never once did they let us down.

Poor or rich, they despised their masters and declined their bribes. Each one, although suspicious of us, bravely sheltered and fed us from their meagre stores. I felt we ought to have exploited our luck further and boldly asked them for a boat for our crossing to Sweden. I feel sure it would have been forthcoming; instead, we preferred (or should I say, suspicion forced us) to find the unguarded boat for ourselves.

With this object in view we trudged along the road leading out of town, pleased with our sightseeing but very footsore owing to unaccustomed walking on hard surfaces, and once clear of the houses made our way to the beach again.

The last rays of daylight were fading when we arrived back on the dunes, and our first concern was to find a shelter before darkness set in. We had plodded along the dunes for perhaps a mile when we saw a boat hauled up on to the shingle. It was just the very thing, our luck was holding; in fact, it was ahead of us with everything laid on. We gave it a thorough examination and passed it A1 at Lloyds though stripped of all tackle.

Now a boat without tackle is a useless thing to set out with on an eighty-mile trip across even a swamp, and we had to cross quite an ocean involving two dark nights and one day's voyage, so we looked around for a boathouse. We hadn't far to go but found it locked. The mast lay alongside the shed, which was a lucky find but useless in itself. The door was fastened by a simple padlock, and after searching among the outside junk we found a weapon and forced it open.

We both simultaneously voiced our disapproval of this vandalism; as Bill expressed it, "We're no better than the blasted Germans," and I could only agree. I would have liked to leave an I.O.U. for the damage and the boat but I might just as well have surrendered to one of the sentries on the bridge as done that. We eased our consciences in the hope that the owner was covered by insurance.

Inside the shed we found everything we should need; sails, oars, rigging ropes, tiller, and all sundries. First we carried down the mast and rigging ropes, set up the mast and braced it. I knew little about the job, but Bill had been a keen yachtsman, and under his expert guidance we soon had it braced and roped ready for the sails. We then returned for the oars and sails; there were several sets of sails so we spent some time sorting out in the dim light which appeared to be best, and loaded up.

I was in the lead carrying the oars, and when I breasted the last dune, there was the figure of a man standing by the boat not more than ten yards in front of me. I instantly dropped to my knees and sank behind the ridge for cover motioning Bill to do likewise. He crawled forward close to me and I whispered what I had seen. It was a sticky situation! We wondered how long he would stay there and who he might be, and more to the point what were we to do about it.

In a tussle we might easily have overpowered him, tied him up and left him in the shed, but if we were later caught, the penalty for an escaping prisoner using violence to resist capture, was certain death in front of a firing squad. That was good law, and we must avoid it at all cost.

We both peered cautiously over the ridge just as our visitor was leaving the boat and making for the boathouse on a course directly towards us. We crawled back hurriedly behind the next ridge and scurried off, keeping low, among the dunes, leaving our plunder just where we'd dropped it. Fortunately the sand muffled the noise of our hurrying footsteps or he could not have failed to discover our presence.

We had slunk in this fashion for possibly a hundred yards when we suddenly realised we had abandoned our rucksacks in a hollow about ten feet from the boat.

The rucksacks contained all our worldly possessions; two loaves, a piece of cheese, one small piece of bacon, and our water bottles. We just couldn't leave them behind. They had to be retrieved whatever happened, for without them we were lost, and trusting to the darkness and the sand ridges to cover our movements we crept stealthily back. It was an advantage that we knew of his presence and his whereabouts, while he would be blissfully unaware of our existence. As we closed in on our objective we could hear him rummaging in the boathouse so we quickly grabbed our belongings and made off as fast as the moving sand would permit us.

We considered it would be sheer madness to seek shelter in the immediate neighbourhood in case our unwelcome visitor raised an alarm. Were he to do so it would require very little analysis to decide that whoever went to the trouble we had taken, could have intended only to put to sea, and as no local would have any cause to do so, there must be escapers in the district. And a determined search over a given area must end in our capture.

It was too horrible to contemplate. So we tramped north along the beach for a full two hours before deciding to lie up for the night. We had very little choice of site as the darkness limited our vision to a few feet, yet we managed to stumble into a dense patch of scrub. Here we scratched a hollow in the sand, crawled into the shelter and lay down – I'm afraid I can't add – to sleep.

It was probably our worst night out of doors; we slept only for minutes at a time until we became so cold and hungry we crawled out in the early hours and began swinging our arms and stamping our feet in an effort to bring warmth to our bodies.

"Never mind," said Bill cheerfully, "We're still free!"

Soon dawn brought the rising sun and we began to feel better. We took stock of our surroundings, and as far as we could see we were the only inhabitants in the district.

We made a hollow in the sand between two ridges and with a few pieces of dry wood started a small fire. After smoking and frizzling our last piece of bacon, we made two dainty sandwiches, a good two inches thick, for breakfast.

It was then we realised that in the excitement of the previous evening we had forgotten our suppers, which would account to a large extent for our sleepless night and our frozen bodies the next morning. It had always been our rule to travel on the lightest breakfast and sleep on the heaviest meal our resources would permit.

This desolate stretch of coastline had served our purpose well in so far as it provided the perfect hideout at night, but we debated seriously whether it would make us the more conspicuous during the day.

For concealment during the day, the busy streets would provide our best cover, but we were also concerned with finding a boat and that would only be possible if we kept to the dunes.

We reviewed the circumstances which had contributed mostly to our success so far, and unanimously agreed that luck had been with us at every turn of events. We decided each to toss a coin: heads we kept to the dunes and the coastline, and tails we kept to the crowds.

We both returned heads, so off we went with the proviso that should we spot a suitable unguarded boat during our daylight walk, we would then join the crowds and return to the boat at dusk.

It was a sunny day and we thoroughly enjoyed our walk along the beach. We saw no sign of human activity and only an occasional track led townwards from the dunes. It was about mid-day when we saw a few houses ahead which looked like a small fishing village. On consulting our map we concluded the place must be Saraiki.

Thinking it best not to make any contacts at this stage in our quest for food supplies, and that our presence among the dunes might arouse some curiosity among the fishing community, we decided to turn inland and circle round the back of the village.

We crossed a small stream on our way back to the dunes and then continued along the coast when in the late afternoon we saw it – our boat! It was lying in a similar position to the "one that got away" the previous evening.

We went casually towards it, made an inconspicuous examination as we walked past it, in case we were under observation, continued a little farther, took rather a long turn with our eyes skinned for any building that could hide an alerted watcher, then walked away from the dunes searching for the boathouse. There it was, just about as far inland from the boat as the other had been. We were naturally worried in case the same thing happened again, so we worked the area up and down making a little farther inland with each turn, looking for a dwelling that might harbour the owner of the boat.

Our apparently aimless wanderings carried us into a belt of pines, and at the far end we could see a small farmhouse with its outbuildings. After a further inland search we felt sure the farm was the only inhabited house in the neighbourhood and concluded the boat must belong to the farmer.

We would still have to wait several hours for nightfall so we returned to the dunes and settled down to eat half our remaining bread and cheese. We would have given anything for a cigarette but our small stock had run out several days ago.

While waiting for the last rays of daylight we made our plans. We estimated our position as thirty-five miles north of Libau and opposite the large Swedish island of Gottland about eighty miles west. As there was an off-shore breeze which would be blowing on our starboard beam, we plotted to sail on a course of 300° anticipating that any drift would consequently come from the Gulfs of Bothnia and Finland to the north.

Having settled these technical details to our satisfaction it was now dark enough to get busy rigging the boat. Taking a good look round to make sure there was no-one watching our movements, we made a couple of false approaches to the boathouse to draw any enemy movements; each time we waited by the door for five minutes then walked away with every sense alerted for a reaction.

Nothing happened.

We had noticed the door was fastened by means of a wooden peg through a hasp and staple. On the third approach we removed the peg, threw one of the double doors wide open, walked away and waited under cover for a few minutes, then boldly entered in search of the necessary gear.

We had previously carefully examined the boat and found it an exact replica of the other; an open type about fifteen feet long with a step for the forward mast. The owner must have been a very tidy kind of boatman, and had placed the whole of the equipment together in one corner near the door. We silently thanked him for his forethought and carried the lot to the boat in one trip, carefully closing the door before we left, as Bill remarked, "To keep the rats out."

We surprised ourselves at the speed with which we managed to rig the boat, fix the sails, and ship the oars aboard ready for off. I suggested it was due to our previous night's rehearsal, but Bill playfully assumed all the credit. However, our troubles were far from over; we still had shingle instead of sea beneath the keel and there were thirty feet of it before reaching the water. It would be a sticky business getting it across that thirty feet of shingle to launch it. A fifteen foot boat is a formidable object for two weary men to push that distance into the sea!

We pushed and shoved and heaved for some time without making the least impression. I began to fear the worst. If Paddy had been with us we could have managed fine, but Paddy wasn't there – and the thought of him raised a lump in my throat. We returned to the boathouse hoping to find something to give us a bit of leverage. Again we were lucky. We found the very wooden rollers that the owner would use.

Each carrying a couple of these rollers on our shoulders we smiled and nodded our heads at each other like a couple of congenital idiots as we made our return to the boat. No doubt we both thought our troubles were over and were crediting ourselves as a couple of clever lads. And as things turned out our troubles were over, for when we used the rollers under her keel, she made a rush into the water as though she were glad to be in her proper element. We pushed off and jumped in. We had timed it for complete darkness, exactly nine p.m. Seaborne at last!

We could have shouted for joy.

"Pity we couldn't have hired the village band to give us a send off," remarked Bill.

"I'd plump for a thermos of coffee," I replied.

Without further back-chat we hauled up the sails and set them to catch the breeze, and setting our course with Bill at the tiller we got under weigh – like the owl and the pussy cat we sailed away, only our boat wasn't a pea-green. The inshore sea was quite calm but we picked up the breeze and bowled along at something like five knots.

Sensitive to this new luxury we sat back to enjoy our new mode of travel; it seemed too good to be true. One minute we were land-locked, hunted animals of darkness with but one object in life, asking no more than enough bread and water to maintain the strength in our bodies to gain our freedom; the next, freedom was in our grasp.

To us, freedom meant everything in life worth having. To gain thus far in our bid for freedom we had accepted the standards of living of many of the lower animals. We had burrowed through the earth like moles, run the gauntlet of the huntsman's bullets, scavenged like rats, begged like hungry little robins, stolen like foxes, slept in the open like pariah dogs, travelled avoiding human contact like the hyena and jackal.

And never once had we considered it any price to pay. Never once were we despondent or without hope. Never did we feel heroic or even clever. We just could not accept imprisonment. We claimed only the inborn urge to be free; our hardships were the means to gain that freedom.

True, we had so far only escaped the terrors on land. The sea held many dangers, we had yet to test the seaworthiness of our boat and our own amateur seamanship, we had food and water for only one meal and it might be several days, even weeks, before we reached the shores of Sweden. We should need sleep. The Germans would send motor boats to seek us. We paid no heed to these terrors, even if we ever thought of them. I don't recall that we ever once said a prayer, but we liked to think that God was taking care of us and our thanks were in our hearts although unspoken.

We had earned the right to feel a little jubilant now that we were riding the waves with a nice little boat carrying us merrily away on the last lap to freedom. Anyway, we argued, even if our navigation went astray and we missed the island of Gottland we could not fail to hit the Swedish mainland sooner or later.

The shoreline soon receded into the darkness and the sea became a bit choppy as we left the land behind us, but not enough to cause us the least worry.

Satisfied with our luck and happy in the prospects before us, we sailed merrily on until just after midnight when the breeze died on us and the sails went limp and useless, leaving the boat wallowing in deep water. We voiced our disappointment, calling it a dirty trick, the first time we had audibly criticised our luck. It was no use moaning, we got out the oars and set to in earnest to face the hard task of rowing. My oarmanship would never have won me a position in the Oxford boat, but with Bill as stroke we teamed up well and got along without my catching too many crabs.

It was back breaking work for our unaccustomed muscles and we were obliged to take frequent rests. Our poor physical condition now began to reveal itself and we moved slowly; but however slow our progress, provided the farmer did not miss his vessel for a few days, we had all the time in the world before us.

If only another breeze would spring up and release us from this toil! But at last, dawn crept up to find us still heaving at the horrible wooden oars that were already blistering our hands. I began to hate the very sight of them and tried to distract my mind from the discomfort by fixing my gaze on the back of Bill's head and counting the times his head went forward and back again with each stroke.

We fancied we could feel a slight movement in the air and hopefully held out the sails, but there was not enough to fill them, so we decided to take a short rest and eat a mouthful of food.

We estimated we were close on thirty miles out to sea, and although we ought to have been fifty miles out had the breeze not gone on strike, we were satisfied with our progress. Time itself meant little to us. We could have contented ourselves with sleeping away the time with the knowledge that another breeze would get up by nightfall and save our blistered hands.

But one cannot dictate to the wind, and there would be enemy shipping about which would take us aboard. We needed darkness at this moment in the absence of a breeze.

After a conservative raid on our small supply of bread and cheese followed by a short rest, our flagging energies revived, and we were preparing to move on again, when the sound of an aircraft engine came faintly to our ears. In seconds it quickly materialised into an enemy scout plane flying at a fairly low level on a northerly course about five miles astern. At first sight we thought it would miss us, but as it reached a point almost dead astern it turned and flew directly over us.

Thinking to allay suspicion we adopted the pose of earnest fishermen. It circled above us at a very low level forcing us to take notice. We gave it a cheery wave as a further bit of bluff and continued with our pretence as hard working fishermen. It finally headed off in a south easterly direction which we knew meant disaster for us – we didn't wish the crew any harm but we did hope the blasted engine would conk out over the sea.

As soon as the plane was out of sight we grabbed the oars and started like mad. We kept going as hard as we could for a couple of hours before stopping for a rest and then anxiously searched our stern horizon for signs of pursuit. We could see nothing, and we began to hope we had fooled them after all.

Returning to our task once more, we went on for perhaps another hour, then when I glanced behind me, I saw it. I called to Bill and we both took a good look.

It was a motor-launch.

It headed in our direction at a good speed. There was nothing more we could do. We just sat and waited.

In a few minutes it drew alongside and stopped. It was a German naval patrol boat carrying a crew of four. The Captain informed us we were in forbidden waters and wanted to know who we were. I told him we were Swedish sailors who had missed the boat at Libau, and to prove it we showed him our passports. Although he seemed to think these were O.K. our tale sounded a bit thin, and he said he was not satisfied and we would have to convince the port authorities before we could proceed.

We were ordered aboard his vessel, our boat was taken in tow, and we headed back to Libau, the port from which they had come.

Speaking in undertones on the return journey we agreed to stick to our tale that we were Swedes in the hope that, with a bit of luck, they might put us aboard a ship bound for Sweden. But on arrival in port we were taken under escort to a large house, used as local German headquarters. I had hoped to be turned over to the Latvian authorities and appeal to them to treat us as Swedes (with a blind eye to the truth) but a sight of the German escort was as good as a one-way railway pass to Hydekrüge.

I knew I'd never talk my way out of German hands. Bill thought we might be handed over to the Swedish Consul for interrogation, in which case we could have told them the truth and probably received their protection. But alas, we were in German hands, and as soon as we arrived at headquarters we were taken to separate rooms and given a third-degree grilling, during which the least punishment they could threaten was death.

I told my tale and stuck to it like a drowning man sticking to a floating spar. Suddenly a big bullet-headed swine yelled, "What's the name of your ship…?"

I hesitated trying to think up a name.

He banged the table, "What are you waiting for? … you lie … you have no ship!"

I hadn't, I couldn't even imagine one. I didn't know a damned word in Swedish beyond the pronunciation of my name "John Svenson" as stated on my passport.

"What is the Captain's name?" he yelled, laying his loaded revolver on the table, and fingering it in a menacing way.

I was beyond thinking by then, and all hope died within me. I told them the truth.

"I'm English," I replied. "A British airman prisoner of war. I escaped from a camp in East Prussia, Hydekrüge!"

They didn't believe that tale either.

"You all lies. You Ruskie saboteur. All Ruskies shot!" he belched at me.

No matter what I said now, they were intent on making me a Russian saboteur. Although what a Ruskie saboteur would be doing in a small boat forty odd miles out in the Baltic I failed to see – unless poisoning fish for hated Deutscher to eat.

Henceforth every question was accompanied by the threat that I would be shot.

They spent two hours trying to extract a confession that I was a Russian. I answered with a flat denial and screamed at them: "For God's sake 'phone Hydekrüge, they'll tell you. I'm not such a bloody fool I don't know whether I'm British or Russian!"

Finally, they gave up in blind fury and the guards led me out. I was taken to meet Bill, looking a trifle pale, but still grinning. I asked him if he would prefer to be shot before or after lunch. His reply was unprintable, and reflected on the parentage of all Germans in general.

We were conducted outside the building, marched off by four guards right through the centre of the town while the people stood and gazed curiously, and away over the bridge to the northern outskirts – quite a trek – where we arrived at a camp. The same old familiar sight, barbed wire all round, searchlights and machine-guns mounted in stilted cabins overlooking the compounds, and the patrolling guards.

We found it filled with Russian sailors – funny, I thought, we must be Russians after all!

We were led into a room adjoining the office, and searched down to the bare skin; here I lost my little compass. I was sorry to part with that, we had come a long way together. Finally they marched us off to the cooler, an ordinary wooden hut with a row of cells on each side of a central corridor. We were locked in separate cells and I was shouting something to Bill next door, when a voice with a strong Irish brogue piped up farther down the block, "Well if it isn't me own two wicked truants away up for a seaside holiday! How are ye now?"

"Paddy, begorra!" yelled Bill and I together.

What the other victims in the cells were thinking I couldn't guess but for the next hour or two we were yelling question and answer across to each other and breaking into howls of laughter that must have sounded very queer to them. Bit by bit we got Paddy's story and related our own adventures in exchange.

After leaving us in the cornfield he had walked along the Libau road as fast as his condition would permit and arrived in the town late in the afternoon. After a tour of inspection around the wharves he decided it would be quite impossible to make a quick getaway by boat, and as his physical condition was so low he could scarcely drag one foot after the other, he gave himself up to the police late the same night.

He appeared to have no regrets, except that circumstances forced him to make the decision. His dysentery, or whatever it was, had plagued him hourly night and day. Often he was caught wanting to evacuate without any privacy at hand and his clothing became so saturated he despised himself. Twice he washed his trousers and laid up in a barn until they were only partly dry.

Instead of food in his rucksack it was filled with hay to stuff into the seat of his trousers and exchange periodically whenever he was overtaken without warning. His groins were so sore and inflamed he was obliged to walk with his feet wide apart. He was truly in a sorry state when at last he surrendered.

When eventually I saw him I was so shocked to see such a fine man reduced to a skeleton I could have wept, although he was still in good spirits and could crack a joke.

The Germans couldn't spare a hospital bed for him but he received a fair crack of the whip at the hands of doctors in medical treatment and food whilst in his cell. His disease had now run its course and with proper diet and care he stood a fair chance of recovery. Poor Paddy! He paid dearly for his spell of liberty. He had been in this camp since he surrendered, and as information of his capture had passed to the authorities at Hydekrüge, he now awaited an escort to return him there.

Two days later an interpreter and one guard arrived to collect Paddy and when our guards informed them of our presence they came along to see us. They were as surprised as though they'd seen their own grandfathers walk out of their graves.

The interpreter was a certain Unteroffizier Schreiber who had been with us since the early days at Barth. A really decent chap was old Schreiber, one of the better type of Germans, and if the truth were known he was anti-Hitler and rather pro-English. Before the war he had been a teacher of some sort, I fancy a professor at Heidelberg University.

He had a magnificent baritone voice and enjoyed nothing better than to join us during our concert rehearsals for a good hearty sing. He could also take a good deal of leg pulling with good grace and a smile – a rare trait in any German.

He came first to my cell, and as soon as he recognised me, exclaimed, "Oh, Mr. Fancy! How nice to see you again. We *have* missed you. I presume your dear friend Mr. Street is here as well?"

Voice from next door: "You're dead right, pal! I hope you've come to take us back?"

"Yes, so do I, Mr. Schreiber. These damned fools want to make us into Russians so they can shoot us. Can you do something about it?"

"That, I will see to, Mr. Fancy. Please have no worry now."

Good old Schreiber, I thought, our identity would no longer be in doubt. He went off to 'phone Hydekrüge for instructions, as obviously he couldn't cart all three of us back with only one guard! He returned a little later to inform Bill and me that we would have to stay here and "be good boys" until another tough party of guards could be dispatched for our "protection".

It was good to see old Schreiber smile as he said "protection". We promised to be good, and gave him our word of honour not to attempt to escape if only we could go back with him. We told him what a terrible dump we were in and how glad we would be to return to Hydekrüge. He was sorry, but explained he dared not take any chances, he would be exceeding his instructions. Orders were orders, anyway, so we promised to behave and wait.

Our daytime cooler guards were Austrians, two quite elderly old gents. They spent hours each day talking with us, telling us all their troubles and showing us photographs of their families whom they hadn't seen for more than a year. I fancied there was method in their madness, that they were afraid we'd escape somehow and get them into serious trouble, so they engaged us in conversation to make sure we would not get up to something we shouldn't do.

They were very confiding and, as they said, they could trust us because we were English. We felt flattered and quizzed them all we could about Austrian reaction to Hitler and his crowd. We gathered that they considered themselves more Hitler's prisoners than we were, and that all Austrians were Anglophile and terrified of the Germans.

But our night guards were of a very different type. They were young Germans of the unfit class and scared stiff of being sent to the Russian front for the least misdemeanour. They spent the night peeping at us through the spy-holes every few minutes, afraid that if left unguarded for long we'd surely vanish or do something else. They were probably right, too.

We often wished our Austrian pals could be switched over to night duty because we should have stood a fair chance to make a break, and once outside the cooler hut, the perimeter wire would present no problem. It was only a latticed fence of single barbed wire.

Curiously enough, although the camp was filled with Russian P.O.W.s, the outside patrolling guards were also Russian: Ukrainians, or White Russians as they were called. Although we had no contact with either section of these Russians our friendly Austrian guards told us they hated each other like poison and the Ukrainians would never hesitate to bayonet the Russians inside on the least pretext. It struck us as a queer state of affairs and I wondered what would be the final outcome when the Russian armies marched into the area.

We had spent a vile fortnight in this hole before a party of guards arrived to escort us back to Hydekrüge. And what a party! They would undoubtedly provide "protection" as Schreiber had put it. We were certainly very pleased to see them and I gave them a hearty welcome in my best German. They marched us to the station in the early morning and we arrived at Hydekrüge camp at seven-thirty in the evening.

Although the accommodation was now two men to each cell, and a long queue waiting for the cooler, they found room for us and rushed us straight inside. We rolled up next morning before the Commandant who tried hard, with the aid of his interpreter, to get an admission from us that we had been helped by local residents at various stages in our travels.

We stuck just as hard to our story of living off the land and after a two-hour sweating and bullying interview the interrogation was closed with an award of twenty-eight days in the cooler without the option, adding:

"If you can improve your memories in that time and reveal your helpers, you may escape a further two weeks' solitary on bread and water later."

We now began to learn exactly what had happened on the night of the tunnel break. Apparently the first eight men successfully cleared the tunnel but number nine, a newcomer to underground work and inclined to be of the nervous type, stood straight up as soon as he reached the exit, instead of carefully scanning the area at ground level with only his head exposed. Consequently he almost barged into the patrol as soon as he emerged.

It was most unfortunate he had failed to take the necessary precautions because at that moment the guard had halted right by the tunnel with his attention drawn towards the trees – he may have heard a rustle of something in the bushes – but the sight of an apparition suddenly rising from a hole in the ground immediately in front of him must have given him apoplexy.

Naturally, Bedlam broke loose instantly, and for the next few minutes shots were fired in all directions. It was nothing short of a miracle that no-one was killed or even hurt.

Reinforcements of guards quickly appeared on the scene and the task of extracting the remaining tunnellers began. As one by one they emerged the number soon became an embarrassment to the guards outside the wire and the operation was halted. I think the Goons began to fear they would soon have all the kriegies on the wrong side of the wire, so they left a guard over the hole to prevent the others leaving while they marched those already outside back into the compound and straight into the cooler cells.

Then further reinforcements entered the compound and began searching for the tunnel entrance. I chuckled with pleasure when I was told they were unable to find it. They could hear the kriegies shouting below deck yet they still couldn't find how they got there, until they received shouted instructions from below what to do.

It was after midnight, they told me, before the last man was brought out; then the fun and games really commenced. All the kriegies were hauled from their billets and herded together in one corner of the compound, large quantities of straw were brought in and set alight, hurdles were erected between two huts, and by the light of the bonfires and searchlights the kriegies were passed through the hurdles and counted and checked one by one just like counting sheep.

This procedure was carried out backwards and forwards several times, each time with a different total, and all wildly inaccurate, until by early morning they gave up in disgust, and amid the howls and jeers of the P.O.W.s locked everyone in his billet.

I could just imagine the chaps passing through and then nipping back again time and time again to muddle the count.

The next day, as soon as breakfast was over, a complete identity check was made. To begin the check everybody was locked in his billet. Then two guards were placed at the door of a hut and one by one each man presented himself at a table set up in the compound on which was a file, including photograph and number of every prisoner in the camp, or rather, every prisoner who should be in the camp.

When every hut had been carefully checked in this way the German count showed more than thirty men missing. They knew that couldn't be right, so they began all over again. This time, after each hut had been emptied one by one the men were returned to the hut and locked in.

At the end of this stunt they lost three more men.

They now locked the men in each hut with the scrutineers and documents inside and although there was a roster for each hut, by the time they had checked every hut they had lost another two.

The Commandant stood in the middle of the compound waving his arms and blasting the guards to Hell, Hull, and Halifax while the P.O.W.s laughed at them from the windows and set up merry hell banging tins and pans on the hut walls. Eventually the Gestapo were called in and they literally pulled the place apart, but still no two checks agreed in number. The Gestapo and Goons went berserk and gave vent to their tempers by confiscating every unopened tin of food they could find, and of those already open and partially used they scattered the contents on tables and floors, and threw the tins at anyone who came into view.

In the end they arrived three times with a count that agreed correctly with the P.O.W.s' figure. They marched out of the compound to the tune of "John Brown's body ..." sung lustily by the lads.

Incidentally, and the boys all knew it, one more Gestapo agent went out of the compound than came in. Unfortunately he was caught at a later date, but it was certainly a good effort.

George Grimston, and that's the real name of the extra Gestapo agent who walked out, was no ordinary P.O.W. His German was so perfect that all newcomers to the camp thought him a German, planted there to spy on his fellow P.O.W.s. In fact many fools called him a traitor to his face. They never knew what he was ultimately working up to, nor did anyone else.

That the Gestapo party never suspected him, proves the true measure of Grimston's stature, and does not reflect on the intelligence of the Gestapo. Grimston was one too many for a regiment of men. He proved himself one too many for the whole Gestapo system and eventually for the German government.

He actually became a Government servant and functioned as such, at least for several months, until they liquidated him in a Belsen gas chamber.

He was no traitor! He was never bought over by the Germans. In fact I feel ashamed to use the word in his defence. He never needed a defence in our eyes. We eventually learnt the object of his adopted swagger, his recitals of the German poets in German, his German songs, his marvellous vocabulary of German curses and swear words, his blather, and ostentatious friendliness and association with the Germans, his false idealism of the German people. He was acting, and deliberately preparing himself to achieve success in a scheme that only he knew anything about. He deliberately provoked his friends to mistrust him, to encourage the Germans to believe he was their friend. And it worked.

George Grimston's singleness of purpose during our stay at Barth, and later at Sagan, and finally at Hydekrüge where we saw the last of him, had caused many hard things to be said against him by thoughtless companions. I could never understand why he would never join me in my various hair-brained attempts to escape. Only once did he offer the least enlightenment.

"Fance," he said, "when I go, I'll walk out, and they'll never bring me back again."

I always thought he meant he would stay a P.O.W. until liberated. But he had now evidently decided it was time for action, and he was ripe and ready.

The kriegies stood aghast and watched him walk out.

CHAPTER TWENTY–ONE

It was George who, nattily attired as a smartly dressed Gestapo agent, walked out of the camp with the rest of the party never to be seen again. Although we never saw him again we heard plenty from him. Somehow he had given the party the slip on the way to headquarters and was now as free as the birds in the air.

We heard nothing from him for several weeks – and for all this time we had smothered his absence on roll-call.

One day a note reached the hands of the escape committee stating that a certain Herr Somebody-or-other (in fact George) was spending a few days at a local hotel after making several return trips to Danzig, and warning them to be prepared to receive a detailed report of his travels.

There were scores of ways of passing such notes outside and inside the compound. In this case the go-between was a seedy youth in uniform working in the Commandant's office, a German-born boy whose Dutch parents had escaped to Holland and were engaged with the underground organisation there.

Another instance of German stupidity, although the Commandant was unaware of the youth's parentage and anti-Nazi sentiments. The youth lived with the other Germans in the Lager and was treated as the village idiot.

In due course a progress report arrived detailing George's efforts to pioneer an air-tight escape route from outside the camp into

Danzig, with an appeal for more money. Funds were produced from the kriegie bank and George received his pay packet.

Our next intelligence report revealed that George had actually secured for himself the position of Port Inspector at Danzig![1] ... that the escape route via the Polish underground movement was completed and open to conduct escapees from outside the camp at Hydekrüge to Danzig, and from there on board a ship to Sweden.

The only thing left for individual initiative was to get out of the camp and make his first contact – and this first contact was known to the escape committee. From there he would pass from hand to hand.

There must always be a first, and it fell to Paddy Flockhart (his real name), an Irish pilot, to be first to test the route. This isn't the Paddy Flynn who surrendered at Libau. Now Paddy Flockhart was a bit of an individualist and a daring schemer.

At the time the latest news from George was received, work was in progress deepening and widening a ditch which ran through our compound, preparatory to laying an underground drain.

Paddy waited until the excavations reached the section running under the main wire to the outside, leaving a nicely levelled trench four feet deep along which anyone could walk to freedom, if he could evade the watchful machine gunners in their elevated cabins. One machine gunner stood guard over this weak spot, especially during lunch hour while the workmen went to lunch.

The workmen had scarcely left the compound when along came Paddy, almost immediately at their heels, decked out in jackboots, breeches, short leather coat, and wide-brimmed hat, the very person-ification of a German labour supervisor, carrying a long measuring rod.

He walked boldly up to the warning fence, gesticulating and shaking his fist to the sentry in his box, as much as to say "Don't shoot me, you fool," as he passed over the warning wire into the forbidden

---

[1] This episode sounds so incredible that the author would like to emphasise that this – like the rest of his story – is plain, unembroidered fact.

area. All the guard saw was a jovial German civilian with a grand air of authority, apparently one of the gang working on the job.

He gave a nod of assent to pass, Paddy stepped down into the trench and began assiduously measuring his way outside, straightened his back as though his lumbago was troubling him, spoke a couple of words to the guard and continued to measure his way out until he vanished from sight.

That was the last we saw of Paddy!

He made a successful journey to Danzig, was smuggled aboard ship the same night for Sweden and eventually reached England and Home.

All this was achieved by George Grimston, the man who deliberately acted a part for a purpose, and declined to take advantage of his own labours to escape himself.

No-one will ever know how he managed to deceive the Germans to obtain his post of Port Inspector, a key position in the escape route, whereby he was enabled to select his captains and crews to guarantee safe passages for his fellow P.O.W.s.

Some time later a link in the Hydekrüge-Danzig escape chain snapped, suspicions were aroused in official quarters, and a trail of searching enquiries led to a certain Port Inspector at Danzig. George was on the run, a hunted man fleeing for his life. Despite his own personal danger he managed to close the route and send word back to Hydekrüge to halt the traffic indefinitely.

We received our end of the news through the grapevine, but of George we have heard no further word from that day to this. Rumours through the Polish underground placed him at one time in the Belsen horror camp, where we believe he ended his days in the gas chambers.

I knew nothing of his family and friends in England; I knew only that George Grimston spent his days and years a P.O.W. alongside me and that he was an extraordinary man. He used every moment of his imprisonment to study the German character, prising open every hidden crevice in their facade and system with a single secret purpose in his own mind. That purpose was to clear an escape route back home to England for his friends and many of those who were not his friends.

I admired George: he possessed that rare brand of courage which set personal safety at naught to help others.

I still possess the watch he left in my safekeeping and should he by some miracle ever reappear, I shall be the happiest of men to return him his own property. On the other hand, should any member of his family care to contact me, I would be delighted to hand it over to them in remembrance of a brave man.

While Bill and I were still in the cooler, and I'm certain it was our presence back in camp that gave the Commandant the idea, he instituted a further reprisal. You will recall that we had used quite a quantity of bed-boards to shore up our last escape tunnel. Well, he ordered the confiscation of all but five of every kriegie's bed-boards, the barest minimum required.

We witnessed the scene of this enactment from our cell window. A wagon similar to the one used at Sagan for carting away the soil during the conversion of a spare hut to a concert hall was brought into the compound drawn by a motley team of one ancient horse and one ox, complete with an old farmer as driver and one guard.

All the kriegies were ordered to carry out their surplus bed-boards and pile them on the compound. This they did most dutifully to the letter, and up to a point everything went according to plan. When the wagon arrived they were ordered to load up, but as more and more boards were loaded on to the wagon from one side they disappeared at the other, and while the pile on the ground got lower the pile on the wagon got no higher, and a steady stream of kriegies could be seen staggering away hugging several planks under their greatcoats in front of them.

The guard watching the loaders on one side suddenly noticed this peculiarity and dashed round to the other side to see what was happening.

He caught a couple of fellows and made them return the planks, but during his temporary absence the fellows on the other side were piling them under billets to be restored later on. As soon as he returned, the procedure renewed on the other side.

He got so mad in the end, in desperation he climbed the wagon and mounted on top of his reduced load and stood with his rifle at the ready bawling at all and sundry to the accompaniment of wild cheering from the assembled crowd.

Muttering ponderous German curses he eventually left the compound sitting on top of the salvaged remnants, leaving the krie-gies in peace … and with a pile of planks they had stacked on the ground under his wagon!

It was during this particular spell in the cooler that the conveyor belt was improvised. Naturally, we were not allowed cigarettes, although a few were occasionally smuggled in, but as the occupant of one cell had no official contact with the others it was difficult to share out our smuggled luxuries. However, we were allowed cotton and wool and other materials for mending and darning our clothing, and this gave birth to a bright idea.

Each cell window could be reached from the outside by the next door neighbour holding a bed-board at full arm's stretch through the grill. A rough sketch was drawn and pinned to a bed-plank with instructions and passed along outside.

The fellow in the cell at one end was instructed to pass a large darning needle through a bobbin of cotton, pinion it firmly to the window frame, and return the plank so that the reel would freely rotate. Then he was to attach the end of the cotton in a split at the end of his plank and pass the plank to his neighbour; this passed from hand to hand until it reached the other end, where the chap would pinion an empty reel in similar fashion. He would then pass the cotton round it and return the plank with the cotton attached. Finally, number one received his bed-plank and tied the two ends of the cotton.

Thus we had an endless belt with the cotton reels acting as rollers serving, if I remember rightly, nine cells.

The operation was now quite simple. When a chap managed to procure some cigarettes either by barter or arrangement with a co-operative guard, or smuggled in by one means or another, everyone of us got a smoke. The bloated capitalist lighted his cigarette, took a few puffs and then, by means of a safety-pin, attached it to the conveyor belt. His next door neighbour pulled gently on the thread until the cigarette appeared opposite his window, took his ration of puffs and passed it on down the line. When the chap at the end had had his puffs he returned it to the donor who then sent it in the opposite direction to the other people. If any cigarette remained it returned to the original owner.

Many other lightweight articles were distributed by the same means. The erection and manipulation of the contraption could be carried out only after dark, and then only with numerous interruptions while a guard patrolled outside the block. The reels were taken in after each nightly session as they would have been seen in daylight. The cotton line, looped over the darning needles, we left outside, trusting to escape detection in daylight. It worked perfectly for the remainder of our period in the cooler.

On one dark night we were operating our conveyor belt for the usual community smoke, when a more than usually alert – and windy – guard, saw a small red glow travelling mysteriously along the wall from cell to cell. He let out one blood-curdling yell and dashed to the guardroom.

All the guard turned out with rifles and fixed bayonets, and hastened to the rear with torches to investigate the strange occurrence, but fortunately the windy guard's yell had warned us and by this time we had dismantled the whole thing and nothing remained to be seen.

We kept out of sight and enjoyed listening to the outside conversation, but had to nip smartly into our hard beds when they all trooped in to search the cells. They drew a blank, of course, and the mystery remained unsolved.

A few days later we were released from the cooler, and with an air of innocence, I enquired of our old friend Schreiber what all the commotion had been about.

He explained that constant night duty had turned the poor fellow's brain and he began seeing things. "He was sent on sick leave," he remarked, adding, "which means he will find his way to the Russian front. The new Reich doesn't like madmen." I thought it a splendid idea and wished they would send a few more of the meddlesome Goons to the same destination.

About a week later another amusing incident took place which we christened "The Deutschers' Folly". It happened the day after the Commandant spotted me taking my daily tramp, for exercise, around the perimeter in company with Bill. "Ah, Fancy, so the 'Mole' is out of cooler again?" he queried with a benevolent sneer, and went on to warn me, that if I brought him any more reprimands from authority he really would be obliged to have me shot.

The Goons entered the compound with a powerful mechanical road-roller and began slowly driving it around the perimeter inside the warning wire. The idea, of course, was to reveal any tunnelling which might be in progress.

All the kriegies gathered around and watched the operation with amused interest, and from all sides offered annoying advice on where and where not to drive. But the Goons had gradually become immune to the jibes and nagging of the irrepressible kriegies after several years of close contact with them – they had long since written us off as quite mad – so they ignored their tormenting spectators and continued their leisurely course round the compound until they reached a point behind the latrines close to where I had dug my last escape tunnel.

Then it happened! The whole thing sank gracefully out of sight leaving only the driving cab and the engine bonnet visible above ground.

Quite naturally we cheered this performance to the echo, and if such could be possible, the Goons left the compound with very red necks, cursing and threatening us with every possible unpleasantness conceivable to the German mind.

The thing remained there for more than a week, during which time we robbed it of every working part we could and buried them in the latrines. At last, lifting gear arrived and it was hauled out to ground level, and engineers began to start the engine.

As soon as they discovered its main parts were missing all hell broke loose. The Goons rushed in and tore the billets apart, scattering our personal kit in every direction in the hope of finding the bits and pieces.

The cause of the subsidence was the section containing our soil disposal chamber which the boys had wisely thought not to fill in. We now had to set to, under the personal supervision of the brutal chief Goon who had clouted my jaw with his revolver at one time, and make the hole safe and solid.

Our return from the cooler had coincided with the closing in of winter in that locality, and we settled down to the usual round of concerts, plays, bridge, and a variety of educational lectures, not forgetting a spot of Goon-baiting whenever opportunity occurred. We had the inevitable ice hockey blood matches on the flooded compound attended by the usual crowd of German spectators and their comments on the mad English.

The plays that were produced revealed some first-class acting and the general standard of entertainment was maintained at a very high level. But alas, our winter entertainments came to an abrupt end when one night in the early spring the theatre was gutted by fire. The high-light of this disaster was a comedy provided by the German fire brigade.

They came dashing into the compound accompanied by a great clanging of bells, ran out their hoses with traditional speed and stood poised for the attack ... nothing happened! Not a trickle of water issued from the nozzles. The firemen yelled at the guards and at each other, still nothing happened. I never learned why, possibly the hose-union was the wrong size to fit the hydrant or something equally stupid.

The Germans are an amazing people, clever but stupid. The funny side of it appealed to us and we had to have our laugh, although it had serious consequences from our angle; we lost almost all our musical instruments, music, costumes, stage props, and much other property we kept stored in the building. The building was burnt down to ground level. When it was almost too late we were called out in our night clothes to fight the blaze with bucket chains, but we could do little towards saving the theatre, and in the end concentrated on cooling the surrounding huts which were already blistered and smoking with the heat. The cause of the fire was never discovered, and we went without entertainment for the remainder of our stay at Hydekrüge.

This stay would not last much longer, for with the improved weather the Russian steamroller began trundling westwards, and ever nearer to us, at an increasing pace.

With the vast advances in the west there were correspondingly large-scale Russian movements in the east seriously threatening East Prussia, and rumours were rife that the Germans were planning to evacuate us into Germany itself.

I did not like the idea of moving west into Germany as it was a common belief among the P.O.W.s that when Germany became faced with the certainty of defeat, either the Army or the civilians would slaughter all prisoners remaining in their hands. It was an ugly prospect so I decided to go east and risk being collected either by the Russians or the Americans who were sweeping round apparently to join hands with the advancing Russians.

We had no idea how much advance notice the Commandant would give us of the date for our evacuation so we approached the escape committee with a plan to be put into immediate operation. Three of us were involved in the scheme; Neil Prendergast, an old diehard, Jock Sterling and myself.

There were two wash-houses; one we had used for our previous escape tunnel, and another opposite, which had so far escaped the attentions of the Goons. In the latter there were two large brick-built boilers, and it remained a question of finding a ready means to get underground with a suitable cover for the entrance.

There was a deep and fairly wide ash-pit under the less conspicuous boiler in one corner, and we found it possible to squeeze head and shoulders inside to enable one of us to break through the concrete floor and start digging downwards until deep enough to begin tunnelling.

I am of the greyhound breed so I undertook the job of making the initial opening. This meant removing several bricks from the side wall of the ash-pit, sufficient to give me leg room, so that by twisting my body into a letter "L" I could wriggle inside the brickwork casing and work unseen. This made just enough room for me to squat in a crouching position while I broke through the concrete flooring and began excavating.

The sand was dumped next door into the latrine itself by willing helpers until I reached the underground wall dividing wash-house from latrine cesspit. A rather horrible business.

Nevertheless, I broke through this wall making a hole large enough to throw the excavated sandy soil direct into the latrine and provide my tunnel with air; hardly the sort of air to recommend for a health cure, but then, beggars can't be choosers; it would serve our purpose.

We could now operate entirely underground. At this point, we noted the feverish activities of the German administration above ground – large cases arriving and being carted away by civil railway wagons, obviously laden with documents and office equipment – indicating preparations for an early move. We decided to abandon the tunnel project and go ahead by carving out an underground room, large enough for us to sit in comfort, and if need be, lie down to sleep.

The completion of this chamber would provide a two-way means of escape. If orders arrived for a sudden evacuation we could dive below after roll-call and remain there while the others marched away. Afterwards we could pop out for a scout round and if the Germans had gone, too, simply walk out, either as we were or disguised as Germans – anticipating a few items of uniform being left behind. If any guards remained, we could continue our tunnel beyond the surrounding wire and escape that way.

We had just completed our underground chamber when it was officially announced the move would take place in forty-eight hours.

CHAPTER TWENTY–TWO

We promptly laid in a store of anything the escape committee decided would become surplus; tinned food of many varieties, biscuits, jam, cheese, bread, and anything else available including a small Primus stove and a quantity of fuel. We were now ready!

The announcement warned it was to be a complete evacuation; each man would have to carry his own load of whatever he wished to take, including stores and personal kit, as no transport was being provided. Anything and everything, including stores and personal belongings not carried in person, would be left behind.

It was evident the whole area was being cleared of P.O.W.s and possibly civilians, in preparation for turning it into a battle area to meet the Russians.

After roll-call on the evening prior to the move we collected our blankets, a supply of fats for our lamps, a few magazines, some cans of drinking water, and a pack of cards. We were doing ourselves extremely well, and after making arrangements to smother our absence on the next morning's roll-call, and for a couple of pals to brick in the boiler wall behind us and leave everything neat and tidy, we dived below and were sealed in for the night.

I recalled the day when I was about ten years of age and my parents went off for the day. Hoping to give them a fright on their return I dug a small cave, and my sister and I hid ourselves until late at night, when the police were alerted and found us fast asleep surrounded by food we had filched from mother's pantry.

I felt a real childish thrill in this adventure as we did some cooking on our primus and ate a meal fit for a Mayoral banquet. We then spread our pile of blankets, put out the lamps and went to sleep.

Early next morning we could hear our pals dashing in and out of the washroom for a quick wash. Several of them shouted a last "cheerio" and then all went quiet.

We imagined them lined up with their belongings and the shuffling from place to place to cover our absence, and then heard the guards shouting and hunting for skulkers. We could hear the rattle of their rifle butts as they banged and poked around, then they, too, departed and silence once more descended on the compound. We then got the primus going, made some good strong tea and had breakfast.

Another half-hour went by then along came more searchers; the Goons this time. We could see the light of their torches reflecting through our air-hole, comforted by the knowledge they could not see us, as they searched the latrine.

They spent quite a time banging about, and at one point we could even catch their conversation: they were bemoaning that they had no means to swipe and carry away the large quantity of Red Cross tinned food and other luxuries our fellows had been obliged to leave behind. Finally they pushed off and we were once more left in peace, so we settled down to a quiet game of cards to while away the daylight hours.

During the afternoon we heard looters rummaging around the huts, and judging from the noise they made, they seemed to be having a right royal time of themselves; some of them visited the wash-house but as there was nothing worth looting they soon cleared off. It was sufficient evidence for us to realise that, as yet, the civil population had not been evacuated.

We had been earlier warned over the grapevine that a rearguard party would be left behind to pick up any prisoners who, despite the close check, had managed to evade the evacuation. Their job was to tear the place apart to reveal any possible hiding place, and although we could hear them in the wash-house above we could not imagine any reason for them to disturb a brick-built building.

Hence we considered ourselves fairly safe. But had they demolished the place we would have been in a sorry plight indeed. As soon as the looters departed – no doubt driven off by the wrecking party – we could hear them tearing up the hut floors, so we took the precaution of temporarily blocking our air vent leading into the latrine lest they tackled the uninviting job of pulling out the seats and woodwork and came across our hole.

They certainly entered the latrines and spent a short time poking around and from such remarks as we could hear they had no taste for further investigation, and by late evening the camp was left in complete silence.

We then cooked a deferred hot supper – deferred because we dared not cook during the day in case the smell attracted attention – and continued our oft-interrupted card games until a late hour, then settled down to sleep for the second night.

We were safe enough here and decided to take no chances by making any untimely move, but to stay put until the evening of the following day in the hope of finding the whole district cleared of both guards and civilians.

We began the last day of our self-imposed imprisonment in our self-made stinking hideout with a hearty breakfast, and then continued our patient routine of reading, card-playing, eating, and generally trying to occupy ourselves while the hours ticked away towards nine p.m. – the hour of departure.

We then had a wash and shave in hot water – the first since tenanting the chamber – and a rollicking good feed although in spite of bulging tummies we still had to leave some tins of food behind, much to our regrets. Now we were ready to leave.

I hauled myself up under the stove, smashed away the bricks and crawled out. I waited a few minutes to make sure everywhere was silent, then our travelling kit and food including the little Primus was handed out followed by Jock Sterling and Neil Prendergast. We dusted ourselves down and thus began our journey to the Russian front.

The scene that met our eyes when we left the wash-house and walked into the compound was a complete shambles; books, Red Cross supplies in battered tins, clothing, old letters, and the thousand and one almost sacred bits and pieces hoarded up by men living under such confined conditions, were scattered not only within the huts but all over the outside compound.

Much of the stuff lying about was in some way intimately connected with the lives of our men who would have treasured every bit of it and, but for the necessity to preserve their stocks of food and other necessities to keep body and soul alive, would have carried it away with them. We pondered whether to light a fire and burn such things, but again there was enough stuff to form a pile that would burn for hours and as this would endanger our liberty and even our lives, we left it for the plunderers.

The compound gates were open and we could have walked out without trouble; instead, we scorned the idea. No! We would cut our way through the barbed wire just for the fun of it.

So we returned to behind the wash-house and cut a gap through the wire in the northeast corner as an expression of our contempt and independence and walked out the hard way.

We headed straight for the river and walked upstream along the bank for three miles until we came to its narrowest part where a footbridge leading to a farm spanned the stream. We had passed several apparently abandoned farms on our way without seeing or hearing even an animal – all seemed very quiet. We crossed the bridge making for the border which we crossed at approximately the same point as before.

I began to feel like a well-travelled tourist and be damned I was acting like one, pointing out to Neil anything I remembered from my last trip. We then set a course a little more south of east hoping to avoid the vast bog which had delayed and almost exhausted us on our last trip.

Fortunately, this time, we were much fitter and able to keep up a good pace, so that we were crossing our first road by the early hours.

We continued our tramp until seven a.m. and then called a halt for breakfast. The manner of our departure from the camp, the unexpected factors which simplified our going, and the amazing surplus of foodstuffs available, had enabled us to bring much more food than would otherwise have been possible, so with our first meal we ate without stint.

During the meal our thoughts wandered back to our fellow P.O.W.s and above all to the Chief Goon and the Commandant. I conjured up in my imagination the moment it became certain that we had dodged the evacuation. I enjoyed picturing the Commandant cursing and swearing at his Chief Goon as he reported our absence – "That damned Fancy, Prendergast and Sterling, again! After all our searches they've gone again! How the devil did they manage it?"

I could visualise his neck getting redder and redder while the Chief Goon was swearing to make it his personal duty to strangle me, if ever I showed up there again. Oh, what a laugh we had! I've no doubt that at the last minute the Goons had been warned to keep a tag on me, yet after all I'd given them the slip.

When all is said and done, I'd certainly tried their patience to put it mildly. What wouldn't I have risked to be able to overhear their rich vocabulary of German swear words at this minute, and how I'd have liked to hear higher authority dressing them down. I began to hope they'd both be on the Russian front if ever I was returned there.

Our future plan was to walk east until quite close to the "Battle Line" and then lie low and let the Russian front roll over us from the other side. We estimated from the latest news before leaving Hydekrüge that the eastern front was one hundred and fifty miles away and rapidly closing in at about ten to fifteen miles a day. From now on we would be guided by local conditions and by the sound of gunfire on the direction for our next move.

After breakfast, followed by an hour's rest, we commenced to travel directly towards the Russian front and shortly afterwards passed through a small village on the banks of a stream.

There wasn't a sound to be heard and no sign of life in the houses; whether the people had been evacuated we couldn't guess, nor did we stop to investigate. We crossed the stream by means of the stepping-stones and found ourselves in a country with fairly open stretches of cultivated land interspersed by scrub and common grazing land.

We were resting under a hedge at the side of a country road having lunch about one o'clock when along came a farm cart driven by a young man. There was no time to collect our things and hide so we brazened it out. When he reached a point opposite our picnic place he suddenly stopped, and after looking at us for a few seconds, remarked in perfect English, "You are Englishmen." Up to that moment we had taken little notice of him, but this pronouncement simply staggered us, we just gaped at him.

How on earth could he tell who we were? We hadn't spoken a word to him! We admitted we were English, and he told us that if we cared to follow him he would take us to his uncle's farm. So off we went and after about a mile reached a small farm, to be greeted by an elderly man who led us into the house and presented us with glasses of milk. He asked where we were going, and we told him just what we intended to do.

At this he was visibly shocked and warned us that we would most certainly be killed by the first Russian soldier we ran into. They never ask questions until you're dead, he explained, and a civilian's one chance is to remain in his house with a sign in Russian welcoming them as liberators. They usually drop pamphlets ahead of approaching troops warning the people to remain indoors with a white flag outside, front and back.

Finally, he suggested we should stay with him and he would fit us out with clothes and we could help him on the farm until the Russians arrived. I asked him how he knew all this, and he told us the Russians always choose one man from each village they occupy to follow the German's retirement and warn the people not to leave with the Germans, and several had already passed through his village.

We considered the matter and thought the idea was a tempting one, but in the end I thought he was banking on our presence on his farm to stand him in good stead when the Russians arrived.

We finally decided it would be better to move farther ahead in case we might have to wait here several weeks which might extend to months, and if the Germans decided to make a stand along this border line anything could happen to us.

It was one thing to play the fool with the Germans behind their lines, but soldiers fighting in the front line haven't the time to ask many questions of lonely strangers such as we. A bullet and four feet of earth is more economical and settles the question for all time.

In the light of future happenings we were crazy fools not to have accepted his offer, but at this moment we were free and our past long period of captivity had filled us with the urge to be continually on the move – it was a driving force we could no longer ignore.

We spent the rest of the day on the farm – mostly sleeping – then as evening closed in we thanked the farmer and the lad for their kindness and moved off, travelling straight across country. After walking for a further three hours we struck a road which appeared to lead more or less in our desired direction so we marched along it for several miles, when suddenly, looming out of the darkness a few yards ahead we were confronted by a sentry box.

It was too late to take avoiding action, it would only create suspicion if we suddenly dashed off across country, so we marched boldly forward expecting every second to hear the command "*Halt*". But none came, so giving the guard a friendly greeting by a wave of the hand we continued on our way, perspiring freely.

When a few minutes later we arrived on the outskirts of another small village we discovered the purpose of the sentry. There in a field at the side of the road was a German horse transport column bivouacked for the night.

It was quite dark and I'm sure we could have walked by without noticing a thing, only at that moment a horse indicated its presence by rattling his harness and we suddenly halted ready to react to circumstances. At that moment a guard poked his head over the fence and wanted to know who we were and where we were going.

Neil, who spoke the best German, went across and explained that we were Polish workers on our way to a job at Siauliai, a town we had heard of somewhere ahead of us, and before the guard could continue his interest in us Neil sidestepped further questioning by cheekily asking how far it was.

The guard fell for it as easily as downing a whisky on a cold night, informed Neil it was forty-three kilometres, and then chattily wanted to know if we intended to walk all the way. Neil smiled with a Continental shrug of his shoulders and assured him there was no other means of getting there, then before the sentry could collect his wits he apologised for leaving him hurriedly as he and his friends might lose the job if they arrived too late; and with a cheerio, boldly left the guard standing there.

To our surprise and infinite relief our inquisitor seemed quite satisfied so we added a word to Neil's goodbye and hurried away.

"Keep going pretty hard, lads," whispered Neil, "I just noticed a burly N.C.O. approaching, that's why I suddenly terminated the interview."

And we did keep going, we hopped onto the grass verge to muffle our hurried steps and pressed along as fast as we could go short of an actual run, trusting to the darkness to hide our sudden hurry. There seemed no end to the transport parked in the field and after hurrying along for half a mile we slipped into the field on the opposite side and eased our pace until well beyond the bivouacs. Then we returned to the road.

"That was a smart bit of work," I assured Neil as soon as I recovered breath enough to talk.

"Yes, poor sod," he replied, "I'll bet he's getting it in the neck from his sergeant for letting us go. He was only a poor kid, just a baby-faced sixteen-year-old. He was scared stiff and glad to see the back of me. I don't suppose he's ever fired a shot in his life. They wouldn't with horse transport, you know!"

We thought this pretty good evidence of the many stories of the Germans using schoolboys as soldiers. Anyhow, it was helpful to us on this occasion, as an older man with more training wouldn't have been so easily bluffed; he would have kept us covered with his rifle while he called for others to round us up for interrogation by an officer.

It alerted us to the possibility of there being more experienced fighting men in the neighbourhood. We could also use the information of forty-three kilometres – approximately twenty-five miles – to our advantage.

It meant we would not have to follow the road much farther before turning off as we had no intention of visiting Siauliai, but it was nice to know where it was as a guide for our course. During the next five miles several motorised columns came along, and having audible warning of their approach we were able to dive for cover in good time. We noticed that none of them carried lights except one mere pinpoint deflected down to the near-side verge which we took to be a sign indicating we must be approaching the battle zone. At the first suitable point we turned away from the road on a course south east so as to give the town a wide berth.

The going hadn't been too bad and by the time dawn began to break we estimated we had covered about fifty miles since leaving Hydekrüge. The question now was, how far had the Russians moved in our direction since we started out.

We had no information upon which to make even a rough guess and as we were tired we began a lookout for a suitable hideout to pass the day.

We soon came across an old tumbledown shack which couldn't have been inhabited for many years; at least it afforded a shelter from the breeze and a place where we could light a fire, so we dragged inside a plentiful supply of wood, which littered the surrounding area, and set a good fire going, had breakfast, and settled in for the day.

We decided we had somehow tumbled into a troop-ridden locality in which it was far too risky to move openly in the daytime, so we would do one more night march before going to ground. At irregular intervals throughout the day we were awakened by heavy transports passing along a road some distance away, but in spite of our observations from various points of vantage we couldn't determine exactly where the road lay. All we knew was that it ran somewhere across our front and that it must be a trunk road to carry so much heavy traffic.

In the evening we heated a tin of meat, brewed some tea, and had a good hot meal complete with toast. We were still feeling very fit, and as soon as darkness descended we dowsed the fire and started off on our last march. We soon came upon the road and walked warily along it for a long way; strangely enough not a single transport passed that way but we occasionally caught the faint crump of what sounded like the fire of heavy guns.

We were speculating on a possible explanation for the absence of night traffic on what appeared a well-used road in daylight, when we stopped speechless with fright.

We had been creeping along very cautiously with our ears tuned for the least sound, when we heard voices not a dozen yards behind us in the pitch darkness; there was no time to hide so we stood anxiously waiting.

At last the voices came nearer, jabbering away in a lingo we couldn't understand, then they came into view ... a couple of drunks in difficulties managing their bikes. What a relief! They greeted us like long lost brothers although they hadn't the faintest idea who we were. To ease the situation, and hoping to quieten them, we pushed their bikes along while they staggered behind us jabbering all the time.

The sound of gunfire now became more frequent and aircraft began to fly overhead, our friends kept mumbling "Ruskie" and pointing in the direction of the gunfire. We eventually made them understand who we were and they showed their delight by hanging round our necks and continually slapping our backs. We accompanied them for a couple of miles when they led us to a small farm invisible in the darkness, and hammered on a door until an upstairs window opened.

A very frightened voice enquired what was happening, to which our friends told some sort of story, and the owner of the voice, a middle-aged woman, came down and opened the door, ushered us inside, and promptly shut and bolted the door. To our amazement she then greeted us in perfect English with an American accent and explained she had been a schoolteacher in America.

I felt like "Alice in Wonderland". Almost every contact we made on this trip had greeted us in Americanised-English, and each one an accidental meeting! After the introduction she brought out a large dish of honey in the comb and a loaf of fresh bread and heaps of butter, and invited us to eat. It was pitch black in the room as it was too dangerous to light a lamp.

What with gunfire rattling the windows, aircraft overhead, eating bread and honey in utter darkness, telling our story to an English-speaking Polish lady whom we couldn't see, and in a foreign country, while she interpreted the tale of three escaping P.O.W.s to two persons we knew were there but couldn't see, and our two drunks, it was enough to give anyone the creeps.

We managed to eat up all the food, but on account of the darkness we were covered in honey from our eyebrows to our feet. It was heartbreaking for three Britons to feel so helpless as our kind hostess and her unseen friends sadly related their fears for the future.

I instantly pictured such a scene way back home had the Germans reached England, and to these poor helpless folk the oncoming Russians seemed to hold more terror for them than even the Germans. I could do no more than advise her to bury in the ground any guns she had on the premises, hang white sheets from the windows before the Russians arrived, do what they told her without offering any resistance, and answer their questions promptly.

She told us there was a village called Celle at the crossroads about a mile farther on, and one of the unseen voices assured us he had heard of no Germans there when he was in the village during the early evening, so we thanked them and decided to push ahead. I think we were all glad to leave the house; the occupants were really terrified of what might be going to happen to them with the exception of the pair of cyclists, and they were still too merry to care what happened.

It was just on midnight when we entered the village, which proved to be quite a large one. We were displaying no special caution in view of having been told that all was clear, when, as we were marching across the centre of the square, we suddenly found ourselves surrounded by a ring of German bayonets gradually closing in on us.

Many sudden and astonishing things had already happened to me but never anything quite so sudden as this.

Yet there they were, coming from nowhere as though expecting us, their bayonets only a few feet away and pointing directly at our tummies like spokes of a wheel with us at the hub. We made an effort to appear casual but it soon became clear that they weren't playing games. We were trapped and things looked ugly from our angle.

We were ordered to put up our hands, and there we stood; there must have been at least twenty of them all standing at the ready; no one moved – least of all we three – until an officer arrived. It was a very ticklish moment, and I could feel a tingling at the back of my neck. Without a doubt, had we made any movement, we should all have had it. I had no misgivings on that point, it was clear to me they were front line soldiers and determined ones at that. Such was our astonishment that up to now none of us had spoken a word.

The officer, a typical fat German, questioned us as we stood there without relaxing the guard for one moment, as though ready to give the order to finish us off on the spot if we failed to satisfy him.

He yelled his questions with a menacing snarl and sneered his disbelief at our answers.

"Who are you?" "Where do you come from?" "Where are you going?" "Are you Jews?" This last he rolled out with the obvious relish of anticipation. For anyone admitting to that nationality would have been committing suicide for certain.

This went on for fully half-an-hour without his once ordering the troops to remove the bayonet threat, and finally he led us away and told us to sit on a form outside the inn where they were billeted for the night.

We had unluckily blundered into a collection of stragglers and undesirables being escorted from behind the battle front back into Germany, to what fate I could only guess. Although, within a few hours we knew the fate of many of the poor wretches.

Apparently these unfortunates were camping for the night in the square under the watchful eye of their guards and had arrived there only half-an-hour before us, and of course we just walked right into the middle of them. Can you believe it?

Not a German was near the village until the convoy of wagons arrived with their prisoners just ahead of us. It transpired that sentries had been posted all round the outskirts of the village, and although we had not seen them as we approached, they had seen us and quietly closed in and trapped us in the centre of the web. I could have banged my head against a wall, I felt so mad with myself. The fellow at the farm had been right, there were no Germans in the village at the time, they arrived immediately afterwards without warning.

The next few hours put years on me, for while we were combatants and theoretically, at least, entitled by international law to certain protection against gangster-minded civilians and soldiery alike, and also prisoners-of-war entitled to protection from mob law, here we received neither; we were thrown in with a civil mob of six or seven nationalities, unable to understand a word of their language or to explain our position among them.

One word against our integrity rumoured among that bunch and we could have been lynched – and that word could have been released by the soldiers supposed to protect us; on the other hand, to curry favour with the guard and so purchase their own lives, any one of that mixed crowd could have whispered a cock-and-bull story to the soldiery, supposedly emanating from us, and the Germans would have murdered us.

We seriously considered making a protest, but it seemed pretty clear to us that our jailers were an extermination squad and would have no qualms about exterminating us with the others, so we thought it better to wait and see, and better still to bolt at the first opportunity.

We considered ourselves in the gravest danger; in fact we had never before been in such dangerous circumstances. Only the most careful diplomacy could preserve our lives.

All around us were groups of terrified people muttering prayers, counting their beads, making the sign of the cross; often wailing and moaning, casting mute appealing looks towards their guards and weak smiles at us.

I never want to see anything like it again.

The groups consisted mainly of old men and women. It was a pitiful scene, especially as deep in the eyes of these elderly folk, who might easily have been our own parents and grandparents, one could read their brave acceptance of the fate awaiting them at any moment.

There were some in their teens, looking frightened; some would be sent to factories, and some to their deaths. Quite a lot of happy little children, who innocently wondered why they had been driven from their homes, and were unaware of their absolutely certain fate. It was horrible realizing our impotence.

Soon they were being questioned, especially on their ancestry and anyone unable to give satisfactory answers was segregated from the crowd – all were Jews who could not disprove the fact. And as dawn came these poor unfortunates were led away in batches to a wood outside the village … there was the sound of shots … and the guards returned, alone.

It made us feel sick until we could stand it no longer, and we let them have it hot and strong, officers and troops alike. Then they threatened us in no uncertain manner.

Said one officer, "You three have reduced our food ration. Three bullets or the bayonet point will put us back on a full diet. You count that little." The troops scowled at us and pointed their bayonets every time they came near us. It was enough to tempt a suicidal act from any full-blooded man, we managed to avoid the temptation.

What saved us I do not know. We quite expected to be soon on our way to the wood. But no, we were kept waiting there on the bench, and when the horse-driven wagons filled with survivors moved off a few hours later we were marched alongside. There was ample room to spare inside the carts but they made us march as a punishment for our "English insolence", as the officer reminded us.

Four guards with fixed bayonets at the ready marched behind us; had one of them tripped or stumbled over anything one of us would have bitten the dust for sure and been kicked aside to die. The thing was too nerve-racking to describe. We stuck it out for a couple of miles then made a protest. The officer granted a concession.

"I don't want you to die too soon. You'll be glad to die before I've done with you!" he sneered, then ordered the guards to follow with slung rifles.

Marching alongside the column we were being slowly choked by the dust kicked up by the horses' hooves. It was a consolation to know that the Goons behind us were also suffering the same discomfort. I didn't know where we were making for, but by making a rough calculation from the angle of our shadows it appeared we were travelling in a south-westerly direction, so it looked like Poland.

We were very glad when at about mid-day, two army staff cars stopped alongside and the officers enquired who we were; the officer in charge of the column told them some tale we were unable to hear – I think he was anxious to be rid of us – and bundled us into the cars.

We settled down like blue-blooded Lords and after a two-hour drive were dumped at an army H.Q. somewhere behind the lines.

I don't think the Staff Officers took us out of pity although I'm certain the convoy officer wanted to get rid of us. It is my belief the Staff Officers knew our guards were an extermination squad and saved our lives to avoid a possible stink over our deaths. Not knowing our ranks they may have thought we could serve their purpose better by a close interrogation at headquarters.

Here we were locked in separate rooms and at intervals were brought out one at a time for questioning. Our first questioner was a Russian-speaking German. We found it laughable.

In time he reverted to German and asked us our rank in the Russian army, who was our General, how long we'd been at the front, and which front we came from. Then, offering a glass of pretty good vodka, he started all over again in Russian. I could stand his vodka and replied in the only Russian word I knew, "dobra" as near as I can spell it, meaning "good". This made him laugh. Then I went one better, "Russich naeman dobra," meaning, as far as I knew and can spell, "Russian, no good." Again he laughed, I suppose at my using the German for Russian and my pronunciation of "no good". It became quite a pantomime. He was a very intellectual and aristocratic looking man with an almost British sense of humour.

I discovered his German accent was hardly up to old Schreiber's Heidelberg and suspected he belonged to the old Russian aristocracy. Anyhow, he certainly behaved like a gentleman to all three of us. It shocked me when he addressed me in Oxford English and wanted to know if I knew any lines of Shakespeare.

It was right up my street. I replied "Very well," and went straight through "Henry Fifth before the Battle of Agincourt". He was delighted, clapped his hands, and said, "Bravo, you're English all right!"

He put Neil and Jock through a similar test and wished us the best of luck.

But this didn't quite settle matters, we were brought out time and time again before several very different types of Germans, who were all convinced we were Russians and kept trying to pin the bogey stuff on us of being Ruskie saboteurs. But try as they would we never seemed to fit the picture and all they could get from us was the fact that we were British P.O.W.s. Then when they searched our kit and it revealed nothing but Red Cross tinned food labelled in English print, and a letter in Neil's bag from his father, they decided we must be English, and gave us up as bad eggs. Then they brought us a feed and locked us in together.

After spending the night in these headquarters, we were next day loaded into a large touring car bound for East Prussia.

Our guards kept trying to stuff us with tales of how they were pushing the Russians back to Moscow, but we were overtaking troop convoys, armoured tanks, and heavy artillery, all going in our direction – away from the Russian front – so we innocently enquired if we also were going to the Russian front. They understood our meaning all right, and as this rather took the bounce out of them they afterwards remained silent.

It was late afternoon when we arrived at Tilsit, and drove immediately to the town jail where we were deprived of all our possessions and locked in separate cells.

This was my first experience of a civil prison and I didn't like it in the least; the cell was dark, cold, and dismal and I wasn't even allowed to shout across to Jock and Neil. I did try it once, and once only – the warder came in with a black truncheon in his hand and made things most unpleasant for me, so I lay down on the planks which did service for a bed and tried to sleep. The damned thing was so hard and unyielding that I had to keep standing up for a rest.

At supper time – with the emphasis on "time" and "supper" – they brought me a bowl of some offensive-smelling liquid and a piece of dry bread, one blanket, and a straw-stuffed dirty old sack bolster – that was my lot until next morning. Sleep was out of the question, I spent a most uncomfortable night, most of the time tramping four steps one way and four steps back trying to keep my blood circulating.

When morning arrived, to my intense satisfaction we were allowed out one by one as far as a tap at the end of the corridor for a wash and visit to the toilet. Following this, they served us with two slices of bread and a small cube of rancid margarine, and a mug of poisonous German tea; in fact, I can only suppose it was tea, it could have been some left-overs of tea, coffee, and cocoa warmed up together.

When the warder came to collect my breakfast utensils he stood for a moment facing me, raised his hands as though in prayer, pointed to my heart and said, "You, Kaput!" Now "Kaput" means "done for", "lost", "finished" and I tried to question him in German but he ignored me and closed the door.

I was churning the matter over in my mind trying to reach a meaning, when punctually at ten a.m., all the cell doors were flung open and we were marched outside into the prison yard to find six guards lined up with rifles. We continued our march in single file to the far end and halted with our backs to the wall, facing the riflemen. Here we stood for about ten minutes – or was it a lifetime? I muttered to Neil who stood next to me, "What do you make of this?" He muttered back, "I don't know, but I don't like the set-up."

At that moment an officer appeared and began speaking to the *Unteroffizier* (N.C.O.) in charge of the riflemen. My knees began to give way under me, I felt sure the officer had arrived to superintend the shooting of us.

I thought of the little baby I had never seen and was now never likely to see. I thought of the thousand and one things I wanted to tell my wife. I wondered why we had not been visited by a priest or parson – a privilege granted to the worst criminal before execution.

I heard Jock mutter, "This is plain bloody murder, fellows!" And then the officer stood aside.

"Chins up, boys," whispered Neil.

I prepared myself for the awful, red-hot, sizzling, sudden pain of the crashing bullet.

Instead, the *Unteroffizier* strolled casually across to us, marched us back to the cells, and without a word of explanation locked us in. I flopped on to the shelf-bed like a dying man.

This exact ritual took place three times during our two weeks' stay in Tilsit. It varied only in that once there were eight of us lined up with a firing party of twelve, and once five of us with eight riflemen. It provided the only outdoor exercise we were allowed for the whole period.

We never found the answer. Whether we were taken out in error, or it was a form of German playfulness to break us down, I'll never know. We can crack a joke about it today, it was no joke then. We never knew which day the fun would become reality. There was no relying on being marched back *every* time. You must try it some time. It will change the colour of your hair overnight.

Other than marching to the execution stand and back, our main form of exercise was banging on the cell door to be escorted to the toilet, and while on our way along the corridor shouting to each other to confirm that we were all still in the land of the living. Whether there were any more prisoners in the block besides those who stood with us on the line, I never knew; we neither saw nor heard another.

The food was scarce and unfit for human consumption; the bread was stale and mouldy, the soup or, as they called it, stew stank abominably, the margarine was rancid, and the tea or whatever it was, cold and bitter to the taste.

The hours and days of solitary confinement were a period of indescribable monotony. We sat in semi- or complete darkness with nothing to read or occupy our hands until I felt certain I would soon go mad. You may imagine our relief when one morning our kit was returned to us and we were told to be ready to move in ten minutes.

I could have screamed to high heaven, my nerves had reached breaking point.

There were three guards came for us, one for each prisoner, with an interpreter N.C.O. in charge of the party, who marched us through the streets to the jeers of the mob until we reached the station.

I never knew before that fresh air had a smell. I smelled it and tasted it, it was lovely, even though it was German air. We breathed our fill as we marched along ignoring the jeers, and although the distance to the station was covered in about twenty minutes I could feel the first creeping agony of cramp gripping my leg muscles. Another ten minutes and I would have been writhing in agony.

We found our interpreter more talkative than any we had previously met – he was probably anxious to get in as much practice as possible. He informed us we were going to Thorn in Poland, so Neil slyly enquired if he thought we should get there before the Russians.

He stuffed us with the usual nonsense, but he unwittingly revealed the information we were thirsting to know; namely the Russians' present position. We knew where they were just over a fortnight ago, and even though our interpreter would naturally push them back for our benefit it was enough to convince us that the changed positions indicated the Russian advance was still making good headway, however much our chatterbox tried to minimise the Russian effort.

CHAPTER TWENTY-THREE

We boarded a train packed to capacity with refugees, complete with their goods and chattels stacked to the roofs and on their knees. They were all Germans, we heard the train guard tell our interpreter, and they looked very tired and despondent as if undergoing a miserable time.

I recalled the poor unfortunates surrounding us at Celle before the staff car rescued us, and I felt damned mean towards this crowd, despite their sufferings.

They were packed like sardines even along the corridors and would remain so for the next twelve hours or so. It positively cheered us up a bit to see the cruel swine getting a taste of their own medicine. Naturally I felt sorry for the innocent kiddies, though they had shown no pity for the helpless little mites of other nationals – the mills of God were grinding slowly but surely.

These were the same faces of other days revealing a different mood. They are a wonderful race while they stand with their heels stamping other people's faces into the mire, but it's a different story when their turn comes. They are brutes and beasts at any time and don't ever forget it! It's the first time they've ever felt the real horrors of wars of their own making. 1914–18 was a soldier's war and the German soldiers certainly bit the dust, but their civilians and German property were never soiled to the extent of a broken window. This time they were really getting it in the neck from every angle. It was no longer a case of a broken window, they were hoisted with their own petard, and soon every heart and every window would be broken; and, frankly, I was going to enjoy it.

We found it especially satisfying to have a compartment all to ourselves with room to spare while the rightful owners of the train had scarcely room to breathe.

Our journey lasted all day and it was late in the evening when we arrived at Thorn and were lodged in another civil jail. Were we never to get away from these horrible places? Our question was answered the following morning when we were collected by a new set of guards and marched for a mile beyond the town.

And there ahead we saw the old familiar barbed-wire fences, and elevated sentry boxes of a P.O.W. camp.

We were taken to one of the administration huts in the German Lager for interrogation. Neil went in first while Jock and I waited our turn in the next-door room, but the guards did not keep us company.

There was a window at the rear of the room which seemed to be inviting our attention, so we looked out; everything seemed quiet and deserted on the outside, and not being a part of the prisoner's compound, with only a couple of strands of wire to fence it in from the road, we saw no reason to wait any longer for our interview.

We opened the window and popped outside.

We ambled away between the German staff billets so as to be out of sight of the open window, hoping for time to nip under the single strand wire fence before we were missed. Unfortunately one of the guards had poked his head into the waiting room just after we had disappeared and began yelling blue murder around the place – we guessed we'd had it, and pretended to be washing our hands in a nearby fire bucket outside one of the billets; in less time than it takes to tell we were offering an explanation before the Commandant.

He was very annoyed with us and seemed to treat this latest episode as a personal affront, and very indignantly tacked a further two weeks on to our sentence.

We now faced a two months' stretch instead of six weeks, and instead of dumping us in the compound cooler we were accommodated in private quarters at the Lager. But this was no privilege! These were cells to accommodate German malefactors and if they seemed unkind to British P.O.W.s, they were really brutal to their own offenders.

It was a new experience to have our food brought to us by British prisoners and I fell to wondering how the Commandant could have become so trusting, unless it was his aim to put opportunity our way so he could personally take a pot shot at us. They were army lads, and we learned from them that a lot of R.A.F. P.O.W.s had arrived at the compound only three weeks ago. This was interesting news so we gave them our names and asked them to enquire if these latest arrivals were our crowd from Hydekrüge.

At their next visit, they reported that it was, indeed, our party, and as things turned out we spent only four days in the cells before we were back among them. We were released one afternoon and taken bag and baggage to the compound, a very large one, where we found the remainder of our friends.

Before hearing a word of our story we learned that the camp was being moved again the very next day, and sure enough next morning we were all paraded and marched off to a goods yard outside Thorn where we loaded into our Pullman cattle trucks of old, en route for some place we had never heard of, called Fallingbosthe – as near as I can spell it from the pronunciation.

I thought our journey was never going to end. It occupied three whole days, travelling west all the time, and several of the wits suggested they were taking us home to England because Germany was getting so much smaller every day, with British and Americans advancing on one flank and the Russians on the other. What hopes!

On arrival we did a spot of plotting, and pinpointed ourselves on Luneburg Heath, midway between Bremen and Hanover.

We were to occupy what had once been a Hitler Youth camp, and although these Hitler brats were supposed to be the true *Herren-volk*, the accommodation proved no better than any of our previous camps; it consisted of large brick-built barns containing row upon row of double and treble-tier bunks. We were counted into each barn according to the number of bunks, including us three, although we expected accommodation in the cooler.

As no-one shipped us off to the cells we didn't trouble to point out this omission to the Commandant, but kept very quiet and almost invisible, avoiding all chances of contact with the Germans and hoping they would forget all about us – and that is just what happened!

The so-called German war machine had now reached a stage of impotence from which it could never recover. The signs of disintegration were everywhere plain to see – it was visible on the faces of every German we saw.

Our information within the camp had little basis in fact, and in spite of the bare-faced German lies circulated for our consumption we knew a great deal more concerning the true situation than many of the liars themselves. Their lies were an attempt to bolster their own hopes; they hoped their lies would somehow by a miracle become the truth. We tested their reactions by taunts, jeers, and open insults, and proved they were too demoralised to impose further authority even upon helpless prisoners.

The state of internal affairs within the German Reich was such that authority was passing from the governing class to the man in the street. Things were becoming decidedly sticky. We sensed from our constant flittings and their poor show of discipline within the camp that they couldn't possibly hold out much longer.

Persistent bombing on an ever increasing scale had reduced the cities to heaps of rubble and had disrupted internal communications, and our guards knew that we knew it, or they would never have toler-ated our lousy insolence and riotous behaviour. We complained against our reduced rations and the Commandant let it slip that there were no prospects of receiving any additional food supplies.

As the western and eastern fronts were fast closing in, our guards revealed their jittery nerves and were becoming almost friendly.

At the end of our third week in this camp and still with an eight-week sentence looming threateningly over us we decided on another effort while we still had some stamina left. We gave the perimeter a thorough inspection and decided our best chance lay in working from one of the latrines backing up to the warning wire. This meant digging a twenty-yard tunnel to break out in the local cemetery just beyond the outside wire.

Our intention was to make a blitz effort, but after two days burrowing we were obliged to face up to the truth that we would never make it, we just did not have the necessary strength to do the work.

It was a bitter pill to swallow, but to press on would probably mean one or both of us crocking up altogether, so we abandoned the attempt, consoling ourselves with the thought that if we eased up during the coming winter and conserved our energy we might be fit for another chance next spring.

We learned later that our particular area was to be strongly defended, and if the war continued much farther into the heart of Germany a big stand would be made right here. We knew there was a large S.S. barracks quite close to us and the grapevine informed us it was marked down as a death zone, and any unauthorised person seen moving around after curfew hour would be shot.

CHAPTER TWENTY–FOUR

B y the time winter moved in on us we were a thoroughly miserable bunch of kriegies. Late in November I went down with some mysterious illness and I remembered little of what went on until a few days before Christmas.

Neil, who was sharing my bunk to double my blanket supply and use his body to keep me warm, and Bill, who unfortunately was billeted in another barn, nursed me through my long illness, and the fact that I am here writing this story is wholly due to their ministrations.

On Christmas day I was sitting up and taking notice, and due to someone's ingenuity we had a cake; a part of the bread ration was set aside, dried and ground, and with a few handfuls of sugar, carefully hoarded over several weeks, and then earnestly guarded by half a dozen "cooks" while it baked in our home made oven. Our "sugar cake" was then withdrawn and hoisted overhead, while all those who had contributed to its birth, or rather re-birth, formed a procession and circumambulated the barn until it was cool enough to eat.

It still harboured a faint taste, denoting age, of its principal constituent, yet the result was a pleasant variation in our diet.

Gone were the ice hockey games, concerts, and theatricals; even the cheerful spirits that had always stamped us as the mad English were no longer evident. This was the outcome of food shortages, total lack of medical supplies, and non-arrival of those much appreciated Red Cross parcels and letters from our loved ones.

We were no longer the Goon-baiting, insolent, mischief-loving young men of Hydekrüge, we represented a fair selection of the ancient invalid warriors to be seen at Chelsea. Many of us felt we should not live to see the day of our deliverance.

We economised our movements and hoarded our strength ready for the final day, knowing the troops could make little headway during the winter months – we must be ready to help ourselves when the soldiers arrived, it would be too bad to be cheated by death right at the winning post.

Our hopes revived with the advent of spring. German morale had sunk to a low level; our guards smiled and extended friendly nods and even deplored the hopelessness of their chances of victory. They no longer trusted their officers; poor old Schreiber went so far as to discuss with me his concern for his family.

We frankly discussed the situation; he had the facts concerning the dispositions of all armies engaged in the struggle and he thought his home town – Heidelberg – would fall to the Americans. "I've no doubt the Americans are a civilised people, and will act very correctly," he began, and then to my surprise added, "not like a certain class of my people who are no better than the Huns of old. I could have told Hitler we were doomed the moment American power was launched against us."

I did my best to persuade him to stay with us until British troops arrived, that he would be among friends who would never fear to testify in his favour.

"I am getting old you know, Mr. Fancy. I do hope you will soon be with your dear family. You have been with us almost five years, and you are young, it is a long time," he concluded, and I saw tears in his eyes. I felt really sorry for poor old Schreiber, he was a decent man and I knew his sentiments were genuine.

There was a quickening of the tempo on both fronts and conditions within the German Reich were becoming daily more desperate, until finally, with the crossing of the Rhine, it was decided to remove all prisoners into Southern Germany in the Hartz mountains area nearer Schreiber's home.

There was a persistent rumour that the last stand would be made in this area and all P.O.W.s were to be held as hostages – it seemed to me incredible the Germans would go so far.

Orders were given and countermanded each alternate day but at last the evacuation began.

Each day a party set out on the long trail, but as Bill, Neil, and I, together with many more old hands, were not so keen on organised hiking, we kept well out of sight as each new party was made up, hoping to delay our departure until the very end. Eventually the camp became so thinned out of prisoners we could avoid the guards and Goons no longer, and one cold morning in the last week of March we were rounded up with other chaps into a party about a hundred strong and marched out of camp.

We were a seedy-looking crowd, and, unable to keep formation, we straggled out into a thin crocodile winding slowly along the road, and halting frequently to rest. Even the guards lost heart in the job and none of them seemed to know where we were heading. I fancy they stayed with us only because they had nowhere else to go or felt safer in our company. We covered only about eighteen miles that day and I was exhausted when evening came and we were halted in a small village and billeted, without food, in a large barn for the night.

We were hauled out early next morning and given a slice of bread and a drink of butter milk, a gift from the nearby farm. When the officer in charge ended a conversation with another officer, in charge of some passing transports, he informed us we could go no further – the route to the south had been cut. There was nothing for it but to return to camp.

At this point I hunted for old Schreiber and told him this was his one chance to escape the Russians and fall into American hands where he would receive protection and probably get a well-paid job. I advised him to slide into the fields, make his way to the nearest large town, place himself at the mercy of one of his own class, get into civilian clothes – his age would be his best cover from German soldiers – and stay there until the Americans arrived. He ought to have the name of a small village now in Russian hands ready on his tongue in case he was picked up before he reached the town and had to pitch a tale of escaping from Russian capture. All he said was, "Thank you, Mr. Fancy, you are very kind."

What happened to him I never learnt, I never saw nor heard of him again.

I no sooner returned to my two friends than we began our return trip. Yesterday's march had left us very tired and weary, and with an empty belly my movements became slower and slower until we trailed farther and farther behind, when at last we were left ambling along on our own, just the three of us without a guard or any other P.O.W.s in sight.

As the day wore on we called at a farm for a drink and found several Russians who had been living and working on the farm for several months. And although the farmer was a German married to a Polish woman, he provided us with a satisfying hot meal and allowed us to spend the night there.

The following day, realising our condition could not stand the strain of another escape bid, we made the rest of the distance back to camp, where others behind us were still trickling back in odd numbers.

We held a meeting, with our leader as chairman, next day, and arrived at a decision, that come hell or high water we would stay there until relieving forces reached us.

As our water supply and our main source of food, a potato dump, were both outside the camp, we must do something about them. There was now no organised guard in the camp, so we rounded up the sole remaining German officer, and our spokesman and leader, Taylor Gill, or T.G. as we knew him, told him to order all Germans still on the camp to surrender their arms and clear out.

This they did without a word of protest, and we searched them all. Those with nowhere to go were allowed to stay with us on the camp, the others were told to push off within the hour.

We then organised our own pickets both inside and outside the camp, with a few specially picked from our heftiest blokes to guard our food and water supplies. These were valuable commodities both for ourselves and the people of the local village of Fallingbosthe. As we considered we had a prior claim on these supplies we denied them to anyone except the villagers.

This was the situation on the morning of the nineteenth of April 1945 when a lone British Army jeep rolled into camp driven by a Padre. The most welcome sight I had seen in the past five years.

The Padre was a fine-looking man who shook our hands and hugged every one of us. He was plenty old enough to have been my father, and I could have kissed him. He advised us on no account to stray from the camp as a fierce tank battle was expected to take place any moment with the local S.S. barracks.

Sure enough this developed an hour later. We had a grandstand view of the battle from the elevated guard boxes and watched the shelling of resistance points in the town. The Commanding Officer of the Seventh Brigade of Guards – our relieving force – then drove into camp to receive a tumultuous welcome.

At last! ... we were *FREE*!

Three days later, motor transports arrived, we drove to an airstrip, and after a good feed were flown to Brussels. We spent one night in the city and were then flown back to dear old England. *Four years, eleven months, and one week*, after taking off for what was originally intended to be *a three hour trip* in May, 1940.

No words of mine can possibly describe my feelings as my fellow R.A.F. types surrounded me and dragged me to the Mess hut where we were fed and fêted like heroes. Telegrams to my wife and family were snatched from my hands the moment I had written my message and rushed off to be 'phoned north to my home. I could tell them no more than that I was safe in England, as there would be certain formalities before I should be able to get leave to meet them.

First I had to be interrogated by intelligence – a mere formality – and then a rather searching examination by the doctors. And here I received a shock. They sent me to hospital as in need of urgent treatment … both my lungs were full of liquid … they extracted pint after pint. After eight months I was allowed to return home.

To all intents that is the end of my story.

But possibly even to this day, somewhere tucked away in Germany's files, the fact will be recorded that *Kriegsgefangeners* Prendergast, Sterling, and Fancy, sentenced each to eight weeks' solitary confinement at Thorn, in Poland on a certain day in August, 1944, still have seven weeks and three days of their sentences yet to serve.

Should any old kriegie browse through my scribblings, no doubt, he will recall to mind many of the humorous situations that arose from time to time, as well as the many trials and tribulations of prison-camp life.

The amount of forbearance shown one to another by so many men under such conditions and in similar circumstances and over so long a period of time has never ceased to amaze me … I raise my hat to each and every one.